DATE DUE

HIGHSMITH 45-220

Getting Elected in Canada

by Tom Brook

With a Foreword by Allan Blakeney

THE MERCURY PRESS

ACKNOWLEDGEMENTS

The publisher gratefully acknowledges the financial assistance
of the Canada Council and the Ontario Arts Council.

Cover design: TASK
Production co-ordination: The Blue Pencil

Typeset in New Baskerville and Gill Sans by TASK.
Printed and bound in Canada.

THIRD PRINTING, 1993

Canadian Cataloguing in Publication:

Main entry under title:

Brook, Tom
Getting elected in Canada
ISBN 0-920544-84-3
I. Elections – Canada. I. Title.
JL193.B76 1991   324.6'0971   C91-094563-2

———————————————

Canadian Sales Representation: The Literary Press Group.

The Mercury Press is distributed in Canada
by University of Toronto Press,
and in the United States
by Inland Book Company (selected titles)
and Bookslinger.

The Mercury Press
(an imprint of Aya Press)
Box 446
Stratford, Ontario
Canada
N5A 6T3

Contents

Foreword

There is a well-known story that is part of political folklore, about a southern United States politician who offered this statement when asked where he stood on alcohol:

"If by alcohol you are talking about the elixir which brings ease of conversation and convivial undertakings among people who might even be strangers; if you are talking of the alcohol that employs men by the hundreds, and makes good use of the fruits of our farmers' labour, then I stand for it."

"But, if the alcohol to which you refer is the vile liquid that breaks up families, leads to hardship and hunger for children, and ruins otherwise good Christian lives, then I am totally opposed to it."

I sometimes think that most people have a similar attitude toward elections. Elections are viewed as the very basis of a free society– the essential ingredient in the functioning of the democratic institutions by which free people govern themselves. At the same time, elections are often regarded as exercises in political chicanery, masterminded by cigar-chewing men in smoke-filled rooms, mysterious and vaguely disreputable.

Tom Brook, who has organized dozens of political campaigns at the federal, provincial and local level in most parts of Canada, has set out in this book to take the mystery out of the electoral process, drawing on his own library of stories about the turns and twists that campaigns seem to generate.

Brook deals only fleetingly with the broad sweep of nationwide campaigns. His book is written from the perspective of the individual constituency and the individual candidate.

Brook takes us through the election process, commencing with how to become a candidate, going on to how to carry on a campaign– the speeches, the money, the publicity, the crucial role of recruiting volunteers, and more. He then moves on to how to stay elected and, finally, explains when politicians should retire from elected office.

The book is conveniently divided into chapters, each dealing with a specific aspect of a constituency campaign, and covers some special issues, such as the problems faced by women in getting nominated and elected.

The book is a treasure trove of useful information on how to run a constituency election campaign; it is virtually a campaign manager's manual.

Brook's book is laced with anecdotes of the successes and failures of candidates in dozens of elections. Elections are about people attempting to convince other people, and the personal element comes through.

I was reminded of some of my own campaigns. Brook recalls how during Alberta provincial campaigns, NDP leader Grant Notley needed a steady supply of oranges. On my own provincial campaigns, I used to carry a feather pillow with me, so that after an evening rally, when the adrenalin pumped as I tried to sleep in a strange bed, I didn't need to spend the night fighting with a foam rubber pillow.

This book will be of special interest to anyone who has ever taken part in a constituency campaign, or think they might. But its anecdotes about politicians, past and present, and its comments on such topics as polls and polling, "dirty tricks," and the problems of political families, give the book a wider appeal.

Canadians apparently believe that a democratic political system is one of the most precious things any country can have, that Canada has a political system as good as any in the world, that the Canadian electorate is among the most intelligent and best in-formed in the world, and that the people we elect to office by this system are bumbling incompetents.

At a time when it is fashionable to criticize politicians and the political process, it is good for many more people to understand the processes by which we choose our elected representatives.

Getting Elected in Canada is a valuable addition to the tiny library of books which tell us how elections in Canada are carried on.

Added to this, Brook's book is a good read.

— *Allan Blakeney*

1. Taking the Leap: The Stuff of a Good Candidate

"The revelations of politics come
not from example, but from
experience." *Dalton Camp*

It is no secret that the general public is becoming more and more cynical about politicians and their role in society. To some extent, this cynicism is justified. An examination of the issues around candidacy, what is happening to candidates and their handlers, and all the steps that take place in electing our politicians, may not dispel hard feelings that exist today, but it may help us understand our political environment a little better.

During federal, provincial and municipal elections, countless hundreds of people from all walks of life offer themselves to their fellow citizens for close scrutiny and approval. They are judged for who they are, what they say, and who their friends are. Most are rejected. Why do these people do it? What goes into making the decision to be a candidate?

To begin with, prospective candidates have to ask themselves a series of important questions before making the decision to run for office. Without truthful answers to these questions, a budding candidate will be walking into a mine field from which there may be no return. The old saying, "many are called and few are chosen," may have been written with political candidates in mind.

There are two common paths to political candidacy. Some candidates are completely self-motivated. They are attracted by the prospects of political power and excited by the race. They have a singular determination to enter politics and win. Some candidates are persuaded by others to seek political office. One method of entry is as valid as the other, and there have been as many successes as failures among people who have become candidates by either route. The important consideration for candidates is not how they have come to the point of decision, but whether they have the "stuff" that will make a good candidate; and then, whether they can adapt to elected life and all the demands that puts on personal lifestyles and family life.

Let's look at what many feel are the qualities required of a good candidate.

Does the candidate have an inventory of experiences that will tell voters: "here is a person who can represent us well"? Are there examples of personal abilities demonstrated through work in community organizations or leadership in a profession or business? A candidate who has worked hard to bring about a community recreation facility or a stoplight at a critical intersection has demonstrated that he or she can get things done.

No experience is as valuable as having already served in an elected position. Many successful provincial and federal politicians have earned their stripes by service in municipal governments. This is easier in smaller towns and rural municipalities where there is not as much competition for local office as there is in larger urban centres. Regardless, experience on school, library and hospital boards can always round out the political resumés of candidates, and give some issues about which they can speak with authority.

Candidates need to have the ambition and drive to want to do something good for the people they seek to represent, some "fire in the belly." They have to feel that by serving in an elected assembly they can have a positive impact on the course of events. And, most important of all, others need to see that burning desire and feel a need to share it.

The public wants to know that candidates will represent them and stand up on their side. After all, that is what our system of democracy is all about. We have a representative democracy. When people become disillusioned or cynical about politicians, it is largely because the public feels politicians are not representing them well, not doing or saying the kinds of things that voters feel they would do or say in the same circumstances, or because politicians do not seem to be listening to public opinion.

Charisma is an important quality for a prospective candidate. The ability of a candidate to make people believe in his or her vision forms at least an element of charisma. Style, class, and flash are all words used to describe charisma, and, like it or not, some element needs to be there for a candidate to attract workers, money, and votes. As an old American political axiom of "Uncle Joe" Cannon goes, "you can't beat somebody with nobody."

Candidates have to be comfortable in front of crowds. In our age of electronic politics, nobody expects today's campaigners to be a Tommy Douglas or John Diefenbaker style of orator, and fewer judge a politician's ability based on public speaking, but a candidate should not look like an idiot on the podium either. Fortunately, there are many sources of information and training on public speaking, so this asset can be acquired.

Public speaking for a candidate these days means being able to say a few words at a luncheon, making some remarks at a candidates' debate and speaking at party functions. Half hour speeches several times a day are no longer a part of most campaigns; only party leaders are expected to perform flawlessly from the platform all day long.

Having a high level of self-esteem is important for anyone entering politics. Self-esteem gives a candidate that air that seems to border on arrogance, but it also makes it easier to stand in front of crowds, put a reputation on the line or ask complete strangers for votes and money. Self-esteem gives a generalized expectation of success, and, at the same time, also gives candidates the armour they need to deal with failure. A high opinion of one's own self is a definite requirement to bear up under the heat of battle and, if necessary, rationalize a loss.

A little more difficult to handle is the ability to meet people well. Every candidate who hopes to win must get out and meet the people. This means more than going to various events; it also means meeting voters on their turf, door to door. A lot of candidates "don't feel right" asking people for their support in an election. My advice to these candidates is always very simple, "If you can't do it, then who do you think will do it for you?"

Being known or having a high level of name recognition is worth at least 5% of the vote. In a campaign where there are few issues, it can be worth a lot more. Candidates must take time to assess how well they are known. Do they enjoy support from a large cross-section of their community? Have they received favourable press over the years and do the local media know them?

In one constituency where I did some polling, the press had

covered a story about the candidate; students in his class had been given tickets to sell for a raffle sponsored by his party. When confronted with the issue, he tried to pass it off as a minor matter. It probably was, but he took so long to deal with it that it became a local issue. Even though it passed out of public view after a short while, not many people, when polled later, could remember why he had been in the news; those who did, only knew it had had something to do with young kids. Asked if this made them feel more or less inclined to support him in an election, about 5% of those who were inclined towards his party said "no." The end result was that he lost the seat by less than 3%. He should have apologized for the indiscretion immediately to remove the issue from the public's mind, instead of having it linger in the press and become a negative part of the public's perception of his otherwise strong credentials.

You can't say that this alone caused his defeat, but what little name recognition he had established was for negative reasons. A candidate should be known, but it should be for positive reasons.

Politics are played out in a rough and tumble manner. Candidates need to examine their backgrounds. Is there anything in their past that would embarrass them if it were printed on the front page of the local newspaper? No part of a candidate's life escapes scrutiny. The American habit of wanting to know everything about their office seekers has become a part of Canadian politics. Candidates can expect all kinds of stories to be used against them on the doorstep, over the telephone, or along coffee row. Sometimes these matters will be raised by their opponents, but just as often by the media or outside organizations.

As an example, marital status no longer has much impact on a candidate's chance for success, but a criminal record is a negative influence. Often, matters which can be explained easily or have yet to be proven can be just as damaging as a documented incident. Unfortunately, it is the impression left with the voter that is more important than the facts themselves.

An Alberta Conservative candidate was named in a half-million dollar lawsuit, along with two law partners. The suit formed part of a complicated deal involving a development company, and the charges included dishonesty, bad faith, and breach of duty. Subsequent news articles indicated that this was the sixteenth civil action brought against this person in the previous four years. Needless to say, this candidate didn't stand a chance in the ensuing election. Where her party had lost the seat by 700 votes in the previous election, she lost by nearly 4,000 votes and a good deal of the failure can be credited to the negative publicity about the lawsuit.

You can bet that once this case has been dealt with in the courts, and particularly if this person is found innocent of any wrong doing, little space will be taken up in the press to report the final outcome of the story. Elections have the effect of providing a focus for these kinds of things, and it is likely that the story would never have made the papers and news magazines under any other circumstances.

Does the candidate live in the constituency he or she is seeking to represent? At one time, this was an important consideration for a person seeking a nomination, but it is becoming less so, in urban constituencies at least. In rural ridings, the candidate almost always lives in the constituency or has undeniable roots there.

In his first bid for the Norwood seat in Edmonton, Ray Martin, the Alberta NDP Leader, lived outside Edmonton, in the suburb of St. Albert, and lost his bid for a seat. When he tried, a second time, to get elected, he had already moved into the constituency; this made a big difference in his ability to communicate with local voters on issues that directly affect them. Ray could certainly afford to live in a much more exclusive part of the city, but when he decided to upgrade from his Norwood home, he moved two blocks over and one block up.

It takes a special kind of person to be successful in electoral politics; each person seeking office needs to ask if he or she has the right mental and physical stuff to make it over the long haul.

Candidates need a terrific sense of humour. Self-deprecating humour, properly timed, can always earn a lot of admiration from the general public. Politics is serious business, but politicians should never take themselves too seriously. If they do, the low times will seem even lower, and the good times will have a little of the genuine excitement taken from them.

Politicians also have to be tough-minded, even bloody-minded at times. There are times they have to say "no" to what seems like a legitimate request for help, or have to support a position in public that they are uneasy about because of the rules of caucus solidarity. This is harder than it sounds, and many hours of sleep have been lost because of it.

Candidates have to be healthy. They require physical stamina. An average work day can be twelve hours or more under stressful conditions. A candidate must work longer and harder than the hardest working volunteer. Without that personal commitment, candidates can hardly expect volunteers to do the same on their behalf.

Smoking and drinking are coming under increased public criticism. Candidates who smoke should consider quitting for the sake of their image in today's health-conscious world, even if they are not concerned with their own well-being. The days of cigarette-wielding politicians died with René Levesque.

A candidate who drinks should also consider giving that up, at least for the campaign. A close friend of mine who enjoys a drink or two with friends gives alcohol up completely during a campaign. He loses weight, looks great, and is sharp under all conditions. After the campaign is over, all the media interviews are complete, and the thank you cards are put in the mail, however, he makes up for lost time.

There are times when drinking, or at least the culture that surrounds social drinking, can help with a campaign. During the 1977 Ontario election, I complained to Bud Germa, who was the popular MP from Sudbury, that our canvassers were having a lot of difficulty finding people at home during the first warm evenings of spring. After looking over the voters' lists to see in what neighbourhoods we were having this trouble, he declared, "I know where the buggers are." Every evening, after normal canvassing and other campaign activities were over, we consulted the list of bars and taverns we had put on the wall and visited each bar in order. We handed out literature, buttons, had a few drinks and a lot of fun meeting those voters that were not at home during our regular campaign period. Sudbury is a special place and this type of campaigning is not recommended in more sedate communities.

The late Walter Dinsdale, who was MP for Brandon Souris for many years, campaigned in beer parlours in a slightly different

Tom Brook

manner. A Salvationist, he would often lead the band through Brandon beer parlours, passing out Salvation Army literature.

Unless a candidate is seeking a municipal office, there will come a time when the structure of the party becomes a factor. Since the first test of a candidate will be with those who are members of the same party, candidates should ask themselves whether their service to the party has been positive and attractive to party regulars. This usually means certifiable service to the local party constituency association such as having been an election worker, fundraiser or membership recruiter. The more the prospective candidate has engaged in activities that others are loathe to volunteer for, the more likely they will receive the gratitude of the local party leadership, who in turn influence the voting membership.

Bud Germa once explained to me that being a candidate was just one of the jobs a good party supporter performed. In his case, he had put up signs, served as sign chairman, canvassed, and organized in elections before he became a candidate. He served a short while in the House of Commons, was elected municipally and then sat as an MPP. Even as a candidate, whenever the weather would not allow canvassing, Bud could be found silk screening signs or bundling leaflets or boosting morale by regaling the volunteers with political war stories.

These days, more and more parties search out their candidates, and internal party experience is less important to the party brass, but when it comes to a nomination fight, those with long-term local loyalties will certainly have an advantage.

Candidates have to be able to explain why they want to be elected representatives. A candidate who cannot answer in 25 words or less why he wants to run for election, and make it believable, will have a real problem convincing voters and the media that he is a serious candidate. Ted Kennedy's presidential bid was torpedoed by his inability to make a short and concise explanation to Roger Mudd on national TV as to why he was running. The indecision and stumbling killed him and made him appear unprepared and insincere.

A candidate has got to do some arithmetic as part of the decision making process. Can she or he actually win? Winning is never completely out of the question in any democratic contest, and

15

there are countless stories that detail the upset victories of candidates in difficult circumstances, usually when their party sweeps another out of office. Regardless of these dreams, a candidate still has to ponder the numbers well in advance of an actual election and often, well before the events that will shape the final outcome of a campaign have taken place.

If a win does not seem possible, then what other reasons are there to run? A candidate might run to build credibility and experience for the next campaign or for a race at a different level of politics, or simply to raise his or her profile among those who hand out patronage.

The late Henry Tomaschuk, a former labour leader in Alberta, and a great political warrior, once ran on a slogan of "Next Time—Henry Tomaschuk." It was catchy, but it didn't work. The voters didn't support him in that election, nor did he do all that well in the next one. He liked to say he finished just ahead of spoiled ballots.

We often see candidates who run in order to advance a particular idea or because they believe so strongly in the platform of their party that they feel it is important that this agenda is placed before people regardless of their own personal chances for victory. Or, they may be on the ballot at the pleading of the party leader or organizers. True martyrs all. This explains why people will offer themselves in situations which seem nearly hopeless, such as a Conservative in Quebec during Trudeau's days. Every vote gained in these circumstances is one more vote towards forming a solid base that will provide the level of support that will ensure victory when times and attitudes change.

Some people who are a little more cynical about the motives of candidates may feel that those who enter a near-certain losing situation may be trying to advance themselves in terms of future appointments to boards and commissions, or to influence government policy. There is no doubt that some of this goes on, but it is quite a bit of personal punishment to take in exchange for an appointment that may pay very little. Which is not to say that there aren't several political appointments that are very lucrative and pay more than the salary of an elected person, carry as much prestige and don't require re-election.

One piece of arithmetic that seems to escape a lot of candidates is figuring out the pay. Can they afford to be elected? I am often amazed by the fact that during long discussions with me about candidacy, hardly anyone has raised the matter of money. Almost always I have to lay out the pay, allowances, benefits and perks. It is usually the spouse that shows the keenest interest in the financial rewards.

There is a story that is told of former Winnipeg MP, Cyril Keeper. On the evening of his first victory he approached veteran parliamentarian David Orlikow and wondered just what exactly he was going to do for money now that he was elected. He was more than pleasantly surprised to learn that being an MP paid a great deal more than what he was getting at his job at the time.

Generally, provincial legislatures pay elected people relatively well, or at least competitively. A teacher with ten years' seniority will likely suffer little or no loss in pay. Professional people, such as lawyers, will lose some money, but most of them are able to continue some practice, or still make profits from their firms, either as partners or because of their potential to draw additional clients.

Fortunately for us, most who seek provincial public office are bound by a common thread: they are willing to make some sacrifice because they feel they can make a difference.

Municipal politicians are notoriously underpaid in most jurisdictions and should not give up their day jobs on election.

Members of Federal Parliament are the best paid. The perks are generous and legendary. The prestige is great and the responsibilities, particularly those of backbenchers without a lot of committee or legislative assistant activities, are not much of a burden.

Pensions for many elected officials are excellent and some legislative bodies will also include service in other elected houses and the armed services in calculating years of pension eligibility.

Defeated MPs are now able to line up for unemployment insurance and severance benefits. The same is true of more and more provincial houses as well. Adjustment to civilian life after the wars of politics is made that much easier. An MP defeated after one term can live very comfortably for several months while waiting for the right job offer to come along.

Living arrangements should be considered: the politician who lives in or near the seat of government will have no problem, but, if a candidate lives more than a commute away, then decisions about having another residence or moving from the present home need to be made. When the decision to run comes to the family for consideration, this question will have to be met head on.

The catch-22 for a winner can be that one of the contributing factors in his or her success may be local popularity. That popularity can suffer if the politician moves away lock, stock and barrel. It's a complicated problem. Unless matters of residency and living conditions are considered when making a decision to be a candidate, they will become a source of uncertainty and stress in the future.

A candidate needs to take all these personal assessments and answers to the important questions, along with some determination of the strengths and weaknesses of the main opponents, and begin to make a decision.

An organizer's rule of thumb is that people lose 40% of their common-sense when they run for a nomination, 60% more if nominated, and another 50% if elected! In my experience, anyone who begins contemplating a candidacy begins to lose objectivity almost immediately, well before a final decision is made. The advice of others is important.

Who should a candidate turn to? Close friends are liable to say only what they think a candidate wants to hear. Political activists will couch their comments in ways to protect the position of other possible candidates or to advance or protect their own political interests. Business associates are likely to consider the whole notion bizarre. Those who are true friends and have the candidate's best interests at heart will be bloody-minded enough to give honest answers to the basic questions.

When candidates ask friends and associates the question, "Should I run?", they also need to add the second question of all those who give a positive response which is, "Will you help me?". The second answer should help restore a bit of real world consideration to the final decision.

Regardless of the level of office a candidate seeks, the whole process of deciding whether or not to enter the political arena for the first time is an excruciating one. On one hand, a candidate has abstract and ideological desires to serve in public office; has a deep commitment to issues; knows the need for effective community leadership; feels strong loyalty to a party, if he or she is seeking a partisan office; and knows the weaknesses of the opposing politicians and has the certain knowledge the opponents can be bested.

On the other hand, there are serious drawbacks. Candidates need to have a strong sense of their self-worth, tempered with the humility to ask others for time, money and ideas. There is the risk of having a good name and reputation dragged through the political mud. Time with family and other personal pursuits will have to be sacrificed and promising personal careers can be thrown into jeopardy. And if all this is not enough, there is no certainty of winning.

A candidate's family needs to be involved in the decision to run. A candidate needs the support of the immediate family. Nobody expects, or should expect, a family to drop everything to work in politics, but candidates need to know that those who are the closest to them understand what is happening, and the impact it will have on their lives.

There are four basic types of political families or spouses.

There are those who could be called participatory. They take on the job and challenge of politics with as much relish and commitment as the candidate, sometimes more. There are other families which help as much as possible. They approve of the candidacy and take on extra family duties to make the job easier for the candidate. Other families simply approve of the entry into politics, provide money and advice if requested, but offer no direct involvement. At the other end of the spectrum there are spouses or family members who are jealous of all the attention paid to the candidate and fear the prospect of the family growing apart; they may be angry because of increased public scrutiny of their private lives.

Families can become great political casualties if they do not feel they have a say in what is happening. They actually bear more of the 'slings and arrows' of campaigns than do the candidates. The candidate, win or lose, will have a group of campaign workers and candidates from the same party to provide praise and adulation or aid and comfort as the case may be.

For a candidate's spouse, who carries on normal daily activities in the workplace or among family and neighbours there is no such support group. Children must face school friends and peers who do not understand politics and whose parents do not share the same views. In short, a candidate's family travels in different circles, yet have to deal with people who follow current affairs and will know if he or she has put a foot in it or made some stupid mistake.

For instance, pity the family of the Texas politician who released his ten-point plan for education and was told later by the press that it actually had only nine items. The candidate's family didn't have a press officer or campaign manager to explain the slip-up, or deflect an attack from an opponent, but they were held just as accountable.

There are a lot of different situations in which the family may find itself. Often a decision is made to run when children are not old enough to offer an opinion but later suffer from the loss of a political parent. Ed Tchorzewski, a popular Saskatchewan MLA, tells me that his family is involved in every decision he makes. They were consulted at length when he was considering running for his party's provincial leadership, and they take an active role in making the decision for re-election bids. But, he adds, this is a new phenomenon; it wasn't until he lost an election, after 11 years as an MLA, that he discovered he did not really know his family and was not a part of it during his intense involvement in politics. Re-elected in a by-election in 1985, he is no less a powerful force in provincial politics, and has an enviable family life as well.

What about the candidate's job? Politicians are often criticized because they tend to over-represent certain professional and business occupations. In many cases, this is simply because they are their own bosses or have to deal only with some partners who are essentially equals. In these situations, lawyers or small business operators create time for campaigning at their own peril, but with little risk to a career or future employment prospects.

Employees are expected to keep regular work hours unless they enjoy the favour of an understanding supervisor or the protection of a progressive union contract. They will find time to secure a nomination and particularly the amount of time required to mount a viable candidacy during an election a hard thing to come by without taking vacation leave or using up other accumulated leave benefits.

As a minimum requirement, candidates also need to know that there is a job to return to after a campaign if they are unsuccessful. Many teachers are able to receive unpaid leave to serve as an elected official and then return when they retire from politics or are defeated. Many elected people retain some outside job to augment their legislative pay if they are not serving in a cabinet or on a variety of committees that offer extra remuneration. Farmers sometimes continue to farm, teachers may take on spare duties, for example.

Candidates cannot expect to be successful if they do not have the ability to devote all their time to the campaign itself. Campaign periods are becoming shorter in length, and any candidate who cannot give every bit of energy to a campaign has a serious handicap.

Manitoba NDP leader, Garry Doer, expresses the situation well when he says the reason there are so many lawyers and professionals in politics, rather than real people, is because those with real jobs have little prospect of getting time off to campaign, and have little chance of being re-hired if they leave for a political race.

Before deciding whether or not to run, candidates have to be mindful of conflict of interest. Will previous or present business and professional contacts take on a new meaning when one is sitting in a provincial legislature or the House of Commons? Will there be people expecting favours? Candidates should take time to examine those relationships, and make sure there is nothing that will compromise their positions or credibility as public officials.

Women have a much more difficult time being candidates than men. This comes as no real revelation. Columnist Allan Fotheringham has correctly noted that Canadian politics operates largely as if women were invisible, although they are actually in the majority. In each election, more and more women are elected, but there are still not enough women elected to satisfy a sense of balance in our legislatures.

What are the major barriers facing women who want to enter politics today? One of the most difficult handicaps to overcome is the attitude of the parties. Women are often used to fill the slate; they are put into unwinnable constituencies, while the party uses their numbers as statistical proof of a liberated point of view towards women's issues.

The peculiar thing is that if you walk into the campaign offices of any party anywhere in the country, the key campaign positions, from manager to the most enthusiastic volunteer, will most likely be filled by women. In my experience, there are far more capable women campaigners than men.

One key to determining whether a woman's candidacy can be viable is to consider the level of success women have had in holding elected positions at various levels of government, such as school board, hospital board or municipal council in the same area. This helps to indicate the general degree of public acceptance in the community towards women's involvement in politics and public affairs.

Money is another serious factor affecting prospective women candidates. Contributions for early campaign activities such as organizing to win a nomination, or even for the election campaign itself are harder to come by for women. To fight this, women are forming their own support networks within the traditional structures of the parties to build campaign war chests specifically for women candidates.

In most families, women are the main care givers. This responsibility alone makes a candidacy very difficult. Generally, women who seek office will have no children, or their children will be grown and able to take care of themselves. Those with young families need an especially understanding and capable spouse.

The other major obstacle faced by women in politics today is the general expectation established for them in the public's mind.

A woman needs to know twice as much as a man. Women can expect to be asked tough policy questions that men rarely face. For some reason, we seem to need a woman to prove her abilities in ways that we never expect from a man.

Honesty and integrity are important qualities that most people would say they expect from a political candidate. These qualities are fairly easy to describe when it comes to men, but who defines the criteria for women? Do we demand a different level of character from a public woman? I suspect we do.

The old saying, that in order to be successful in business, a woman has to act like a man, look like a woman, and work like a dog, is equally true about women's participation in electoral politics.

A more positive outlook was expressed by Charlotte Whitton, former mayor of Ottawa: "Whatever women do, they must do twice as well as men to be thought half as good... Luckily, it's not difficult."

When overall credibility is concerned, there is no question that women have to work harder to get it and in some cases, have to demand it. Men seem to have instant credibility in politics. Women have to prove themselves.

Some might say that the level of participation from women in politics may be a result of a lot of capable women saying, "who needs it?". Women might simply feel that they can have as much or more impact on their local community working in less stressful and equally rewarding ways. Working with local environmental, educational and other community-based organizations can bring about real change without major disruptions to personal life.

Thank goodness, the women who have made it intend to stay there and help other women join them. Women like Dawn Black of the NDP, Sheila Copps of the Liberals, or Barbara McDougall of the Conservatives, and countless other public women, are always urging other women to join them. They are willing to help and offer advice in a way that men in similar circumstances would rarely consider.

An important consideration for any woman considering the political arena is that, if elected, they can expect to be 'fast tracked' to the head of the class. Those willing to accept the added responsibility will be offered high profile positions by a party that wants to blunt its male dominated image.

There are a host of other factors affecting women in the public domain and there is a chapter devoted to that later in this book. Our job here is to point out that a woman trying to decide on a political career has as much and more to consider than her male counterpart.

These are the main factors that face men and women in making up their minds to seek elected office. Each aspect has to be considered carefully, and then the total package needs to be assessed realistically. For men or women running for elected office there are a series of choices— deciding to run, gathering a campaign team and the finances necessary, choosing the issues to emphasize and those to ignore, developing an image, and, finally, implementing those choices. There is no certainty that any one choice is the right one, and this uncertainty is compounded by the chorus of bystanders who will second-guess every decision.

We must understand that those who are willing to take up the challenge are answering a higher calling, and every candidate for elected office takes risks. A candidate's name and reputation is on the line; a candidate is open to abuse from the opposition; large sums of money are involved; and defeat is very public. There are always a lot of reasons not to run and certainly that is the safest decision, but as I have told people considering whether to run or not, if they honestly feel that by being a candidate and serving the public they can make a difference for themselves and their community, then they have no choice but to run.

I had the opportunity to play a round of golf with B.C NDP Leader Mike Harcourt, right after helping him in his unsuccessful bid for the Little Mountain provincial seat in 1979. We talked a lot about his future and about seeking the Vancouver Mayor's chair. I told him that if Vancouver could be a better place if he was mayor then he should run. When he did, and won, I couldn't have been happier.

2. The Nomination

"Modesty in the face of ability
is hypocrisy." *Robert Crown, California Legislature*

"Tonight is the real election; election day will only be the coronation," trumpeted a proud PC supporter, at the nomination meeting to select a Conservative candidate for the Beaver River federal by-election that was held in March, 1989.

Not everyone was as certain about the outcome as this loyal partisan. The Tories got whipped by Deborah Grey and the upstart Reform Party.

One of the most misunderstood steps in Canadian politics is the process of nominating candidates to represent the different parties. If we had more understanding of what happens on the road to nomination, we might have a better grasp of the nature of politicians and what motivates them.

It is the nomination process that shapes the future for candidates. Their experiences seeking local endorsement can play a huge role in shaping their public and private political posture. A tough nomination race can turn a novice into a seasoned veteran overnight. Many candidates will not receive as rough a ride from their opponents of the other parties as they will get from their friends in the same party. Every action past, present, and presumed-in-the-future comes under close scrutiny and is the subject of rumour and innuendo. Personal, business, and social life are all fair game.

Even candidates who receive their nominations by acclamation must act as though they were in a multi-candidate field, by actively soliciting the approval of each local party member. For the candidate, the certain knowledge that he or she has earned the party's support can make life on the campaign trail a little easier.

Most people would be hard-pressed to tell you who won a nomination for any party without an election to help focus attention on the personalities. Generally, only political operatives and activists follow nominations closely. But really, we should all pay attention when the parties are selecting their candidates. Knowing a bit more about the personal credentials of the candidates and something about their personal beliefs before these have been clouded by the imposition of party platforms can lead to a more informed vote on election day, one that isn't obscured by the barrage of advertising or the leaders' images.

All political parties welcome nomination meetings. They help to renew and revive the membership and provide unpaid political exposure and activity at the local level.

It's a different story in ridings where there are popular incumbents. The parties don't want to take any chances in constituencies they already hold by introducing unknown commodities. Of course, there are times when a member has been a bit of a maverick or has embarrassed the leader and party by things that the member may have said or done, and the party hierarchy might actively seek a substitute, a display of roadside justice on the way to an election. In most cases, however, this is backroom bluster that most campaign insiders are quite good at, and when it comes time to fish or cut bait, most incumbents face little or no challenge, no matter how embarrassing they may have been to their parties or constituents.

Another instance where the party may try to interfere with the local selection process comes when the expected nominee has lost the riding before, sometimes on many tries. This often happens in a constituency that the party may feel is rightfully theirs, but which has slipped from their grasp for want of the proper person on the ballot. The notion of "letting old Joe have one more crack at it" doesn't find much sympathy among central party planners bent on maintaining or gaining power.

The game from the point of view of the political parties is to show strength and create the feeling of momentum through the nomination meeting. It's in the selection of a candidate that the parties try to convey a sense of enthusiasm and renewal by showcasing new candidates in a large display of community support at a nomination meeting that overflows the local school gymnasium or hotel ballroom.

There are few ready recruits to political life. Not many of those people who have all of the best characteristics of an ideal candidate fit into the category of "having always wanted to run." That is one of the reasons why the political parties have more than just a passing interest in the local candidate selection process.

Lists of potential candidates are maintained by the party leadership and are usually prepared immediately after an election and updated at regular intervals. Whenever an opportunity comes available to discuss a candidacy with these people, the political or administrative party leadership continues to work them over, never really taking "no" for an answer, always leaving the target a chance to think it over.

In one form or another, each of the parties has a candidate search committee that tries to encourage people who, they feel, are appropriate for candidacy. Notwithstanding the personal decision-making process described in the previous chapter, some candidates for nomination are a little more blessed than others. It is not uncommon for party brass to offer special hints, lists of possible campaign workers and other kinds of endorsements to help promote the candidacy of a particular person over another. They can even find a little money to help out or direct the candidate to someone who can find it for them.

No matter what qualities an individual candidate for a nomination may feel are important, the parties are looking for particular things when they seek out a candidate. This list varies little, regardless of the party. No party is really any different from any other when seeking a candidate, only the emphasis might be different. For instance, one party in a given riding may want to emphasize youth because the incumbent is old, while another may want a woman because there are a lot of young families in the area and family issues like child care and education are important to that party. They may also have differing ideas as to what an ideal occupation for a candidate might be, or what elements lead to a strong standing in the community. From the point of view of the political parties, the candidate is simply part of the overall strategy.

They want a person who fits the general profile of the constituency. The candidate should be a member of a dominant ethnic group, if one exists in the riding, and should meet the general profile of the local demographics, attitudes and values.

Parties will examine the attributes of people who have been

successful in the riding to see if the employment record and community involvement of the prospective candidate fits a pattern which has been acceptable in the past. As a general rule, most parties will welcome a professional or high profile business person with the view that these people command automatic respect and recognition in the community.

Parties will not knock down the doors of previous losers. There are always circumstances under which defeated candidates can and should run again, but generally, one defeat is enough for the parties, if not for the electorate. This doesn't preclude some of the more fascinating election races that have been seen in some Ottawa and Toronto federal ridings, where there are PC and Liberal politicians who have served two or three terms, but never in a row.

Those who make a party's short list will likely have strong family roots in the riding and, just as important, will have a spouse with equally deep roots and high standing. Children with strong athletic and scholastic records are a bonus in the eyes of party insiders.

Prospective candidates' credibility is greatly enhanced if they have the right friends. Current or former MLAs or MPs in your corner are a great help. The support of party regulars who are known to be in favour with the party leadership will also boost the stock of the candidate.

Most party organizers would never admit it, but if the candidate has a lot of money, he or she gains in attractiveness. No one expects a candidate to pay for the whole campaign, but one with money can make a generous contribution and there is less concern about having to raise additional funds to pay for lost wages or extra living expenses. A lot of voters think a person with money must know something, and, by some curious deduction, feel that such a person will do a good job of running a government. Maybe the public just thinks that people who are well off are less likely to help themselves to the public purse.

Finally, every party expects some compatibility between a candidate's personal view of the world and the public policy of the party. A "loose cannon" is not only difficult to control but a plain embarrassment. A candidate who has only one issue in his or her arsenal will not be a credit to the party, particularly if it is an issue that is not high on the public agenda. All parties allow a difference of opinion on matters of personal conscience such as abortion, but some, notably the NDP, expect candidates to state the party position as well as presenting their own.

Parties don't always meet their stated objectives when seeking candidates. A story is told of Manitoba NDP Leader Ed Schreyer looking for a candidate for the Winnipeg riding of Radisson that had a large number of workers from the nearby meatpacking plants. It is said that he was looking for a meatcutter who looked like a teacher, but instead, recruited Harry Shafransky, who was a teacher who looked like a meatcutter.

Candidates who face a contested nomination must work very hard. They need an extensive organization that is almost identical to those put together for election campaigns. There will be a manager, people canvassing the party membership for support, fundraisers, and publicity people.

It is the candidate's job to contact all the members and convince them that they should support his or her candidacy, and convince them that it is important to attend the nomination meeting.

Only those who are party members are eligible to vote at a nomination meeting. Every party has different rules about the selling of memberships. There are usually different deadlines for submitting applications for new membership in the party or for reporting the renewal of an existing membership.

Some of the most fierce and dirty political battles take place in nomination wars. There are some obvious reasons for this. Usually the combatants and their workers are well known to each other. Every strength and every wart is plain to all. As often as not, a nomination race will form part of a continuing battle between camps that may be raging over policy or leadership.

Since campaigning at this level is almost completely through personal contact on the telephone or at the doorstep, campaigners can say almost anything they want about their opponent's frailties without a public record of what they have said. If campaigners are ever confronted over a misrepresentation they may have made, they can simply say they were not understood properly or what they really said was something else. And if all else fails, they can simply fall back on the old stand-by... deny, deny.

This fighting usually takes place outside public view. Even when divisions are exposed, candidates often close ranks and put on an act of complete harmony to protect the party's public image.

There are no limits to dirty politics in a nomination contest, and no party is immune from it, because the stakes in a constituency where a particular party's nominee has the best chance of being elected are very high. It is probably in this darker aspect of nomination meetings where the Canadian political system comes closest to emulating those things in the American system that people like the least.

The most effective attacks against candidates that I have seen have taken the form of doubting a person's commitment to important policy initiatives of the party, or pointing to a poor record of involvement in the local organization. Sometimes the opponent is accused of sympathy and previous association with an opposing party. A candidate who presents false credentials and personal history can expect to be the target of vigorous attack as well. The background and reputations of key campaign personnel are just as vulnerable to this kind of attack as those of the candidate.

Raising issues on sexual, racial, or religious grounds backfires more often than not; while they are dramatic and can fuel a lot of gossip, the widespread use of these tactics almost always provides little or no advantage to the user, and can elicit sympathy and support for the accused.

The most common negative tactics used in nomination campaigns relate to the rules about and sale of memberships.

A candidate for a nomination who has control of the local executive can create a playing field that tilts to his or her personal advantage. There have been nomination meetings scheduled for 8:00 a.m., or dates established with only minimum notice to head off a challenge.

Since only party members are eligible to vote at a nomination, campaigners working on behalf of a candidate will do anything possible to get people to a meeting. They will buy memberships for people who know little about what they are doing or why, and they will do whatever they can to discourage and challenge the validity of their opponents' supporters.

Typically, there will be a deadline by which all new memberships are to be submitted in order for the members to be eligible to vote at the meeting. Most candidates will keep secret their new membership sales until the very last minute, in order to keep their strength hidden and minimize the chances that their pesky opponents might be able to talk the new people out of supporting the person they are committed to vote for.

Campaigning for a political nomination is not solely a negative or sinister activity, however. Much is expected of those who offer themselves, and they have to prove a lot, often with few resources.

Candidates for a nomination are expected to show that they can attract public attention, but they are not allowed to show too much flash. Party members do not want candidates who offend their sensibilities. They need to feel comfortable that candidates will show appropriate restraint and maintain a professional air about themselves and their campaigns. Party members want to feel proud of their candidate and want people to think more of them because they are supporters of this candidate.

A tough bill to fill.

When candidates have made the decision to run for office, they have to pay careful attention to their appearance. The candidate has to dress and act no better and no worse than the local banker or school principal. If the candidate is too much out of the character party supporters have established, it is difficult to maintain their support.

One lawyer and provincial representative had a Bentley, and drove it all the time. This offended many socialist sensibilities, even though he could afford it and liked it a lot. This led to the continued feeling that he was just a bit different. When his much publicized fall from grace occurred over alleged improprieties in his law practice, no one in local NDP circles was surprised.

The other area where candidates for a nomination can be a little too cute for their audience is in their promotional material. Party regulars want some substance from their candidates and expect thoughtful literature as opposed to the pap that is usually distributed during an election. While no one expects leaflets to be run off on a Gestetner any more, people are likely to be a little suspicious of the candidate whose propaganda is printed on glossy paper with expensive multi-colour separations.

What kinds of things are expected of the candidate who wants to be nominated? The activities of a candidate for nomination are much less a matter of public record than those of someone who is an actual election candidate. Local news outlets will rarely offer any glimpse into their activities, and only on occasion do they bother offering any reportage outside of the actual nominating convention itself. Therefore, the ways a candidate gets to be known among party members is much more akin to a real grassroots campaign. In fact, many candidates spend more time among the people of their ridings during the nomination process than during the rest of their political careers.

Candidates with positions in organizations or other elected bodies can always use these to get a little extra public attention. Even though the issues will rarely have anything in common with the nomination race, party members take notice of a candidate's ability to get good press.

Since it is the candidate, more than ideas, that is sold in this process, the best tactic available is for the candidate to canvass every member in person, to seek their support, if at all possible.

This canvassing may be the follow up from a phone call or visit by a worker who determines that a prospective voter might be leaning their way, or are undecided; a visit might bring them over. The candidate will also visit those who are committed supporters with a mind to turning them into workers or contributors. In a large riding, this is the best use of a candidate's available campaign time.

Some ridings may have a small nomination electorate and the process requires little money or energy. One nomination meeting I was asked to chair in West End Edmonton in 1981 showed that, sometimes, only a little work is necessary as long as it is the right work. Eight of us gathered in a classroom at the Grant McEwen Community College Campus. There were five registered delegates, including the candidates, an observer, a reporter from the Edmonton *Journal* and myself. The vote was 3-2, and, to my relief, the reporter, if not a sympathizer, certainly was in a charitable frame of mind as he made no mention of the 'crowd' at all in his article.

The NDP now holds this seat, winning it for the first time in 1989 with a different candidate.

Doug Roche, the former Conservative MP from Edmonton

Strathcona, in his book, *The Human Side of Politics*, describes how he built an organization on a small nucleus of believers. Each event like a coffee party was used as the base to build for the next by recruiting more and more willing workers and signing up members so they would be eligible to vote at the nominating convention. He went on to beat Terry Nugent for the nomination on the first ballot. Nugent had been beaten by Liberal Hu Harries in the previous election, but had been a ten year veteran of the House of Commons before that.

Besides personal visits and small events, candidates for a nomination actively work to sign up new members to support them for the nomination. Stories are told everywhere and in all parties of nominations that have been "bought" by recruiting members only for their vote and paying their membership fee. These stories include collecting people who have no certain idea of where they are going or for what particular purpose, out of hostels and homes for seniors. Certainly this happens from time to time, but these are exceptions which make good news but distort the true nature of nomination activity.

Nominations are numbers games, no more and no less.

Candidates with a lot of self-confidence will canvass every door in a neighbourhood where their party receives a lot of support. The numbers are with them and the numbers will indicate that they will receive more positive response than rejection. When they come across party supporters, they can engage them in conversation on issues which they both feel strongly about, and finally, the candidate can try to close the deal by selling a membership, as a way of making the voter stand up for what he or she believes in. This kind of "prospect calling" can also end up helping the candidate in the long run if the nomination is won.

As mentioned earlier, every campaign organization will do what it can to sell new memberships, because these are the kinds of supporters that can be hidden from opponents until the last possible moment. Friends, neighbours and business associates of the candidate and campaign workers are a favourite source of new supporters. Generally, a riding association will make available to nomination candidates their lists of previous supporters and households where lawn signs have been placed in the past. The notion is that these households are prospects for membership, and the candidates for nomination thus become organizational volunteers for the party by involving people who might not be exposed to these things under normal circumstances, in party activities, ideas and membership.

Not that supporters can't come from surprising sources. Imagine the amazement of the Tory candidate in St. Albert, north of Edmonton, when he saw a number of prominent trade unionists and known NDP activists in the crowd to support him for his nomination. These New Democrats had taken it upon themselves to infiltrate the meeting and stack it for this candidate. He won the nomination, but lost the election to New Democrat Brian Strong. This PC candidate was seen as the most vulnerable of the possible nominees, and he won, but for all the wrong reasons!

One of the great causes for the defeat of a promising candidacy is the failure, during the nomination process, to come to grips with the nature of the audience.

As long as the majority of those who will be eligible to vote are partisans of the party, and are not bogus members, the message of the candidate has to be tailored to their sensibilities. This means that they will be more attracted to sharp, rhetorical attacks against political opponents and the forces that stand in the way of the full realization of their party's fondest dreams.

During an election, shrill attacks against an opponent are only useful when a case has already been built to establish that opposing candidate as the main alternative. In a nomination contest, everyone has already decided which party they will support. So the more the candidates can flail away at the hated opponents, the stronger their appeal is to the party faithful.

Voters at a nominating convention are not looking for new policy initiatives, they are looking for winners. They may tend to agree or disagree with a particular candidate's priorization of issues but rarely disagree with the issues chosen by the candidates because they all come from the same party.

Candidates have to convince the voters at the nomination meeting that they understand the history and significant personalities of the party they choose to represent and are worthy to follow in whatever tradition exists. The electorate places little importance on these matters, but a person seeking a nomination ignores the party's history at his or her peril. Conservatives seeking a nomination on the Prairies will want to have a John Diefenbaker story or two at the ready when talking to older Conservatives, but during an election, few people will be interested in the past other than some who are already committed Tories.

Women who seek a nomination face the same problems they do in a general election. Men expect women to be more knowledgable about issues than male candidates, and women voters may feel threatened by a woman who knows too much or seems overly ambitious or a bit too clever.

Louise Simard, a Regina MLA, says that when dealing with women during a campaign she tends to be reassuring, and to show sympathy and concern for issues that directly affect women and their families. It is a highly personal way of campaigning, but the woman who does it successfully can count on strong support from other women in a nomination.

The most important thing a woman has to convince potential nomination supporters of is that she is electable. This, of course, is the quality that everyone is looking for when deciding on someone to support for a nomination, but for women it is a particular problem. The smart woman strategist will try to attract as many prominent community and party endorsements as she can, to create the overall image that she can win an election.

In most regions of Canada, gender will not be an issue in a nomination race unless someone wants to make it one; but a woman should be prepared to deal with it head on should it become a point of debate.

Many candidates work months and even years toward the one night when they must stand and be judged: are they worthy of wearing their party's mantle in the next election? The campaign within a campaign comes to an end with this vote; the nomination meeting will seal their fate, for a while at least.

One of the most common mistakes that will nip a budding political career before it comes to full flower is forgetting to get supporters out to the nomination meeting. Weeks of hard work by the candidate and volunteers end up wasted on the evening of a nomination vote because the team assumes everyone will come out to the meeting; after all, they said they would. Taking your support for granted is fatal.

Every party and all candidates do whatever they can on election day to get their known supporters out to vote, but the principle that support is only good in the ballot box escapes many candidates when it comes to winning a nomination.

It is not uncommon for the turnout for a nomination meeting to be quite a bit lower than it is for a general election. Participation rates among the faithful at nomination meetings are often as low as 60% or less in areas where the voter turnout at election time can be 80%.

For many of us, going to a political meeting that might last three, four or more hours has as much appeal as washing the cat. Therefore, candidates running for a nomination have to work extra hard to convince their supporters of how important their participation and vote is to the success of the candidate. Then they have to be phoned and visited at the last minute to ensure they are going to the meeting. Even then, special arrangements like child care and transportation might have to be organized to get every possible vote.

Sometimes not quite that much work is necessary. A story is told in Manitoba about how former cabinet minister and mercurial politician from Winnipeg, Sid Green, was nominated for the first time.

Sid went after the nomination in the Inkster Constituency against Steelworker Howard Mitchell. Sid lost by a vote of 61 to 3. Mitchell stepped down from the nomination for personal reasons, and, rather than holding a second nomination, Len Stevens, who was a power in the United Steelworkers and in the constituency, handed the nomination to the runner-up, who had only three votes. It was clearly the appropriate decision, as Green mounted huge majorities during his political career and represented Inkster well until he left the NDP.

Nomination meetings are a real circus. They are really leadership conventions for the common man. Where a leadership convention for a party is restricted to two or three thousand delegates from across the country or a province, a local nominating convention can involve even more people, with all the excitement and drama of ballot after ballot, but without the big hotel and bar bills.

The Conservatives and Liberals in particular tend to hold rambunctious meetings, complete with banners, posters and live entertainment. New Democrats are coming along, but still tend to have the precious knack of being able to turn a fancy ballroom into a church basement.

When nominations go into second and third ballots, the same intense lobbying for support and endorsement from losing candidates occurs that we witnessed on national television at the leadership conventions that chose Jean Chrétien, Brian Mulroney or Audrey McLaughlin.

When I lived in the remote northern Manitoba community of Norway House, I attended the nominating convention for the Churchill Federal NDP in Thompson for the 1972 general election. My friend Steve Galan from Norway House, and I, supported a school teacher from Cranberry Portage in the four-way race. Our candidate came in third on the first ballot with about 17 votes.

Rod Murphy, who is now the MP for Churchill, came to us after the first ballot and asked us to get all our supporters to vote for Don Duff, a United Church minister who was the candidate for the Thompson establishment. The top two candidates were very close to each other and a long way ahead of us. Our candidate decided he would withdraw without remaining on the second ballot, as he was entitled to do. Steve and I got up and walked through the hall and met at the back of the room.

"Well," he asked, "did you tell our people to go with Duff on this ballot?"

"I don't know who the hell they are, do you?" was my reply. He didn't either. Ironically, Murphy's candidate got 17 more votes on the next ballot to win the nomination and Steve and I were heroes with the Thompson bunch.

The agenda for a nomination is pretty much the same for any party. Here is a typical one:

7:30   Call to Order
7:32   Ratification of Committees
       Balloting, Credentials
7:35   Introduction of Special Guests

7:37   Explanation of Balloting Procedures
       Balloting Chairman
7:45   Credentials Committee Report
7:50   Nominations and Candidates' Speeches
       – 5 minutes for nominator(s)
       – 10 minutes for each candidate
       – 5 minutes for demonstrations for each
         candidate
9:00   First Ballot
9:15   Introduction of Guest Speaker
       Guest Speaker
9:45   Financial Appeal
10:00 Announcement of First Ballot Results
       Further Ballots as Required
10:30 Acceptance Speech
       Adjournment

Depending on local tradition, candidates may be required to have one nominator, and sometimes two or more. Often, a candidate will try to show his or her general appeal by having several people representing various ages, sexes, occupational backgrounds and ethnicity say a few commendatory words about them. Usually, this approach backfires; you can almost always count on one of the nominators going on too long or saying something regrettable. There is just too much room for error.

Candidates need to know in advance what their nominators are going to say about them to avoid serious embarrassment. It is certainly not uncommon to hear a friend of a candidate recount personal history that is not true or relate uncertain stories about the candidate's past that would have been best left unsaid.

Former Edmonton MP Doug Roche has said that speeches are not important at nominations; supporters are. People who attend a nomination meeting have generally already made up their minds as to who they intend to support. An undecided factor of even 10% would be high for most nominating conventions. Eligible members who haven't made up their minds about their votes usually don't bother to show up.

While that is true, the other maxim that a speech might not win you a nomination, but it sure as hell can lose you one, also holds a great deal of validity. If a candidate's performance on the dias is below expectations, if the candidate slips or falters in delivery, or touches on issues that offend a lot of listeners, that candidate can lose critical votes at a nomination.

It can also hurt if a candidate fails to live up to expectations with a speech. People may be expecting a "barn burner," and then be put to sleep instead by a front runner who wants to play safe. On the other hand, a candidate who does much better than expected can raise his or her stock in the eyes of the delegates.

Although it was not a nomination meeting, the leaders' debate during the 1988 federal election is a good example of the dynamics of public expectation. Most did not have expect John Turner to have the spirit and fight he displayed, particularly since his campaign had been reeling from stories of inside intrigue and attempts to dump him during the early stages of the campaign.

On the other hand, Ed Broadbent performed below most people's expectations. His answers were thoughtful and well presented, but, in part as a result of the kinds of questions he was asked, he failed to inspire in the way that had come to be expected of him.

Although most people attending the meeting will be committed for the first ballot, they may be less certain who they will support in subsequent ballots, if there is no winner on the first one. This makes the speech critical to the growth potential of the candidate.

Every candidate hopes she or he will get a chance to make a second speech later in the evening to accept the nomination once it has been secured. This speech also requires some special thought and preparation.

If the campaign has been hard-fought and possibly bitter, the winner will want to provide a vehicle for healing between candidates and their workers.

Healing begins with compassion. The winner needs to acknowledge the abilities and experience of those who fought and lost and invite the workers of the other factions to take an active role in the campaign to come, maybe even reserving a key post or two on the campaign committee for these other workers.

There is a lot at stake. No candidate can afford to alienate potential workers, campaign funds or votes by continuing the skirmishes after the battle is over. And yet many do. It is often reported that riding associations are irreconcilably split after a nomination. This often affects a potential candidate's image in the community and certainly lifts the spirits of opponents.

Today, nominations are far more open than in the past, when placing candidates was often the responsibility of the leader, and plum ridings were passed out to favourites. More people, representing more points of view and divergent backgrounds, are seeking to enter politics than ever before. This cannot help but be a good sign for the health of our system of democracy and will breathe fresh air into parties that can become too stale, too easily.

Yet, the potential for renewal in personalities and ideas at every level of Canadian politics is still subject to the dangers of public apathy. The percentage of eligible voters who take a direct interest and involvement in internal party activities is dropping every year. This should be a danger signal to party leaderships to examine their methods of operation and implement strategies that will make larger numbers of people feel welcome in taking a larger role in political affairs. Nomination meetings are one way to do this.

The key to attracting more public participation in grassroots political activity is the nomination of men and women who reflect the attitudes and ideas of the local community and do not represent the group-think of their party's leadership. The local candidate, once elected, is the person who will represent the voters in parliament or the legislature. Too often today, these people are expected to be a representative in reverse. They are expected to represent their party to the electorate, apologizing and explaining policy and issues rather than raising them on behalf of their constituents.

Finally, there is a growing cynicism among members of the general public about the motives of politicians. Public opinion continues to rate politicians very low on the scale of honesty and integrity. Until this trend is changed through better selection of candidates, and then MPs and MLAs whose performance in office can remove this feeling, the idea of being directly involved in the political process, by participating in a nomination meeting or being a candidate, will remain alien to most Canadians.

3. The Pre-Election Period

"The candidate is the party's
standard-bearer, cherished and
adulated by his supporters, a
worrisome threat to his opponents."
Safire's Political Dictionary

"He who snoozes, loses." That's an old saying in drag racing, and it certainly applies as well to political races. Candidates cannot get started with planning their campaigns soon enough.

The political parties, ever full of imagination when it comes to turning a clever phrase, call the period of time before the call of an election "the pre-election period." Many elections are won or lost long before an election is ever called. It is during this time that candidates and parties position themselves on the important issues and have the opportunity to become known by the voters without the pressure of election deadlines.

Opposition parties should always be in pre-election mode. They don't have the luxury of sitting idly by while their opponents in government strengthen their position. The governing party has the benefit of some warning before the issue of an election writ, and can pace its political preparations. Challengers have to assume that an election call will come at any time. As a result, they must always be in some stage of election readiness.

Any incumbent politician should begin working towards the next election the day after the last one. With offices, staff and money to prepare and distribute propaganda provided by tax dollars, the sitting member is always doing work that will help improve his or her chances of re-election. These funds are provided for the purpose of servicing the needs of constituents, but they do double duty by making the incumbent appear accessible, as well as enhancing future electability by building a positive local profile, all at taxpayers' expense.

For the newly nominated candidate, not yet elected to office, the job ahead is formidable. Once the excitement of the nomina-

41

tion has died away, the candidate faces two critical tasks before the election is called: the candidate has to become known to the voters and, the tactics and strategies for victory in the campaign have to be prepared. It is at this time that the candidate can feel quite alone.

People who were hard workers in the drive for the nomination will want to attend to chores and tasks left undone during the contest. The urgency has passed. Their commitment and sense of purpose has to be renewed. The desire they once felt becomes diminished now that the message has to be taken into the uncharted waters of public opinion instead of to the faithful in the party membership. In those safe waters, workers knew they were still talking to people who shared the same beliefs, even if they supported different candidates.

By the time the last of the streamers are swept from the floor of the meeting hall where the nomination was held, few real voters will know who was chosen as the nominee. The candidate's primary goal must be to build name recognition.

Those who study voter behaviour have built models to describe the ability, or maybe it is better stated as the desire, of average voters to remember anything about their political contacts. It is widely held that the thing most likely to be remembered by voters, when making a decision about who to support, is the name of the candidate. The second thing remembered is the candidate's party affiliation; and the last thing is some form of policy information: more likely issues voters did not like, than ideas they found attractive.

Name recognition is the single most important factor when most voters choose a candidate to support. This does not mean that a campaign cannot turn into a mini-referendum on an over-riding issue like Free Trade, or massive giveaway programs, or be a test of the popularity of a government leader. Under ordinary conditions, however, name recognition remains a vital key to vote determination at the local level.

Candidates need to come into contact with as many constituents as possible, wherever people gather. This is how a candidate will come to know what people are thinking, what they expect from their politicians, and what they are likely to support and oppose in the way of public policy. Of course, this also allows voters to get to know them. Candidates keep a file of all public events and attend as many as possible. Showing concern and support for community events will not go unnoticed with voters, and it is an easy way to become known and to get to know the people.

Canvassing door to door is the single most effective way of building lasting name recognition.

When he began preparing for a possible by-election to re-enter the Saskatchewan Legislature after losing his rural seat of 11 years in 1982, Ed Tchorzewski set the goal of visiting every household in his constituency of about 13,000 voters. Not only had he visited them all by the time the by-election was finally called, but by the time the vote was held he had been through every poll twice. Workers reported that wherever they went in the constituency, people knew Ed and were prepared to support him, as much because they felt they knew him personally as for his party or platform.

This intensive form of canvassing gives the voter the impression that, "Here's a politician who really cares, will work hard on my behalf, and will be there to help if I need it."

One politician from Minnesota went even further in his canvassing. He canvassed every door on his first swing through his district. He then came back and went to every second door, while a volunteer went to those in between. He then came back one more time, going to every third home while two volunteers visited the other voters. As with Tchorzewski, even when leaflets were dropped in the mailbox by volunteers months later, voters had the impression that their representative had just been by for a visit, and they had missed him!

The next best thing to the candidate's canvass is the candidate's spouse or another member of the immediate family going door to door. By canvassing, they show that the candidate has family members who care about each other, and that they share a political commitment. The feeling left with the voter is the same as if the candidate had visited.

There are a variety of tactics used by politicians to build name recognition while canvassing. Carrying a notebook to write down concerns people have about issues or local conditions allows the candidate to respond to issues that concern voters. The smart politician writes back to voters in a few days, acknowledging the conversation and offering some ideas about the issue discussed. If it concerns some government matter, the candidate can write to the appropriate department seeking a remedy and send a copy to the voter, leaving the impression that he or she is a doer and willing to take people's problems to those who can do something about them.

Tony Penniket, Government Leader of the Yukon, carries a tape recorder with him when he is canvassing, and uses this to keep his notes for each visit. When his canvassing is completed, he uses these notes to write letters that help to build his deserved reputation as an able and concerned politician.

A typical follow-up letter received after a visit from a politician might begin with, "Thank you for taking the time to share your ideas with me when I visited your home last week." It might continue by recognizing the specific issue raised in the following way: "I agree that taxes are out of hand today. Many of your neighbours in this constituency feel the same way." The letter would go on to say something bad about the opponent's position on taxation, and continue with a positive statement about the candidate's position. It would close with a thank you and an invitation to call or write the candidate should the voter desire further information on this or any other topic that might be of concern.

A letter like this seems innocuous enough, but when it is addressed personally to the voter, recalls something about the previous meeting, and promises some sort of action on a pressing problem, it becomes a powerful tool in building name recognition and credibility for the new candidate.

An additional aid for building name recognition through door to door canvassing is to have a letter dropped in mailboxes from the constituency president, or some prominent local citizen, announcing that the candidate is going to be in the neighbourhood in the coming week or so, and saying a little about the candidate's credentials. This way, even if the voters are not home when the candidate calls, they at least know the candidate is out and about. When the candidate does call and no one is in, the candidate will likely scribble "Sorry I missed you," or a similar note on a calling card or leaflet and leave it in the mailbox.

If I am canvassing on behalf of a candidate, I leave the same note on the leaflet just to help in building the candidate's profile.

In the simple act of canvassing in a constituency, a politician makes quality voter contacts which won't be easily forgotten.

"In a sense," says freelance writer Bob Sweirczek, "door to door campaigning is television in the flesh." It gives candidates the opportunity to show their capabilities and display a little charm. It also enables new candidates to anticipate and forestall any accusations of lack of experience.

An effective positioning tool used by challenging candidates is to announce that they will act like the MLA or MP for the constituency, and invite people to contact them about matters they might otherwise see the current elected member about. This is particularly useful if the incumbent has a reputation of not doing his job well.

Most candidates use the offices of elected people of the same party to help with questions of workers' compensation, pensions, unemployment insurance and the like. In effect, the candidate becomes an ombudsman, undertaking an advocacy role and cutting through red tape for voters. A growing file of successful casework becomes a great source of workers and endorsements.

An important part of political activities during the pre-election period is checking every issue of the local papers and sending cards and letters on births, deaths, and anniversaries. Obviously, there has to be a limit to the numbers included in this exercise, but once criteria are established, they are usually followed very methodically. After all, each card and letter is a potential vote harvester.

Even sad events are not immune from the politician's presence. The former Mayor of Regina and MLA, Henry Baker, was as common a fixture at funerals in Regina as the hearse. For him, this was an important way of keeping in touch with the voters; his attention was always appreciated.

In addition to family events of note, keen candidates might keep a record of outstanding scholastic and athletic achievements of people who live in the constituency; these achievers then also receive cards or letters from the candidate.

The pre-election period is the time for candidates to get to know the leaders of local special interest groups, and to let them get to know the candidate. Differences over policies are less likely to become an issue during an election if each has had a chance to become familiar with the other's position. If nothing else, this familiarity will make it more difficult for groups with opposing viewpoints to work actively against the candidate.

Opinion leaders are important to the success of any campaign. Many candidates make the mistake of ignoring those people who have the potential to influence many voters because they feel they already have the support of the person and their organization, or because they feel they could never gain their support. Both attitudes take too much for granted.

One thing is certain: candidates are not likely to get support from people if they don't ask for it.

Grant Notley often spoke of the importance of "defanging" the opposition. He said the President of the Chamber of Commerce would be a little less likely to speak ill of you if he had seen with his own eyes that you really didn't have two heads.

When Ray Martin (Leader of the Opposition in Alberta after Grant's death) first became a candidate, he made a point of visiting the many Catholic priests in his constituency. This gave him the chance to explain his position on issues like abortion without the pressure of an election. He developed some hard and fast friendships from this exercise that stood him well in the large Italian and Portuguese populations in his Norwood riding.

Service clubs, unions, occupational associations, community, social and athletic clubs, senior citizens and farm groups are all examples of the kinds of organizations that become a candidate's target for outreach activities. These can become excellent sources of workers and lead to good contacts for fundraising.

If candidates ingratiate themselves with the leadership and members of an organization, and also help it achieve some of its goals, by obtaining government help, for example, they have gone a long way towards building meaningful community credibility and visibility.

Gordon Taylor, who is now a PC Member of Parliament, but was also Minister of Highways for the Alberta Social Credit government in a previous political life, provides a good example of the kinds of rewards that can come from paying attention to the needs of different groups. While highways minister, he arranged for a portion of the highway known as 16X between Edmonton and Sherwood Park to be blocked off for the use of local drag racers. He also allowed the Capital City Hot Rod Association use of the Highways Branch Headquarters as a monthly meeting facility for the club. The result was a large number of young people, who probably shared little in philosophy or lifestyle with Taylor, who were forever grateful.

A similar example is that of Ian Waddell, a B.C. Member of Parliament. He fought a successful battle on behalf of the local Chinese community to overturn a decision of the city's health inspectors prevented the traditional marketing of Chinese barbe-cued meats, including hanging the products in shop windows without refrigeration. This led to the support of Chinese voters in Waddell's first election against Liberal incumbent Simma Holt. There were over 12,000 Chinese voters in the Vancouver Kingsway constituency, and their support played an important part in form-ing his election majority.

Another way of building permanent name recognition is to seek a gimmick. Not many Canadian politicians work hard at this, but they should. Gimmicks can add some fun to politics and put a bit of a human face on an otherwise humdrum process. There is something about Canadian political life that makes us pull back at any sign that we are making fools of ourselves. There is nothing in the make-up of American politicians to restrain them.

The Canadian public may well be in a more receptive mood towards politicians who stand out from the crowd. The less candi-dates appear typical, the more appeal they may have for an electorate that cares little for more traditional images.

One Democrat in New Mexico vowed he would shake 1,000 hands a day during his campaign and by all counts he did. He even tried to set the world record for most hands shaken in a 24 hour period, but he failed in this. He lost that election against a popular incumbent, but when a new district was created in the next election, his name recognition was a big help in his getting 64% of the vote.

3. The Pre-Election Period

Walking or bicycling everywhere and similar ideas have been used as gimmicks to get news attention. Just about anything short of wearing a dead chicken on the head is used to attract attention in the States. The big advantage to this is that it makes people talk about the candidate without the candidate having to take sides on specific issues.

Joey Smallwood of Newfoundland had a unique way of getting people to remember his name and think of him in personal terms. Richard Gwyn tells the story in his book about Smallwood.

At an outport rally, where children were gathered around the front of the stage, Joey stopped in mid-speech and declared with an air of irritation, "Ladies and gentlemen, I am going to have to stop. I cannot continue. I cannot go on. That boy down here in front of me, has just called me Joe Smallwood. My name is not Joe Smallwood." The crowd felt sorry for the child, but they shouldn't have: it is hard to inflict pain on someone who does not exist. Smallwood kept the crowd in suspense by saying, "I will not be called Joe Smallwood, I will not allow it. Neither will I be called Mr. Smallwood. My name is JOEY Smallwood." He didn't have to repeat the story many more times before the legend was feeding off itself and people came to know him on a first name basis.

The important element for those who use a gimmick to help build name recognition is to be sure they are also trying to get out a message. Their actions have to be compatible with what they are trying to say. Candidates must also be sure that the point is clear to more than just themselves and a small group of advisers, and of course, that this message is being received in a favourable light.

An example of an attention-getting idea that also served to convey a message was that employed by Florida Senator Bob Graham while he was running for the governorship of Florida. He embarked on a series of 100 "work days." On these days, he performed ordinary jobs, such as working on a loading dock, helping on a farm, acting as a teacher's aide, pumping gas or what have you. After each of these work days he held a press conference and talked about the kinds of things he learned, and how he would be able to help people who worked in those types of jobs if he became governor.

Through this technique, Graham was able to leave the positive impression that he was hard-working, earnest, and caring, and that he understood people. The important thing for candidates to keep in mind is that the message of the gimmick has to be clear, or it will only be seen as showmanship, which leaves a negative impression.

Finally, candidates have to be sure that any method used to gain attention has a highly visual component, i.e., that it will make good TV or newspaper pictures. This, combined with word of mouth and radio reporting, adds a dynamic component to the activity.

Pre-election campaigning does not only make good sense as a way of getting the candidate known, it also makes good financial sense. Spending limits during the campaign period are becoming more strict, as inflation is increasing more quickly than adjustments to legal spending limits are made. Money spent outside the campaign period is not included in those limits, so that billboards and leaflets, for example, designed to introduce a candidate to the constituents before the election writ can be prudent expenditures.

While the candidate is beginning to create name recognition, the pre-election period is also the time to begin laying plans for the election campaign itself. The candidate and the election team start fundamental research on the nature of the constituency they have chosen, plan strategy, and consider tactics for the battle that lies ahead.

Even if a candidate was born and raised in the constituency he or she seeks to represent, one of the first important things to be done is to travel through the area, to walk up and down some of the streets and see how people live. Candidates need to become familiar with where the schools, playgrounds and shopping centres are located.

In a rural riding, this is even more critical. The candidate needs to know how long it takes to drive between towns for very practical reasons. Each town will have its own history and the politician should become familiar with that history in order to better understand the voters and their values.

In my experience, driving down back alleys can tell you a great deal about people who live in a particular neighbourhood. You learn how many cars they have, how much pride they have in their property, and their level of affluence, since this is where all the toys like campers and swimming pools are found. And, if at all possible, I like to take the time to drive along the boundaries of the constituency to get a feel for the size and natural features of the area. All of these things help to bring a little life and texture to maps and poll boundaries.

One pre-election exercise that most candidates do not like to participate in is a cold-blooded assessment of strengths and weaknesses of their own campaign as compared to their opponents'. The candidate has to show objectivity, something she or he is fast running out of as the campaign draws nearer.

Listing the various strengths and weaknesses of the competing candidates and parties develops a pattern that will show what attributes require emphasis and what should be left alone. This process can also help determine what styles opponents might use in their campaigns. It is just as important to know what the opposition's campaign style and most likely strategy will be as to have a firm plan of one's own.

Candidates had better be doing this; they can bet the opposition is busy doing exactly the same thing.

To begin to plan a successful campaign, a candidate needs to know what the electoral history of the area has been. The results from previous elections at the same level and other levels of government are an important source of information for planning strategy and the deployment of scarce resources such as the candidate's time, volunteers, and money.

Previous election results show areas of strength and weakness for the candidate's party. The other important factor to include is the number of voters for each poll and the traditional level of voter turnout for each poll. From this information candidates are then able to priorize polls from best to worst from the point of view of their party.

Voting statistics are not always what they seem. For instance, a poll in which you might get 65% of the vote can be a lower priority than one in which you might get 50%. Here are the factors planners consider in such a case.

One poll may yield 65% of the vote with a turnout of 75% of the voters, but there might be only 200 voters in the poll. Therefore, under normal circumstances, you can expect around 90-95 votes.

Another poll might give you only 50% of the votes, but if there were 400 voters in a 70% turnout it would yield 140 votes. Putting extra effort into the latter poll will yield more benefit since more votes are available by increasing the turnout or converting more opinions.

It is not uncommon to find a poll with poor numbers, right in the middle of several good polls. Often, this is the result of sloppy organizational work in the previous election. The weak poll might not have been canvassed well, or the effort to get the vote out on election day may not have been very effective. This simply means that poll priorization is not a simple scientific exercise. Some subjectivity has to play a part.

Once all the numbers have been reviewed, the campaign team usually colours maps of the constituency to show the good polls and the bad. Maps are also produced which highlight the strengths and weaknesses of opponents. Campaign teams determine their own campaign tactics, but they also make their best guess as to where the opposition is most likely to concentrate their efforts. These maps and charts become the single most important reference point when organizers are allocating volunteers.

It might seem strange, but one strategy I have found to work well is to do as little as possible in polls where there is little prospect of doing well. The theory behind this strategy is that by showing little visibility, there is less reason for supporters of the opponent to get out and work and contribute money. When the opponent's supporters do not perceive much threat to their candidate, they are less motivated to turn out and vote. This strategy is particularly effective if it is already known who most of the supporters are in these poor polls, from identification in previous elections. A campaign following this plan would then contact only these known supporters, and leave others alone.

I used this strategy in the campaign to re-elect MP Les Benjamin in Regina West. The result was a drop in the turnout in our worst polls, which led to our winning most of them.

This priorization of the district becomes the bible for the campaign. It is used to decide which campaign tactics will be applied where. For instance, a poll that is high in the priorization might receive two visits from volunteer canvassers, a canvass by the candidate and some telephone canvassing of undecided voters as well. A poll of lower priority might only receive a drop of literature in mail boxes and a telephone canvass.

Most campaign strategists use the rule of working from strength in a campaign and working from weakness in the pre-election period. This stems from the belief that most minds are made up by the time an election is called, and that the time to change the opinions of people in the weakest polls is in the period before an election is called. This leads to a never-ending argument between those who maintain that elections are not the place for political education, and others who say that if only people hear the word they will be moved to support the candidate. We'll look at this argument later.

It is always easier to find votes in a friendly environment than in a hostile one. Once home territory is protected, then it is time to consider an invasion of the opponents' strongest areas. This may not always take the form of visible action on the streets within these weak polls, but might include appearances in front of organizations that are not considered to be traditional supporters of the candidate's party, or keeping a low profile, by using the telephones and mail.

A Conservative might decide not to speak to a local women's action group because of an assumption that "They're all socialists." Well, they likely aren't, but even if they were, if the Conservative spoke to a room of 100, it is likely there would have been little support before going in, and picking up even a handful of votes would be better than what he would have gained had he not gone to the meeting. The same candidate speaking to 100 Conservatives might actually lose votes because of something that was said.

Every campaign committee spends time scrambling trying to find the records from the previous election. The results of the door to door canvassing, lists of places where signs were put up, records of who worked and contributed money to the election, are usually found in someone's basement or garage. Sometimes they aren't found. These lists take weeks to build and without them a campaign is dealt a serious setback. Electronic storage of this data makes it a little easier to retrieve when it is needed, but a diskette is even easier to lose than two or three apple boxes full of records.

Part of preparing for an election is getting to know the law. Gone are the days of limited rules for the conduct of election campaigns. Today each jurisdiction has its own set of rules that define the way in which the vote is going to be taken and what is legal and illegal activity for candidates. In addition, the laws governing the receipt and expenditure of money are more strict. This is in part due to the fact that in many cases there is some public funding of candidates and/or parties, and the taxpayers need to be guaranteed that there are some controls. Actually, few people realize how much tax money is involved in direct transfers to candidates and parties, as well as in tax credits for contributors. It could add up to nearly $50 million a year, and might be more, if a lot of elections take place in the same year.

Campaigns can no longer be run with cash out of a benefactor's back pocket. The source of funds has to be accounted for and there are definitions of proper campaign expenditures. When these laws were first enacted in federal elections, the Chief Electoral Officer was pretty easy going about proper reporting, as candidates and parties were beginning to familiarize themselves with the law. With each subsequent election an increasing number of candidates are investigated for possible violations of the law. The candidate bears the ultimate responsibility in these matters.

Penalties can be stiff and can apply to both the candidate and the chief financial officer of the campaign. They can include fines, jail, and disqualification from voting, as well as ineligibility for candidacy in future elections; infractions can also result in the loss of a legislative seat, in the case of a winner caught breaking the law. The penalty for exceeding federal spending limits, for instance, can be a $5,000 fine or five years in jail.

Most federal jurisdictions have permanently appointed returning officers; provinces and municipalities will likely have a chief of elections. The friendship of these officials should be cultivated during the pre-election period. Many candidates make the mistake of being antagonistic towards a returning officer, based almost solely on the fact that they may have been appointed by another political party. There are few returning officers who can't be won over with a little charm and a helping attitude. In the heat of an election, when a campaign wants its copies of the voters' lists in a hurry, a good working relationship can save hours and maybe days for the campaign.

Although we will take more time later to examine the relationships between the press and a candidate, at this point the candidate needs to begin to become known to the local media. The first step is to make a list of all the media outlets that serve the constituency. The candidate needs to find out who on each staff is responsible for political reporting and go to meet them, taking along a biography and a current photograph. When local media can put a face to a press release there is a better chance the campaign might get some air time or ink. In large cities, candidates shouldn't be too hopeful about getting much pre-election media coverage, but in rural markets there is more of an opportunity to place articles in local newspapers, particularly if the story has a local twist.

I counsel rural candidates to take a press release that might have been released centrally by the leader and change the emphasis to their local region or town. That will go a long way in helping obtain coverage.

Once a non-incumbent candidate becomes known to the local media, the media may be more inclined to turn to this challenger for comment on articles or stories about political affairs. This will have the effect of establishing public credibility for the candidate.

One final item of pre-election preparation, often overlooked by candidates, is building an adequate photo file. A candidate cannot have enough pictures. Black and white shots with family, friends, seniors, farmers and women need to be taken well ahead of the election. The candidate needs pictures taken in front of important landmarks or recognizable features in the constituency. Each set of pictures should help to reinforce basic themes that the campaign will use. If these pictures are not arranged for ahead of time, there will be an impossible scramble during the election for adequate photos for leaflets and print ads.

I have often been a part of campaigns for even veteran campaigners, and got a shrug when I asked for the photo file. At best there will be a fairly current head and shoulders picture and little else. Often the portrait shot is so old that you can imagine the brown checked bell bottom trousers that are being worn. What current pictures there are may have been taken by a well-meaning friend with a trusty Brownie box camera. Without time and money spent with a professional photographer who can be told exactly what is required, designing an attractive and eye-catching brochure becomes nearly impossible.

Here is a brief list of the kinds of items that the major Canadian parties outline in their manuals as things to be done between elections and in preparation for a coming election. This list refers to items in a riding where there is an incumbent MP, but the principles apply to all candidates in any party at any level of politics.

1. The voters' list from the previous election should be stored in a safe place; each poll captain should keep track of people who move in or out of the poll; they should also find out their politics and record this information.
2. In every poll, there should be a competent, knowledgeable poll captain and poll team. These front line workers are the most important people in your constituency organization.
3. Effective fundraising structures should be maintained in the riding.
4. Lists of volunteers, workers, scrutineers, enumerators, DROs, drivers, canvassers, etc. should be kept up-to-date.
5. Keep your MP informed about local issues, and about birthdays, anniversaries, etc.
6. Make friends with supervisors in apartment buildings. As new people move in, send them a card.
8. Know the opinion leaders. Keep your MP informed when any of these offices are changed.
9. Keep abreast of changes to poll boundaries.
10. Stay in touch with the returning officer so that you know when changes or revisions are made.
11. Colour code a poll map that shows your party's, as well as opposition support, in each poll. Clearly mark polls won or lost by 5%.
12. Review past voting results to see what can be done to strengthen weak polls.
13. Try to do some membership work, canvassing for issues and money; stay familiar with attitudes and opinions in the constituency.

14. Know your party's record in government and spread the news.

15. Keep the fellowship and social aspect alive. People who know and like each other can create winning teams.

There is no substitute for hard work for any candidate who wants to take advantage of the pre-election period to prepare for the campaign to come. It is a chance to make plans for winning votes and raising money without pressure and deadlines. The candidate can meet voters in a casual atmosphere and spend time answering their questions and responding to their concerns and simply getting used to the idea of asking people for their support. And, most important of all, the candidate can use this time to become known. The limited amount of time available during the election period is no time to try and build name recognition.

So far, we have seen the elements that form the basis for making a decision to become a candidate, and have taken a look at the nomination process and what needs to be done to prepare for the election. The next step is to assemble a campaign team, money, volunteers and an effective campaign strategy. Then, and only then, can a candidate be ready to run a competitive race.

4. Gathering the Team

"A person who acts as his or her own
campaign manager has a fool for
a candidate."
"Political campaigns are too
important to be left to the
politicians."
Anonymous

When it comes right down to the crunch, it is always the candidate who ends up winning or losing. It's the candidate who is quoted in the press, whose name is on the lawn signs, and whose picture is on the front of the brochures. And it's the candidate who will go on to sit in some legislature, the House of Commons, or council chamber and shall come back seeking votes again. The candidate is the star of the show.

That's the way things appear to electoral spectators. However, anyone who has volunteered a little time during an election or knows people who have, will know that there is a small army of people involved, and these people do incredible amounts of work on a host of different tasks.

Have you ever walked by a campaign office and wondered who all those people were, what they were doing there, and why?

The campaign team that is assembled for an election comes from all walks of life. Some are party regulars who always serve in some capacity or other at each election. Others have been attracted by the candidate or by some issue that the party has been talking about. Still others may be paid professionals assigned to a campaign by their party headquarters.

In addition to the people who are responsible for specific campaign functions, there are legions of volunteers. A respectable campaign needs volunteer time from a minimum of 200-300 people, and there's not a campaign manager alive who isn't looking for one more volunteer, regardless of how many are signed up and out on the streets.

We'll leave a lengthy look at volunteers until later; what we want to examine here are the 10 to 15 management level people who are part of a winning election team. These are the ones who look after the candidate's time, see to it that voting intentions are identified, organize election day activities, run the office, see that leaflets get out, take care of the advertising, and raise and account for the money.

Every campaign has some version of an election planning committee. This committee is composed of officers of the local constituency association and key campaign personnel as well as the candidate. Depending on the level of democracy in a particular riding association, this committee may also report to the local executive on plans being made for the election. In the pre-election period, a campaign can afford a bit of democracy and needs input from as many people as possible in the initial planning stages.

Great care must be taken in selecting the members of this committee. It is too easy to end up with people who are great theoreticians but have little practical experience about how strategy and tactics are applied to build a winning campaign plan. This committee acts as a sounding board for campaign plans and should provide focus and balance to the campaign.

Once the campaign has started, the basic plan will be in place. It is then up to the campaign manager and a much smaller group of functional specialists to see that those plans are put into action and to make the daily decisions that move the campaign towards its final objective.

An election is no place for democracy.

The campaign manager is in charge. Even though all major plans and decisions need to be run past the candidate, to make sure he or she is comfortable with the ideas, the ultimate responsibility for applying tactics to the strategy lies with the campaign manager.

When I act as a campaign manager, I always make a point of letting the candidate know everything that is happening with the campaign so there will be no surprises later on. It is important that candidates know how we are doing at identifying potential supporters and what problems we might be having with workers, finances, or getting our message across.

I never ask a candidate to solve any problems during the

campaign. If I want the candidate to do everything necessary to win, she or he can't be doing my job as well. Keeping candidates "up to speed" makes them feel they know what's happening and that's important because they can be full of self-doubts. They need to know that everything possible is being done by the campaign team to maximize the resources that are available. If this is not done, the end result may be a strung-out candidate losing confidence in the people who should be counted on the most.

Although it is difficult and time-consuming to go back to a large election committee often during an election, there is still need for a steering committee to meet frequently during the campaign. This group is convened by the campaign manager; people on this committee usually include: the finance person, candidate, a couple of the key organizers and one or two others chosen by the candidate. The campaign manager needs to be in charge of this committee. It is very dangerous to actually put a steering committee behind the steering wheel. But life can be equally hazardous for a campaign manager who decides a campaign can be run from beginning to end without any outside advice.

The campaign manager is ultimately responsible for the actions of all campaign workers, from organizational staff and committees to the volunteers. Simply put, the campaign manager makes sure that people are doing their jobs. It can be tragic if a campaign manager does not know what people's jobs are supposed to be.

In my experience, campaign managers often take for granted that other organizational staff know what they are doing and assume they are making the best possible use of all the time that is volunteered to the campaign. It is often too late by the time the manager finds out that an organizer really didn't have the people skills to manage volunteers, or didn't have a firm grasp on his or her duties, or how the organizer's job fit into the overall effort.

The campaign manager has to summon common sense and objectivity in order to make sure that all the important issues have received a thorough and proper analysis, and then see to it that those messages that will do the most good are heard by those voters who need to hear it. A one-issue campaign manager can be as debilitating to a campaign as a candidate with only one issue.

At one time, the campaign manager travelled everywhere with

the candidate. Campaigns have become very complex, and today, it is necessary for the manager to be on hand at headquarters most of the time, to deal with emerging problems and issues. But the campaign manager should always accompany the candidate to events that might cause the candidate to be nervous or apprehensive, such as TV interviews or town hall meetings.

The typical relationship between a candidate and campaign manager is complex. A campaign manager needs to deal with all the misgivings, fears, and crazy ideas of the candidate. This has to be done in an earnest and thoughtful way. The competent campaign manager literally becomes the candidate's confidant and surrogate parent, leading, cajoling, and coaxing the candidate along. The manager will offer simple praise or good-natured scolding whenever it is warranted. No matter what the circumstances, the campaign manager must never criticize or ridicule the candidate in front of other workers, in public or private.

The fact that the candidate has so many sources of advice and counsel can be a big problem for the manager. Family, friends, business associates, other candidates and people met while campaigning all have advice for the candidate. The poor campaign manager has to deal with all these external influences while still trying to maintain credibility with the candidate.

Candidates are always looking for the quick fix, the one button to push that will make all their opponents disappear, or at least make them call up and concede the election. Unfortunately, it doesn't work that way. Only hard work and careful application of a sound strategy and proven tactics lead consistently to success. The campaign manager's job when dealing with the candidate is to make sure that, above all else, the candidate also knows that.

Long after the campaign budget has been approved, and funds committed, candidates will argue that if only there were some billboards or signs on buses with their pictures on them, the campaign would be in the bag. Hang the paltry few hundred dollars more it would cost. More than one temper tantrum has begun with that kind of blast from a candidate. One campaign manager I know, Delaine Scotton, has a simple reply for that kind of candidate: "If you don't smarten up, we're going to use Plan B!" No one has ever asked exactly what Plan B was, but considering her tone of voice, few would be brave enough to press her about it.

The campaign manager has to keep pressure on the opposition and give no quarter, whether it is in negotiations over the format for a debate, the studio setting for some free time on cable television, or using various strategies to build public momentum for the campaign. You can not let up the pressure for an instant, because every time you do, you lose ground.

I have often been involved in campaigns where every subjective and objective sign pointed to a very comfortable win for my candidate, and yet the opposition would not relent in their campaigning; and neither should they, if for no other reason than personal pride.

I have also seen the other side of the same situation, perhaps too often. I recently helped out in the federal by-election in Beaver River, Alberta. It was clear even before the by-election was called that we were going to lose, and that we'd likely finish third or fourth. It would have been easy for me to leave the campaign in the early days, when we had trouble getting workers or enthusiasm from old supporters, and go and help prepare for the provincial election which was subsequently called for one week after the by-election. But, after meeting the candidate, Barb Bonneau, I did not want to leave her all alone; I knew that if I didn't do what I could to help her campaign, no one else would. Candidates deserve some help if they are prepared to stand up in public for what they believe. We forged ahead. We spent all the funds we had available on regular radio and newspaper ads, mailings, leaflets and signs. You just never give up, and never give the opponent an easy ride, ever. We lost badly to the Reform candidate, but we had a campaign that contained all the elements that would have allowed us to take advantage of any opportunity that came up.

The campaign manager has to be ready to communicate with all kinds of individuals and groups, explaining policy and discussing issues, always looking for new support and endorsements. At the same time, the campaign manager has to make sure that promises or commitments are not made by the campaign that could eventually be compromising or damaging. If a group that wants to have the candidate attend a meeting has to be told that the answer is "no," the campaign manager has to do that. Candidates only say "yes."

While doing all this, the campaign manager needs to keep in mind that your enemy's enemy is not necessarily your friend. Often, people who are upset with the way an opponent became nominated, or who feel slighted or mistreated by the opponent, will come to a campaign manager with stories that seem to leave the opposition vulnerable. The information in cases like this is almost always exaggerated, if not entirely false. The details have to be checked closely, and the best rule is "If in doubt, don't use it. Get someone else to use it." That way, any potential damage to the candidate can be averted, and set-ups avoided.

The campaign manager is not responsible for raising money, or even accounting for it, but he or she has to manage the finances. The time will come when others will want to overspend or underspend what had originally been budgeted. Spending plans made in the cool of the pre-election period should not be changed in the heat of the campaign, unless there is some over-riding reason. To the campaign manager, finances are just another resource, like volunteers or the candidate's time.

Every campaign has people who help with publicity and advertising, probably operating as a committee. The campaign manager needs to know what they are doing and make sure every ad or leaflet carries the themes and messages that have been decided on for the campaign. Often, the publicity people will get too cute, using words, ideas or images that do not enhance the campaign. The campaign manager makes sure that all messages, from every source, paid or unpaid, are consistent with the battle plan, and that they make sense.

It is among media people that I usually encounter the most persistent problem, identified by American consultant Joe Napolitan as "the impassioned amateur." These people may have some expertise in the area they are dealing with, but likely little or no knowledge of how an election campaign works. They haven't the experience to put the campaign in the right perspective. As a result, they have difficulty getting a grasp of the big picture and the role of publicity in a campaign.

Political parties take central control of most of the advertising and campaign marketing functions, presenting a completed package to their candidates. The opportunity for local campaigns to exercise individual creativity is somewhat limited.

Campaign managers have to learn to "keep their cool." A lot of things will happen during an election, over which the manager has no control; it does no good for anyone to get upset. Once, during an election in Ontario, the car I had rented was driven through the front window of the campaign headquarters by one of the organizers. There wasn't a lot that could be done about it after it happened, so there was no point in getting too upset.

Being a good campaign manager requires more than a mastery of technique and strategy; the job is as much about human relations. Internal public relations can take up as much time as fighting the opponent.

Probably the most important and trying part of a campaign manager's duties is keeping everyone on track and happy, and fighting the opposition rather than each other. The collection of personalities that come together in an election campaign would be the envy of any good clinical psychologist. There will always be times when a manager becomes a referee between warring parties. When people are thrown together in the intensity of an election campaign for four weeks or more, something is bound to give.

In my experience as a manager, I have found that I have to be friends with everyone, but close to none. It's important to stay cheerful without appearing addle-minded; and if you can't say anything positive about a given situation, then say nothing at all because campaign workers are looking to you for leadership. If you don't provide that leadership, volunteers and middle management types will find someone else to follow, and that's when things really start to break down. If you can't build and maintain respect, you will never be able to enforce decisions or get the most energy from everyone involved.

A campaign manager's personality is somewhere between Osmond-like optimism and the Dark Prince.

It is often necessary or desirable to designate someone as campaign chair in a titular position. I will often invite an MLA, in a federal election, or an alderman or similar high profile community person to chair a campaign. This gives a bit more credibility to the campaign. I don't expect the chair to do anything in particular, and don't want them to, but they are useful for issuing releases on the progress of the campaign or assisting in recruiting workers or donors because of their profile. No one knows who I am, but the public will know a popular local personality and that can lead to added support for my candidate.

This figurehead position is also helpful when I am managing a campaign in a riding where I am not well known. The campaign chairman can help bridge the gap between the regulars and someone like myself who might be parachuted in to help the riding.

Although it is the job of the campaign manager to set the tone and direction of the campaign, there is more to building an effective team than just this one person.

To start with, there are two people particularly involved with money in an election campaign. One raises it, and the other accounts for the funds and authorizes payments. It's best that these jobs are not done by the same person. The personalities and abilities required to do these jobs are so different that it would be a rare person indeed who could manage the double duty in a serious campaign.

The person chosen to act as the financial officer needs to instill a sense of stability and trust in people who are contributing to the campaign. People want to feel the financial officer will look after contributions as if it were his or her own money; a suitable person to look after the warchest is one who does not have the reputation of being a spendthrift.

Depending on the jurisdiction of the election, the financial officer will have some sort of responsibility to report revenue and expenditures to a government agency. There will be strict legal requirements which define the deadlines for winding up the business of the campaign and may require reporting the names of contributors.

There are a variety of official titles given to this keeper of the treasury, usually something like Chief Financial Officer, Business Agent, or Official Agent. Most election acts require this person to be responsible for the financial conduct of the campaign, to ensure that all contributions are from allowable sources, and that all the expenditures are made on items that are prescribed by law.

Doug Trace of Edmonton has served in this capacity for dozens of candidates, and is a model of the type of person who should do this kind of job. A retired teacher, he makes sure that you understand what the law calls for and what needs to be done. An accountant, he has no problem dealing with record keeping. As a former member of the RCMP, you know all hell would break lose if you slipped a couple of bills into the pile that were not previously budgeted.

Legend has it that there have been antitheses of Doug Trace: one treasurer, for instance, who stood up at meetings of the party and held out both hands like a scale. One hand was designated as payables, and the other hand as income; their relative positioning, suspended like the scales of justice, served as the financial report.

This is not considered the greatest way of building confidence in contributors.

The fundraiser is an entirely different kind of person. Often referred to as "the bagman," he or she has to be fearless when it comes to asking for money, and should never feel self-pity at a little rejection.

The good fundraiser can bring together a team representing a real cross-section of the community. Ideally, this person will already know a lot of the potential donors and be able to establish a level at which canvassers should ask for money from each potential donor. Motivation is an important job for the fundraiser; that person must make everyone feel enthusiastic about asking for money.

Fundraising is not a job for the timid, weak-hearted, or apologetic. The fundraiser and the financial team have to be prepared to go to the well time after time. If people have contributed once, they will likely do so again.

They shouldn't prejudge how much someone can afford to give. As an example, people in a $200,000 house may live well, but have very little cash. All their disposable income may go towards paying bills while those in a modest home may have much more money available for a contribution.

People like to be flattered by being asked to contribute too much rather than being asked for too little. If you ask for $200 and the person or business can only afford $50, they'll tell you, but if the situation is reversed, then you have lost some money.

The fundraising team should be well-armed with information. They should be carrying the campaign budget or some sketch of it with them so that they can show potential donors what the need is, and how funds will be spent. Contributors will give more if they know the extent of the need and that the money is going to pay for important campaign costs like literature or advertising. I even like to provide information such as the cost of a 1/4 page ad in the local newspaper or 30 seconds of radio or television time.

The second most-important thing to convey to contributors is what might be in it for them. Of course, there is the satisfaction of helping to elect a good candidate or promoting issues that are important to the community, but in many cases there are good financial reasons for making a contribution to political parties or candidates. Tax credits are available for financial contributions in most jurisdictions. These are direct credits to tax payable, not a deduction for lowering taxable income. Credits have been a real step towards involving more people in financing election campaigns, removing at least a little of the influence of large corporate or special interest contributors. When these tax benefits are explained properly, they are a real aid in maximizing the level of contributions.

In 1975, just after the federal Election Expenses Act was brought in, I attended a meeting in Basswood, Manitoba. There were 22 at the meeting besides myself. After discussing the agricultural scene, the good Schreyer government and the bad Trudeau government, I started to explain the new Act, pointing out that a contribution of $100 created a $75 tax credit, and outlined how it all worked. When the hat was passed, there were 22 $100 cheques in it. I should have used a larger sum for my example!

Every team needs people to apply campaign tactics to the strategy: a group of itinerant campaigners, usually known as organizers, who can best be described as campaign managers in waiting. They run many important aspects of a campaign, such as identifying the vote and getting it out on election day.

If words like zany or madcap hold any meaning today, they are best applied to these campaign organizers. They work too hard, sleep too little, usually drink too much, eat the wrong food, and some smoke entirely too much. How these people can last a month or two of intense campaigning, let alone come back to it time and time again for little pay and a lot of abuse, is completely beyond my understanding.

Being in a room of organizers is bedlam and comedy. It is more entertaining than putting three candidates in a room with only two mirrors. The campaign stories never stop coming; each one more outrageous than the first, and none are doubted, even if they have been heard before many times from entirely different people in other versions.

One of the stories that keeps making the rounds in one form or another involves a door to door canvasser who felt the canvass organizer doubted the accuracy of his canvass, because he received an intense grilling when being debriefed after each canvass was finished. The organizer kept asking what people said to make the canvasser sure they were supporters. The canvasser was intent on making sure this doubt did not happen again, so on his next round of the poll, he made each voter sign his canvass sheets if they agreed with his assessment of whether they were supporters, undecided or whatever.

The other ageless story is about the canvasser who, when told that leaflets were in short supply and to be careful with them, took only one into his poll. He waited on each doorstep as the voter read it over, and then retrieved it for his next call.

When I first started working on elections, all the tasks which needed to be done on a campaign were usually performed by the same person. You were called on to manage the campaign, organize the canvass, and put scrutineers and drivers in place for election day. Like so much of life today, an increasing degree of specialization is coming into play in our election campaigns as well.

The most important organizational task is coordinating the door to door canvass of the constituency for supporters. Depending on the particular strategy, this organizer must recruit enough people willing to canvass door to door two or three times in all or most polls.

Getting the first 30 or 40% of the necessary canvassers is not too hard. They will have done it before and prefer this task. The rest will have to be coaxed into the job. They may have tried it in the past and didn't like it. Usually their reluctance stems from receiving poor training or not being treated well, and the canvass organizer has to assure them that things will be different this time around.

Almost every person who walks in the front door of a campaign office is a potential canvasser. An organizer who, moments earlier, may have been kicking a garbage can in frustration over the lack of workers, suddenly has to turn on all the charm it is possible to muster in the hope of capturing one more canvasser.

The organizer constantly deals with the disappointment of people not showing up or being unable to complete a task they had undertaken. You can't fire volunteers, but you can grumble under your breath.

Even the great and near great are not immune to causing an organizer anguish. An MP canvassing on behalf of Bud Germa explained he could not hand in his canvass kit with the results. When asked why, he said his car had been hit from behind while he was out canvassing, and his kit was lodged in the trunk which could not be opened. Nobody bothered to question why his kit was in the trunk if he was canvassing at the time; it was just one of life's mysteries. At least he livened up his story by telling us how he used this accident to tell people at the scene how important it was to vote for the NDP, because they were in favour of no-fault, publicly-owned automobile insurance.

The organizer becomes the conduit from the voter to the candidate and campaign manager, providing timely information about what voters are saying about the candidates and issues. The feedback is practically instantaneous. The organizer debriefs canvassers daily and knows what people like or dislike about the campaign and the issues from the reports received from the street.

For example, during the Regina West campaign in 1984, it was easy to tell when the city water went bad. On July 28, canvassers stopped reporting that the important issues were jobs and the economy. People's main concern was "the goddam water." We knew we would have to respond to this emerging issue quickly.

A lot of pressure goes with the responsibility. Campaign managers and candidates are always checking on the progress of the canvass. Usually it is laid out for all to see on charts on the wall that show only too vividly those polls yet to be covered or those workers who have taken out a canvass kit and literature, never to be heard from again. Some Regina organizers once took to slotting names like Ben Johnson and Elvis Presley on the canvass charts on the wall to help fill them in, making the volunteer forces look greater than they really were.

Whether it is by convincing someone to work in more than one poll or getting someone to canvass when all they really wanted to do was put up signs or leave literature in mail boxes, good organizers get the job done, even if they have to "hit the bricks" and do some of it themselves.

Another type of organizer who is becoming more prevalent in election campaigns is the telephone canvass organizer.

As it becomes increasingly difficult to convince people to campaign door to door, more voter identification is taking place over the telephone. Telephone canvassing has become useful in polls with a lot of apartment buildings which might be hard to get into, and once in, hard to find anyone at home. You don't wear out much shoe leather going back to the telephone to catch people at home. Telephones can also be used in polls that might not be safe and are certainly good in inclement weather.

One of the great benefits of telephone canvassing is that it allows a campaign to use volunteers who are unable to take a public role because of their jobs. Other good telephone canvassers are older people who do not want to walk door to door any more, but who know the importance of identifying the vote. Telephone canvassing is also a good job for people who are perfectly able but are a bit eccentric in appearance, such as having orange hair, which is not a hanging offence in itself, but still presents an image best not highlighted during an election.

But the telephone is no magic cure for a campaign that is "worker poor." It still takes a lot of administrative work looking up phone numbers and keeping track of results. Telephoning is not a good "stand-alone" campaign tactic. It produces the best results when used as a backup to work on the street, by taking one more shot at undecided voters, or if it is complemented by follow-up direct mail.

The big problem for telephone bank organizers is keeping workers. A lot of people rank this work as less important than canvassing, and, "Nobody will miss me if I don't turn up," seems to be the attitude. Those with a lot of experience with phone canvassing know that in order to have 10 workers on a given evening, 15 usually need to be recruited. If they all show up, there is still a great deal of work to do, looking up telephone numbers or transcribing results onto master lists; no one will be left without a job.

But if, in the face of all the adversity, the organizer can stay cheerful and enthusiastic, and keep people happy and feeling they are really needed and doing important work, the reward will be a solid cadre of devoted and committed campaigners who will be ready to go to the wall at the command of their organizational leader.

Specialization in election campaigns has led to the addition of direct mail experts as part of the campaign team. Usually these people have some kind of computer experience and understand mail-merge computer programs and how to manipulate data bases to produce personalized letters on issues that concern individual voters.

These people are usually volunteers who are computer nuts. In the United States, this type of campaign activity is a big business, since there, they rely less on personal campaigning to deliver political messages.

Direct mail pieces are based on issues that are identified by door to door canvassers or on the phone. They are mailed or hand delivered to voters who are undecided or leaning towards a candidate. The letters might be standard for each issue raised by the voter, or they might be "boiler-plated," which means that two or three different paragraphs are patched together from a larger selection of issues to make one letter. If the voter has not specified an issue, then the letter will likely contain some mention of an important issue and an endorsement of the candidate by the party's leader or some prominent local person.

The whole idea behind this form of direct mail is to provide one more voter contact. It is effective because it is personalized and targeted to an issue of concern. As a campaign tool it is light-years ahead of the old stand by, "Dear Friend" letter, which does not carry the weight of a personal letter. Therefore, those who have the talent to execute this kind of voter contact are valuable additions to any campaign team.

Actually, campaign professionals are continually wrestling with the role of computers in elections. Computers are valuable for list maintenance and performing tasks such as the direct mail function. They can also be very helpful in preparing lists to phone for volunteers if those lists can be prepared in a way that prevents the same people being called repeatedly. But, the problem with computers is that it takes time to input all the data necessary to make them effective, and often, that time is not available in an election campaign. Also, people can become slaves to the computer, devoting all their energy to its needs and losing sight of the campaign.

A couple of years ago I was discussing the whole business of technology in elections with a long-time organizer friend, Joyce Nash of B.C. At one time, high-tech managers had their own portable electric coffee pots. She told me how much she would like to get a personal-sized photocopier to take to campaigns. If we were holding the same conversation today, I am sure we would be talking about loading a fax machine and a lap-top computer in the trunk of the car before heading out to a campaign somewhere.

Election campaigns are actually divided into two distinct parts as far as organizational responsibilities are concerned. The canvass and telephone organizers are putting together a machine for the single purpose of identifying those people who will definitely vote for the candidate and those who may support the candidate. All of this support is of little use unless it is translated into votes in the ballot box. It's the job of the election day organizer to see that every committed supporter gets out to vote.

The election day organizer starts preparations two or three weeks before election day. This person has to recruit enough volunteers to ensure that every poll has scrutineers monitoring the voting. Actually, those scrutineers that can be seen in the polling station on election day are doing a lot more than protecting the candidate's interests and ensuring that there are no infractions of voting procedures.

A big part of their job is to keep track of who has voted and pass this information to a second group of poll workers commonly called outside scrutineers. These people visit any voters who are supporters but who have not yet voted to remind them that it is election day, that every vote counts and that the polls will soon close. If rides are required, they will arrange them; they will sit with the children if necessary; in short they will do anything to ensure that each vote gets out. This friendly persistence usually pays off. Without it, four weeks or more of hard campaigning can be wasted.

Election day organizing is an exacting job that requires military precision to pull off. The "E-Day" organizer doesn't have the luxury of waiting until the next day if everything is not completely ready. For the election day specialist, there is only one day and only one chance. Many elections have been lost by no more than one or two votes per poll. That is how critical this job can become and how low the tolerance for error.

No campaign can function without a strong office manager. This person makes sure that the office is staffed with volunteers whenever there is work like stuffing envelopes or preparing leaflets for delivery. The office manager also sees that appropriate systems for taking care of messages and the flow of information among the various staff members are in place. And if all this were not enough, office managers usually act as receptionists.

Probably the most important function for an office manager is to make people who walk in from the street feel comfortable, and if they want to help out, make sure there is something they can help with. Nothing can turn off potential campaign volunteers more than to offer some time and find that there is no work organized for them to do.

Publicity people are a necessary element for any election team. We'll examine the whole craft of designing and delivering political messages in detail later. Even though we noted earlier that the parties are taking more central control over much of the campaign publicity in order to ensure uniformity among all their candidates, there are still many jobs for local publicity people to take care of, such as local press relations and material to build name recognition and credibility for the candidate.

Signs are an important election tool in campaigns. They have to be erected and maintained once they are up. This is one more job that needs a person in charge. Signs are used to show a candidate's strength and momentum. Each sign is placed to represent a household of supporters, hard evidence that the campaign enjoys the support of real people.

The sign chair is responsible for gathering a group of volunteers who will put up signs on the property of those who have requested them. And once up, the sign crew makes sure they stay up, by inspecting sign locations and repairing damaged signs, or replacing those that have been hit by a little "sign rot" or vandalism.

Signs are used early in a campaign to provide dramatic evidence that a candidate is well-organized and ready to win. Sometimes former sign locations are re-confirmed, and signs are distributed ahead of the election call; people are asked to put them up when they hear the election is called in order to provide a surprise to the opposition. Derek Fox, the MLA from Vegreville in Alberta, had many of his signs up within a few minutes of the election call in 1989. It had a lasting effect on voters and a demoralizing effect on the opposition, and helped turn what many thought was going to be a tight race into an easy re-election for Fox.

The world's best sign strategy won't do much good if the candidate's name is misspelled, or, as in the unfortunate case of one Manitoba MLA, the name of the riding is misspelled.

The impact of signs in an election diminishes somewhat over the course of the campaign, unless the sign war is highly noticeable, with signs going up in new locations on a regular basis.

When Len Evans first ran for his Brandon East seat in 1969, signs had not been a typical sight in Brandon elections. Literally hundreds were erected for Len in that election, many of them four feet by eight feet in size. Each day, canvassers returned with new locations. Sign crews actively solicited sign locations on corner lots and major thoroughfares. After a period of time, everyone, or so it seemed, wanted an Evans sign. It got so that Tory and Liberal canvassers were seen turning away from many streets because of the forest of black and red that confronted them.

There was an area of Brandon East known as "the Flats," where Len Evans' support was extremely high. It seemed that NDP signs were on every lawn, but right beside the entrance to the Brandon Golf and Country Club was a huge PC sign. Next to this sign was a small handmade one. On the cardboard sign was an arrow pointing to the offending Conservative monster and the words,

"This sign represents the views of only one man. The four women in this house are voting NDP." The sign campaign was becoming infectious.

These are some of the kinds of people candidates need to gather around them and the kinds of jobs they do. They are a collection of dedicated professionals, enthusiastic volunteers and political junkies. The candidate may be the star of the show, but there is no show without supporting actors and crew. These people are an important part of our democracy and bring human values and interest to an otherwise technique and goal driven process. No party or candidate can expect to be successful without them.

5. Electing Women

"We are the majority, but we leave
it up to others to represent our
interests and fight our battles.
Who better to represent the
majority of Canadians than women?"
Sheila Copps, MP

Issues that are important to most women form a major portion of the budgets of most levels of government. Matters like health care, education, child care, social support programs, the environment and opportunities for young people are all issues for which women consistently show more concern than do men. Yet it is no secret that the ratio of women to men in our lawmaking bodies remains deplorably unequal.

This is not the place for statistics; numbers change every day. But there are a couple that help to make the point about the low participation rate in politics by women. Allan Fotheringham has pointed out that in the fifty years prior to the mid-1980s, there were 6,845 people elected in provincial and federal elections. Only 68 of them were women. During that time, 2.4% of all the candidates who ran for those 6,845 seats were women.

But the situation is just as clear without looking at the numbers. As Fotheringham has noted, it is only necessary to survey any Canadian council chamber, from the House of Commons to local school boards, to observe that men have been able to keep mainly to themselves the power to make the laws that govern us.

There are a host of reasons for this gender inequity in our legislative bodies. Where men might only face one or two factors that impede their chances of being elected, such as running for the wrong party, or insufficient experience, women are held back by the combined weight of a variety of forces. Any candidate may face obstacles, ranging from problems of raising money, devising strategy, utilizing networks, finding staff and volunteers or establishing credibility. If you think of all these problems and then multiply them by at least two or three, then you will be close to having some idea of what usually faces a woman as a candidate for public office. That is because compounding these common forces are all the problems of entering what has been traditionally considered a masculine world.

Some people offer the simplistic explanation that women do not hold many elected positions because they have only recently had the right to vote. This doesn't hold water any more. The franchise was extended decades ago, more than enough time for women to become used to the power of the vote. The real reason, from a historical point of view, is that only recently have nominations for the political parties become open and democratic enough to allow any challenger an equal chance at candidacy. Not that long ago, candidates were selected by the parties' leaders or local power-brokers, and only under the most unusual circumstances would they feel there would be any political advantage in promoting a female candidate. Even formal nominating conventions were under the control of the party bosses.

This is less of a problem today. Winning a nomination is now more of an organizational struggle, and although the process is still not completely fair, women have a better chance of succeeding than they did even 15 years ago.

One reason why there are not as many women in provincial legislatures and the House of Commons may be that they see no relevance in those bodies; if you spend any time watching proceedings on television or following current affairs in the media, it is hard to determine just what influence any individual legislator has on the affairs of the country. Many women find that there are more opportunities to have a positive affect by being involved at the local level in municipal and school board or hospital board politics.

Local government does allow women to participate without the disruptive absence from the home or community that is required to perform most of the duties of a provincial or federal politician. Local government is also a next logical step in community involvement and volunteerism. In fact, there are usually more women candidates running locally for school board or councillor positions, than run for election to the corresponding provincial legislature. The success rate is much higher as well. And although local politicians don't get much opportunity to deal with government policy in areas such as pay equity or health care, they do get a chance to advance and apply these important principles and others to local administrations. At the same time, local bodies do decide on such things as parks, libraries, recreation, education and many other matters that are important to everyday life.

Still another reason for so few women in political life is that the electorate has often placed different values on experience and backgrounds when deciding who to support in a party nomination or election. Education and socialization are linked to adult roles, and most winning candidates come from a professional or business background. There are not yet enough women with this kind of background ready to enter politics. Women have been less often trained in fields from which men typically move easily into public life. Many women who do have experience in the professions do not have the "right" kind. For instance, voters will give a male lawyer more credibility than a woman who is a teacher. It also follows that a woman who works in the home will be considered by many voters as having no experience useful to politics, unless she develops her credentials and following by outstanding volunteerism in the community.

In the same vein, men tend to decide on a political career much earlier in their lives than women do. Men often make conscious choices about their future professions in order to build a path that will take them into public office. I once worked with a thirteen year old Ontario organizer who told me he intended to become a Member of Parliament. When I next met him, he had just finished law school and had elected to work for an MP in Ottawa to build experience rather than entering a law firm. I have no doubt that he will eventually show up on a list of candidates.

On the other hand, only a small number of women consider positioning themselves in a way that would advance a future life in politics. Often, women who enter a profession such as law search out areas of specialization that satisfy the need to do good works rather than to make a public name for themselves. For this reason, many highly-qualified female candidates need to be recruited to run for public office; fewer are self-recruited or motivated towards a political career. Without a strong family focus on politics or supportive and encouraging partners and friends, few women can be expected to go out of their way to exploit their professional and community credentials to advance themselves in politics.

The number of women in politics today is also affected by the political "gate-keepers," people who are responsible for fielding candidates or who have a lot of influence within the party structures. They may be reluctant to promote the chances of a woman in a winnable seat, and if they do, it may be only to meet some externally-imposed quota of potential women legislators. The number of women who have endured hopeless situations far surpasses the number who have had a real chance in a competitive riding. There always seems to be a sufficient number of men to fill those spots.

This is not to say that it is always a calculated decision on behalf of "gate-keepers" to deny women the opportunity to contest seats that are winnable. Rather, it is more a result of their being slaves to conventional wisdom about the electability of women when encouraging people to seek nominations. Winning elections is the reason for the existence of political parties, and they will take few "chances" with good seats when the outcome of any election may well be decided by only a handful of ridings. Therefore, those parties that are the most progressive in attracting female candidates, may find it harder to win an election.

A fair chance at a winnable constituency is normally the best a woman can expect. Most safe seats, which a party can only lose in the most cataclysmic situations, are staked out by male politicians and rarely become available. When they do, chances are that a man has been working towards that day for some time and already has a lock on the nomination.

"Gate-keepers" are found at all levels of the party organization and are not limited to the central bodies. No matter how progressive a position a provincial or national party may have towards involving women in electoral politics, the riding level is where the ultimate decision is made as to who the candidate will be, and all the factors that restrict the ultimate nomination of women as candidates are in play at that level.

Other factors that affect the chances of a woman candidate for a constituency nomination include the availability of workers and money. Workers mean support and money means credibility.

The most competent and experienced campaign organizers tend to flock to the person they think will be the potential winner. They want to be where the rewards are, such as the prestige of being associated with a winning campaign and the prospect of future political appointments and jobs. In most cases, they have been conditioned to believe that being part of a losing campaign will not provide them the rewards they are looking for as a result of volunteering their organizational skills.

Money is the "stuff" of politics, and without it, most potential candidacies cannot be viable. Most women candidates are not likely to be able to afford to pay for their own campaigns to gain a party nomination. Contributions for women can be much harder to come by than for men. Party regulars who can always be counted on for a contribution will still give, but there are liable to be fewer zeroes on the cheque. The challenge for female candidates is to find new sources of money to make up for the shortfall likely from the sources traditionally available to her party.

When women offer themselves as candidates, they face a host of obstacles which form part of the conventional mythology of what a politician should be like. A woman's image, appearance, and perceived role in society can all work to her disadvantage. These attributes are part of the package that determines if the voting public will take a candidate seriously and consider her credible.

Today's female candidates are faced with problems never imagined by male politicians, and a difficult collection of paradoxes. The public expects a candidate to be tough and assertive, but, at the same time, will turn away from a woman who does not seem and look feminine enough for them. One woman candidate in a southern B.C. riding was on her way to defeating the male Socred candidate during the 1975 provincial election. She was attractive, mild-mannered and had a firm grasp on the issues in that election. On the day of an important all-candidates' debate that was going to be attended by over 1,000 voters and would certainly be given news coverage throughout the riding, her handlers advised her to get tough with the opponent and bring him to task for his party's policies. Good advice for a man, but poor counsel for this woman at that time. The result was that she was considered shrill and negative and portrayed an image that no one had previously seen. She was reported to have acted like a "fisherman's wife," whatever that is. Even her most partisan supporters began to have doubts, and she lost the election. If she had been a man, her performance would likely have been considered masterful.

Liberal MP Sheila Copps puts it another way when she says that aggression in men is considered a desirable quality, while in a woman it is considered threatening and a sign of insecurity.

Age, height, weight, and clothing are all related to the way the public imagines its politicians, and they all have an affect on the chances women have of being elected. People expect their politicians to look as though they have the experience and wisdom of years, and while the stereotypical male politician is no longer late-fiftyish, the general perception of a politician is someone in their forties at least. Many political women do not seem to show their age as much as males of the same age, and this younger appearance can become a drawback if it leaves an initial impression of lack of experience.

There have been some interesting studies conducted about how physical characteristics like height and weight can have a bearing on the process of selecting a person to support in an election. While there are exceptions, the overall indication is that when it comes to meeting people and influencing their ultimate electoral decision, it is helpful to have an imposing presence. Large and tall men have a lot better chance of being elected than do those who are slight in stature or even of normal height.

This interesting observation first came to my attention when Jean Allard was elected in the northern Manitoba riding of Rupertsland. After deciding to switch from the Liberals to the NDP, he joined the race with only a few days left in the campaign. He was not well known, but he was able to get around to all the communities in the constituency before election day. He was six foot-eight and people found it difficult to say "no" to him.

Women usually don't have this advantage, and a woman who is much taller than average or is heavy-set may be considered un-attractive and less able to gain support than a man with the same characteristics. Even competing with a man of normal height and weight puts most women at a disadvantage as far as physical presence is concerned.

Clothing can also work against women in politics. There is a uniform that is considered standard wear for all would-be legislators. It consists of a dark business suit, dress shirt and tie. But regardless of what the standards of haberdashery are for politicians, most women look totally out of place complying with the code. Regardless of what kind of fashion a woman decides to adopt for an election campaign, her clothes and overall appearance can easily become a source of distraction while she is trying to deliver her message; voters will spend at least some of the first moments sizing her up on the basis of what they see and not what they hear. The grey and blue mass of male politicians in their pin-striped suits, as Allan Fotheringham puts it, works to a man's advantage.

The most dominant factor working against women, however, is the general misperception of the appropriate public roles for women. There is no stigma for a woman with a family who volunteers a lot of time to work on politics or in her community. In fact, it is encouraged. There isn't even any stigma to being active in the hierarchy of the political parties. But as soon as a woman decides to pursue a position as an elected politician, her chances are immediately determined by whether or not local opinion feels that politics is the proper vocation for a woman.

Many voters still consider that a woman should be at home caring for her family or starting a family. Many women who become candidates report that they not only have to face the frustration of dealing with people who are reluctant to support them because of the public notion of the traditional role for women, but they also feel some personal guilt for "abandoning" their families. These are attitudes that are born from deep-seated culturalization and will not go away overnight. Too many highly competent women delay or dismiss political ambitions because of gender roles that have been part of their, and their culture's, set of assumptions through much of history.

The problem is just as intense for those women who do not have "home" as a barrier to entering politics. Those who fall outside the established norm for women of their age have to overcome some level of suspicion about their personal lives. If they are single, divorced, or separated, unneeded issues in the public mindset are created. It is difficult to get a message across in a male-dominated political world where there are no written rules but a ton of conventional clichés about the roles of men and women. At the same time, many male legislators have bizarre private lives which have minimal effect on their chances. Former Conservative MP from the Yukon, Eric Neilson, showed us that in his recent book.

The fine line for female politicians lies between being flamboyant and feminine without being aggressive or abrasive. To win, women need to blend easily into the social landscape of their local communities.

Finally, women are often put into an issue ghetto when they are campaigning. The presupposition is that they will campaign on feminist issues. For a significant number of voters, these are not considered important enough. Therefore, a woman needs to establish her credibility on a variety of other public issues on the public agenda as well. Voters expect her to be far more knowledgeable about current issues than men. They ask questions about policy and philosophy that they would never direct to a male politician. In developing credibility on issues that are not considered to be part of a feminist agenda, many female politicians learn quickly that they end up alienating groups and organizations that could offer support. These organizations can feel that the candidate has turned her back on them in her pursuit of power. It's a tightrope act that every successful woman, regardless of party affiliation, has to learn to walk.

Women are working hard to change the inequities in our legislatures and are successful at convincing the voting public that the main factor in choosing a candidate to support should be competence and not chromosomes. Women are networking and building organizations designed to assist other women in their political careers. Often these networks are less concerned with partisan political lines than they are dedicated to electing women who understand those issues that are more important to women and families. They provide workers, research, and money, but more importantly, they provide a woman candidate with the moral support to make the job of politics a little easier.

All traditional national parties, and some provincial party organizations, now have special funds, controlled by women political activists, to provide extra funding for female candidates. This helps to make up any shortfall in contributions, and pays for extra expenses like child care. New Democrats were the first to recognize this need, but they are not the only ones. This relieves women candidates of some of the financial concerns they may have, and just as important, provides a vehicle for those who want their political contributions to directly benefit female candidates.

Also at the party level, there is a consensus building that more winnable seats have to be contested by women, and while the party hierarchies try not to interfere in the local nomination process, they are beginning to promote and groom women for more of these kinds of seats. This new-found enthusiasm for gender parity is induced, in part, by the fear that the party rank-and-file may begin to insist on some kind of quotas to ensure more women are elected. The party brass wants to elbow their way to the head of the parade on the issue.

The way women conduct themselves in campaigns also works to their advantage. Most campaigns with women candidates are intellectually tough and the spirit and joy over the political battle is infectious. This is due in large part to women being less willing to engage in the negative aspects of political debate; more often they tend to proceed steadfastly with their own agendas.

Audrey McLaughlin's presence in the recent NDP leadership race had a lot to do with raising the intellectual level of the debate and reducing the amount of acrimony between the candidates. As a front runner, her style provided the tone for the other candidates. Whenever one of them tried to make negative statements about other personalities and their issues, he wound up receiving negative feedback.

Women candidates often have an ability to inspire workers to volunteer more hours and expend more energy than the average male is able to, and the sheer enthusiasm of these candidacies has a positive affect on the whole electorate.

The picture for women in politics is not completely bleak. More and more women are being elected, and, where women are competing for public office, gender itself rarely becomes an issue.

Bob Rae's Ontario government has gone a long way in demonstrating that women can and should be a vital part of running a government. After some early freshman jitters, the twelve women in his cabinet are proving an inspiration to prospective women candidates in all parties.

Though not elected as premier, B.C.'s Rita Johnson is doing a capable job of restoring order to a chaotic government. The Social Credits may be too badly discredited to make an electoral come-back, but no one can say that she has not been a positive influence.

On the other side of the country, Nova Scotia's NDP leader Alexa McDonough is impressing more and more people in that province and might well be the first elected woman premier in Canada.

Today, it's a surprise when there is not a woman in a leadership race. It's hard to predict, but it should not be too long before we have a woman elected as a provincial premier or prime minister in Canada.

Maybe the day is not far away when the political parties will begin to practice a system of alternating between men and women leaders, something already practised as an unwritten rule of the Liberal Party, where they alternate between leaders from Quebec and the rest of Canada.

On the non-elected side of politics, women exercise a great deal of influence. Few politicians can honestly say that they didn't have the help of women in their campaigns. Most of the best campaign managers and organizers in the country are women. The executives for the parties at the national, provincial and local level have women members in important positions, making the decisions that guide the parties in their parliamentary and electoral activities. This influence is slowly bringing the parties to adopt an agenda that highlights what are known as women's issues.

Those candidates who do win elections will likely hire female staff. Originally, most constituency assistants were women because the pay was poor: part-time pay for full-time work. Now they are there because of their abilities. In Regina, for example, eight out of ten MLAs' constituency offices are run by women. Legislative caucuses and cabinet ministers hire women to perform a variety of jobs, like research, media relations, scheduling and political organization.

This increase in female participation in the supporting roles of political life means that those women who aspire to a similar career will have women mentors to rely on, rather than seeking out a man to show them the ropes and advance their chances.

Canadian politics needs more women in office. They will certainly go a long way in raising the moral tone of politics and begin to bring new respect to the profession. Aside from one federal cabinet minister's obscene European spending sprees while on government business, and the scandal surrounding Patricia Starr's misguided enthusiasm in supporting her party, women have generally not been a source of embarrassment to other politicians or their parties that men often have. More women in our legislatures will help Canadians feel better about politics and help remove the air of cynicism that shrouds the public view of politics and its practitioners.

Besides, the issues that are central to the legislative agenda of many women, like health care, education, and social programs, do not receive the same kind of attention as they can when there are women to scrutinize those areas. In addition, women legislators often bring a different point of view to the consideration of issues traditionally identified as male, like taxes and the economy, because women can have a far better understanding of human needs and wants, whereas male-dominated legislatures can tend to take the bottom-line as the only rule in these matters.

To the great credit of the women who have been elected over the years, voters are beginning to recognize that a woman will often present a more sincere and honest position on public issues. That is not to say that women in office are not as partisan as their male counterparts, but are simply more likely to consider all relevant points of view. As a result, more people are prepared to vote for a woman when choosing a positive alternative, rather than when registering a negative point of view. As Jan Reimer, Mayor of Edmonton said, "Certainly people have said to me they would like to have a woman for mayor, but I haven't heard them say they don't want a man."

It was nearly four decades ago, in 1952, when Charlotte Whitton faced a campaign for mayor of Ottawa in which the opposition fought on the slogan, "any man rather than have a woman." That campaign was described as a "battle of the sexes" and some men did not run for the office for fear of splitting the male vote.

We live in a democracy, but that doesn't mean that our political life is either equal or fair. Society has erected monumental obstacles against the participation of women in elected public affairs. The chances of some dramatic breakthrough in the next few years, resulting in equal legislative representation for women, is highly unlikely. What is more likely is a gradual increase in the number of women directly involved in the power processes, more women seeking direct political power, and more women and men being elected who will promote gender parity.

This will become more possible as society accepts flexibility in sex roles, in partnerships and in the work world, as male resistance to sharing power continues to decrease, and women's actual power increases. More girls will grow up with the self-esteem and self-confidence necessary to pursue educational opportunities and professional experiences which will provide them with the skills and credentials that will make them welcome to the political parties and the electorate.

6. Getting off the Mark: The First Days

"An election is like a one day
sale... the product (candidate)
in a sale (campaign) is only
available for a few hours on one day."
Joe Napolitan, U.S. Consultant

Once there is a candidate and most of the election team is in place, all working toward putting together a winning effort, the only thing missing is an election to put the "machine" to the test.

Whenever an election seems close, candidates and campaign workers strain to hear every newscast, and keep their radios tuned in to catch the newsflash that announces the beginning of the election campaign.

With the exception of the Prime Minister, or provincial premiers, nobody knows for sure when that call will come with any certainty. Only in municipal elections are the election days set by statute for a specific day, in the same way they are in the United States. The first Tuesday of November every year is the day when Americans vote in national, state-wide and local elections, with only a few exceptions. Without the certain knowledge of when the next election will come, Canadian campaigns are caught up in endless speculation until the date is announced.

Candidates and their parties are always being criticized by their workers for calling an endless string of false alarms. The trick, particularly for those not in power, is to stay in a state of readiness without burning people out emotionally, physically, and probably most importantly, financially.

Opposition parties are at a clear disadvantage in this process; they can only guess at the timing of the vote, and have to find a way to keep their candidates and supporters at peak readiness. This is not an easy task, no matter how important the stakes may be, since many people will have their own idea of when an election will be called and develop their own pre-election timetable based on this. It is an endless source of frustration for party planners to be caught yelling wolf too often, trying to get the troops up, only to find that the government has pulled back again from calling an election at the last moment.

It doesn't take much imagination to understand that this constant waiting is why parties in opposition for long periods of time often call for establishing regular election days as in the United States. Once in government, this reform-mindedness is usually dropped pretty quickly, when they realize the immense advantages the governing party enjoys in our system.

It is becoming easier to predict when an election is going to be called. The media seem to be pretty well tuned in. Their sources are usually close to the action, and they have been pretty accurate in predicting potential dates for election calls. News broadcasts are peppered with speculation when an election call is imminent, and a whole assortment of pundits and analysts begin predicting election dates.

However, the media are not always on top of the preparations. Before they dropped the writ in the 1990 provincial election, the Manitoba Conservatives filmed election ads in a park directly in front of a CBC producer's house, with no one any the wiser.

The government's own posturing and last minute flourishing of positive activity is usually a dead giveaway as well. And finally, there is almost always someone who knows what is going to happen who cannot keep a secret.

Whenever a government is four years into a five year term, an election is quite likely. This does not mean that a government might not go to the people early, to attempt to take advantage of its own popularity or the disorganization of the opposition, but even these "snap" elections are rarely a surprise any more. Elections called out of the ordinary cycle can backfire on a government that seems cynical about the electoral process. We certainly need not look beyond Ontario of 1990 to see the results.

Premier Bob Rae was quick to recognize this fact when he quipped on the eve of his Ontario victory, "maybe a summer election wasn't such a bad idea after all."

One quick election that caught me off guard was the one called by Dave Barrett in B.C. late in 1975. Someone had told me an election was being contemplated for November or December of that year. One weekend, I was going to Dauphin, Manitoba, to raise some money for the Manitoba NDP, and I was told the election might be called that Friday or Saturday. My reply was that an election in B.C. was not very likely, since the B.C. Campaign Manager was Cliff Scotton, and I knew that he was going to be in Regina that weekend, delivering fraternal greetings to the Saskatchewan NDP's annual convention. Barrett issued the writ that weekend.

I had been an organizer for the Manitoba NDP, but Scotton hired me to go to B.C. in January of 1976, to begin training campaign workers and preparing constituency associations for a spring election. I am sure Cliff was as surprised as I was the evening I was in the bar of the King's Hotel in Dauphin raising some money from local businessmen and learned about the impending election on the CBC National News.

Another important clue to an election announcement is the posture and activities of the government. There is a tactic that I call "governing like crazy." Typically, this includes a government making statements of contrition, apologizing for mistakes made in the past, and promising to do better. This is followed by a number of attractive programs and projects. It used to be good enough for a government to simply promise new programs, but now, these are actually put in place and are up and running by the time an election is called. This tactic was developed by Grant Devine in Saskatchewan, and has been further refined by others, like Brian Mulroney and Don Getty; it seems to go a long way in turning around the fortunes of a government that has hit the rocks of public opinion around mid-term, as so many seem to these days. Only time will tell how many times any one government can go to the well with this strategy.

Candidates and their workers find the call of an election a welcome release from the tension that builds with the anticipation. Finally, there is a day to work towards. "The day," as Alberta Opposition Leader Ray Martin always puts it, "when we'll find out what we're going to be when we grow up."

In the days leading to the announcement of the election, one of the important jobs for candidates is to look for campaign office space. Normally, one person is charged with the responsibility of maintaining an inventory of empty space in the constituency, which includes the price, location, and the name of the person to contact to rent it.

As an election becomes imminent, space is secured with an agreement to move in the day the election is called or a short while in advance. It is becoming more common to find many campaign offices fully operational by the time an election is finally called.

The ideal location for an election headquarters is on a main artery of the constituency, where it will be visible to as many voters as possible. It should have a lot of parking, good washroom facilities, and be close to public transportation. The office should be accessible to seniors and handicapped persons. In my experience, campaign offices rarely have an air of permanence about them. You certainly wouldn't confuse them with the opulent offices of a high powered law firm. Even though they are temporary quarters, candidates want them to be neat and tidy and not turn off people who may wander in looking for more information or wanting to volunteer some time to help out with the campaign.

The space should provide for a nice reception area where people can sit with a cup of coffee and have a chat, a work area for organizers and the manager and, with luck, a large area in the rear where the sign crew can store materials and prepare signs. I prefer offices that are open and where little is concealed. I don't like to leave the impression that there are a lot of secrets in a campaign, or that somehow there are things that other campaign workers shouldn't know about. Campaign space with a lot of small offices and hallways contributes to that feeling. It is important, though, to have a separate office or walled off area for use by the campaign manager and the candidate to make private phone calls and hold meetings with some degree of privacy.

I have run campaigns from a variety of locations. These have included a building built on stilts over the water in Kenora, a funeral parlour in Sudbury, a drive-in restaurant in Rosetown, and a collection of service stations, hotel rooms, houses, trailers, and just about every carpet or appliance store that ever went broke in the country.

There is a growing need among candidates to establish headquarters that can accommodate sizeable phone banks. Political telemarketing is the rage among all the parties, and campaign space needs to reflect the special requirements for these new tools. Quiet, comfortable and well ventilated work areas and washrooms are essential for a successful phone bank, or any campaign work space for that matter. Volunteers will cope with poor parking and old coffee, but have a hard time putting up with stale air and tobacco smoke or a dirty washroom.

Campaigns planning on running full-tilt immediately on the call of an election make prior arrangements for telephones. Most phone companies install campaign phones on a priority basis, but if the order is not in ahead of time, an unacceptable delay may result. One advantage to making arrangements for telephone equipment ahead of time is that the main phone number is usually assigned at that time, and it can therefore be included on letterheads, business cards and literature right from the beginning of the election campaign.

Telephones are such an important part of a modern campaign that a lot of thought is required when determining what equipment to rent. A phone system that has all the modern whistles and bells may be impressive, but most of the people using it will not be familiar with the technology, making the system less than user-friendly. Campaigns normally order some kind of easily operated system with a sufficient number of lines: each of the key workers will have a phone, there will be a private unpublished line for the campaign manager to use if all other lines are full; and there should be a number of direct single lines for the telephone canvassers.

Sometimes phone systems can be too simple. In a campaign in Vancouver Kingsway for Ian Waddell, we ran the election out of the Rio Hall, a huge space on Kingsway Avenue. Telephones were at desks along the walls, but they were all single lines; if the phone rang for one of the organizers who was not in, someone had to scoot across the hall to answer it. Good exercise, but not very efficient.

While suitable accommodation and appliances like telephones are very important, they do not, in themselves, put any votes in the ballot box. By the time of the election call, most serious campaign teams have already begun the job of identifying their supporters. Once the race is on, these efforts are intensified. Canvass organizers line up more canvass volunteers, while the publicity team prepares leaflets for these canvassers to use on the doorstep, and the finishing touches are put to priorizing the polls to make sure that no time is wasted in the first few valuable days.

Campaigns often lose the opportunity to seize momentum if these tasks are not started immediately. A week or more can go by before literature comes back from a printer and all the necessary human resources are put into place.

This is one situation where the telephone can be a valuable tool. A smart campaign can show strength and early visibility by using the telephone as a first-strike weapon, getting the candidate's name out, asking for support, sign locations, and money. These early calls usually start with the caller saying how glad the candidate is that the election has been called, by speaking about some general issue and asking for support and opinions from the voter. Even if the campaign hasn't established a phone bank, people can call from a friendly business office or similar space that has a lot of phones. Even though it has its down-side for both the campaign and the volunteer, callers can work from home. Sometimes candidates of the same party share phone banks.

Here is a checklist of many of the important items that need to be considered, items I insist candidates and campaign managers I work with address immediately. The list varies little between parties.

1. Do we have a campaign office?
2. How many telephones do we need? What is the cost?
3. Where will we get inexpensive furniture for the office?
4. How do we decorate and organize the office?
5. Do we have campaign literature and handouts, such as business cards and introductory brochures?
6. Up-date membership lists and worker lists from previous elections.
7. Do we have a budget?
8. Are signs, billboards etc. ordered and a strategy made up for putting them up?
9. What office equipment is needed and can it be donated, or rented at a bargain price?

10. Do we have adequate pictures and biography of the candidate; have they been sent to campaign headquarters and all media outlets?

11. Have you identified who provides central research services and advice on issues?

12. Have you begun to keep an inventory of all public events in the local area? Don't forget to include all the candidate's personal and family obligations.

13. Do you have a complete set of campaign manuals?

14. Are any training services scheduled by the central campaign for key constituency workers?

15. Do you have constituency poll maps and all the records from previous elections?

These matters may seem obvious, but I have often been shipped into a critical constituency, only to find that few or none of these issues have been attended to by the local campaign committee. It strains patience and good relations to have to push people to get caught up.

Of course, candidates have to get rolling as well. The first week or so of the candidate's campaign schedule will have been planned weeks before the election is called. With any luck, it will require only minor adjustment.

A typical candidate's calendar for the first few days of the campaign might look like this:

Day 1
> Get a haircut. Suits to cleaners.
> Press statement/reaction to election call.
> Evening meeting with election planning committee.

Day 2
> Morning— Finalize leave from work.
> Afternoon— Canvass.
> Early Evening— Canvass.
> 9:30 p.m.— Meet telephone volunteers at headquarters.

Day 3
6:00 a.m.— Plantgating.
Noon— Luncheon with other candidates in region.
Afternoon— Canvass.
7:00 p.m.— Campaign H.Q. official opening.

Day 4
7:30 a.m.— Breakfast meeting with campaign committee.
9:30 a.m.— Speak to high school class.
2:00 p.m.— Newspaper interview at H.Q.
Afternoon— Canvass.
Evening— Canvass.

In the first few hours of the campaign, candidates and their managers take time to be certain they still agree with the planned strategy and are comfortable with the plans for deployment of financial and human resources. They also decide on a regular schedule for communicating with each other. Campaign managers get very frustrated if they have to suffer periods of time without talking with the candidate about the latest developments and finding out what is happening in the candidate's world. It must have been more than frustrating to have been Don Duff's campaign manager in 1974 in northern Manitoba. The small plane Duff was travelling in had to put down behind an island on Lake Winnipeg for two or three days because of bad weather; he was stranded without any method of contacting the campaign.

Candidates who are incumbents, or who have established some prior name recognition, are most likely to be contacted by the media for their reaction to the call of the election. They should have prepared statements so that they will know what to say. Nothing can be more frustrating than to have candidates flub their first chance at free election publicity.

As the date for the call of an election becomes imminent, campaign managers want to keep track of where the candidate can be reached at all times so that the most advantage can be had from these first free media opportunities.

Linda Sarafinchan, who ran the by-election campaign for Ed Tchorzewski in 1985, turned this initial opportunity for public presence into a fine art. When the local TV station called for an interview with Ed, she put them off for a couple of hours, being careful not to miss their deadline for the supper time news. She organized the candidate, found a friendly street, which was the one where she lived, and had Ed's signs put up on several lawns. Only after all this was done did she arrange for the cameras to meet Ed on the street, making it appear that he had been campaigning all day. Evening news viewers not only saw an articulate candidate, but one who was immediately in action on the streets. There were even campaign signs on the lawns behind him. This tactic created a positive impression of the candidate for the voters watching at home.

At the same time that candidates are getting their operations into full gear, those people who are charged with the responsibility of conducting the vote itself are putting their administrative operations into place. The returning officers for each constituency have to find office space as well, order phones, get all the appropriate forms in order, and find staff to prepare the lists of eligible voters and work in the polls on election day.

The returning officer's organization chart is not much different than a paint-by-numbers set. Every task is laid out in advance by the civil servant in charge of elections, usually called the Chief Electoral Officer. Each returning officer receives instructions which describe in detail every step necessary to establish polling places, call for the nomination of candidates and prepare the list of electors. Like a paint set, the end result is not always a thing of beauty, but it is neat and standard, if nothing else, as long as the artist stays within the lines.

Candidates must take special note of the requirements for official nomination. If this is not done properly it can lead to a lot of embarrassment for the candidate and party. Nominations close two or three weeks prior to election day; this deadline must be met. There has likely never been a candidate who didn't secretly hope to be acclaimed to office, and who was therefore disappointed to find that others were also nominated to be on the ballot. Candidates usually have to make a cash deposit which will only be refunded if a certain number of votes are received. Also, in most jurisdictions, the name of the candidate's official agent has to be submitted, along with that person's written consent to serve. The official agent has to provide the signatures of a certain number of voters who nominate the candidate. A good rule for smart candidates is to turn in several more names than required, in case some are not eligible.

The political parties work hard to make sure that they have candidates in every constituency. For the party in power, or one that seems to have good prospects, this is not a difficult proposition. For parties in less competitive circumstances, candidates occasionally have to be "parachuted" on nomination day to file their papers. This can get a little haphazard, but everyone seems to get on the ballot; there have been close calls, however.

One of these took place in the 1978 Alberta General Election. A student from Edmonton was sent to be an NDP candidate in the Brooks constituency in southern Alberta, not exactly a hot bed of socialism. He was to visit a party member in Brooks, who would help get the rest of the needed signatures on the nomination papers. When the student arrived in Brooks, the man who was to help him was drunk and unwilling to do anything on the candidate's behalf. When I got the panic call from Brooks with only an hour left before the filing deadline, I advised him to get out on the street and beg for some signatures. He managed to pull it off on his own, in territory extremely hostile to the NDP. There must be a special place in heaven for loyal soldiers like that.

In one Newfoundland general election I was given the job of securing the official nominations for several candidates. Since there were no NDP constituency organizations in most of the regions of Newfoundland, we couldn't leave the official nomination of candidates to chance, in case someone got cold feet at the last minute. I met one man who was far less certain than I was that he was going to be our standard-bearer in a particular constituency. It took a great deal of talking from me and a good scolding and lecture from his wife about honour and carrying through with a commitment to bring him around. Finally, to my great relief, he agreed to go to the Justice of the Peace with me to have his nomination papers properly filled out. I missed the last ferry that night and had to sleep in my car, but at least my party had a full slate in the election.

The returning officer is responsible for ensuring that every person who is eligible to vote is on the list of electors for that constituency. It seems that with every election this process gets less efficient. It's not at all uncommon to find whole streets or apartment blocks left off the voters list due to enumerators receiving poor training or poor instructions, or just being lazy in their jobs. Sometimes the enumerator is reluctant to spend much time in a seemingly unsafe neighbourhood at night, when the majority of voters are home. In some extreme cases enumerators may even be politically motivated, since most are recruited by the parties, for the returning officer. They may choose to omit known supporters of another party or neighbourhoods where opponents have a tradition of strong support.

There is a process for voters to get on the voters list if they are left off; this usually requires only a phone call to the returning office. In some places, voters can simply be sworn in at the polls on election day if they are not on the list.

To be sure that people will vote and not be intimidated by extra forms that might have to be filled out or oaths that have to be sworn, each campaign will be organized to get their supporters on the list if they are left off. That's why an early canvass for support is important. If supporters identified by telephone and foot canvassing are not on the voters list, then they can be put on the revised voters list. Lethargic or poorly planned campaigns that are not in the field as soon as possible will lose this opportunity to secure votes. The results can be disastrous. Many inexperienced campaign managers put little or no emphasis on these details, and don't realize the problem until it is too late.

For most campaigns, one of the big events in these first few days of the election is the official opening of campaign headquarters. It's a great time for candidates to get all the people they want to help and donate to the campaign in one room and work them over.

It's a pretty standard affair. A ribbon is cut, smiles are turned on for the media, and people are recruited to work on the campaign. Other than the possible opportunity of making a press statement on the first day of the campaign to comment on the election call, this might be the candidate's first chance to perform under the pressure of actual election conditions. It's not a time for candidates to take too much for granted. The headquarters are usually filled with strong supporters, but anything less than a completely up-beat attitude will make it harder to convince potential volunteers to spend time working for that candidate.

Often, the candidate will be given the obligatory running shoes or boxing gloves. During the 1986 Alberta election, we used the opening of Ray Martin's headquarters as an opportunity to christen his campaign bus "The Delia Diesel." Sometimes there is some entertainment, and always, endless cups of coffee. These aren't really social affairs, so liquor is rarely a part of the scene. First impressions are too important to be spoiled by a rakish image of the candidate and the campaign team.

Party leaders like to make an early round of campaign headquarters openings while the rest of their tour is being planned. This provides them with a friendly and enthusiastic audience. Although the profile of a leader or some other popular member of the party is welcome, it leads to even more tension. Crowd size becomes the single most important concern, since a large contingent of media will be following the leader. An embarrassment with a small crowd lessens the chances of the leader visiting again during the campaign.

If a politician is visited by the party leader, he or she goes to great lengths to make the most of the opportunity. Svend Robinson of the NDP is one who can always be counted on to figure out the best camera angles and be sure he is in the shots being taken of the leader for print and television news. Whenever I hear that the NDP leader is in Vancouver, I make a point of looking for Svend on the evening national news. He rarely disappoints.

While the opening of campaign offices is pretty much an election ritual, interesting incidents often accompany the practice. I recall one Liberal office opening where a string of twenty dollar bills was cut, rather than the usual ribbon. It is not clear what image the campaign was trying to convey, but if it was frugality or the need for money, I doubt it worked.

That was not as bad as the Conservative candidate in Toronto whose landlord changed his mind about renting the office space at the last minute. Well wishers coming to the office opening participated in an office closing.

The first few days of an election campaign cannot go by quickly enough for candidates and campaign managers. It is sheer agony waiting for details to fall into place. Nothing seems well enough organized. The atmosphere is hot and the mood is tense. This is the time of the campaign when the candidate can make a serious public mistake in the rush to seize public attention. It will be several days into the campaign before any concrete results from all the planning and hard work become evident. Until then, it is nail-biting time for everyone concerned.

7. The Candidate: The Personal Side

"You can't make a candidate
someone they aren't. You
can protect them from someone
they are, or make them more
of what they are." *Senator Norm Atkins*

At the local constituency level, the candidate is generally the main issue. Voters without burning partisan zeal will make their decisions based largely on which of the candidates will best deal with their problems; which one will represent them best. The overall campaigns of the parties and leaders will be a factor in making that decision, but in the final analysis it is the candidate who receives the vote on election day.

Even though polling research shows that voters say the number one vote-determining factor in elections are the issues, rarely are there any true issues. What we identify as issues are usually concerns. People might say taxes are an issue, but is one candidate or party for high taxes and one for low taxes? No. This is really a concern. Most politicians would agree there should be more jobs, better health care, lower interest rates, more support for students, pensions and so on. Voters can identify with these concerns because they have to deal with them in daily life; the candidate who appeals to them most will be the one who shares those concerns. That candidate develops an emotional appeal and attraction based on the way he or she deals with those concerns.

One candidate may call for job creation through grants to business, while another may say more jobs are more likely through increasing the purchasing power of individuals. Most voters cannot identify with complex programmatic solutions to complicated problems because they have no experience with those levels of government. Therefore, they can be expected to vote for the candidate who has appealed the best to their own emotional understanding of the issues and has established credentials in a way that shows it is possible to get the job done. Candidates who tell voters how they are going to solve problems do little to interest voters; but candidates who excite and enthuse electors have a much better chance of getting their votes.

Candidates do their best to stay away from any real issues and address concerns instead. An issue has distinct sides and a candidate who chooses to support one side risks alienating people who support the other. Real issues are matters like abortion, French language rights, military spending or public funding for private schools.

Warner Troyer cites this well-known illustration in his book, "200 Days." It deals with a candidate for a county judge's chair in an election in Kentucky. The major issue was whether the county should pay a bounty on polecats. When finally confronted with this issue in the last days of the campaign, the candidate replied, "Some of my friends, and they are fine people, favour a bounty on pole-cats," said the candidate. "And some of my other friends, and they are fine people too, oppose the bounty. But unlike my good friend on the platform with me, and I speak of the yellow-bellied candidate for the opposing party, I am not going to duck this issue, and I'm not going to run from telling you how I feel. There's only one honourable course open on this matter, my good friends: I stand, foursquare and forever, with my friends."

Bill Vander Zalm was not far from the truth when he said, "The smart candidate avoids detailed policy statements; they rarely help and can do you harm. Your answers should concentrate on style." Unfortunately for him, he has not followed his own advice very closely on moral issues that have clearly established sides.

All of this re-emphasizes the role and importance of candidates in the political process. The "X"s go beside their names and, no matter how extensive a campaign has been waged at the party level, or how much the leaders have travelled and debated, the voters' judgement depends, under normal electoral circumstances, on their impressions of the local candidates.

Therefore, it is the job of a would-be legislator to leave that winning impression. The candidate is the warmest and most effective means of contacting the voter. In some polling research I have conducted, one of the questions asked from time to time requires respondents to indicate whether each in a list of voter contact methods influences their decisions on who to vote for a lot, a little, or not at all. Meeting the candidate is always at the top of the list, and number one by a great margin.

Here is the usual ranking of these voter contact methods when asked in public opinion surveys:

Candidate.
Candidate's family.
Friend or supporter of candidate canvassing at the door.
Endorsement of candidate by persons respected by the voter.
Telephone call from friend or supporter of candidate.
Personal letter from candidate.
Radio, TV and paper news about the candidate.
Non-personalized mail from candidate.
Paid radio, TV and paper ads.
Signs, billboards and novelties.

Serious candidates know that they simply have to see as many voters as possible within the time allowed. Campaign strategists determine which voters take the highest priority for the candidate's time, and allocate campaigning hours accordingly. There are many candidates who are reluctant to go door to door or press the flesh, but few of them ever get elected.

Meeting voters in their own homes leaves the most lasting impression, and if done properly, a positive one. There is a special attraction about a candidate who will work that hard. Candidates do not always canvass door to door by themselves. It is important for them to have someone along who can help them get away from voters who want to monopolize their time, to help them keep notes on each visit, and offer encouragement and motivation to keep going.

Some candidates might take along "beaters" who travel up both sides of a street telling people that the candidate is coming and asking them if they would like to meet the candidate. This has the advantage of eliminating the time wasted waiting for an answer at an empty home. It also reduces the number of voters that the candidate can contact, since when first asked by a stranger, many voters will decline the opportunity to meet a politician. It's really only effective if the candidate is already very well known.

There are lots of little tips to get the greatest advantage from canvassing. A good one that long-time Yorkton-Melville MP Lorne Nystrom offers novice candidates is to walk on the side of the street that faces the traffic. Therefore, people driving by can also see the candidate at work and honk, wave, or offer whatever other gestures seem appropriate.

The candidate's job on the doorstep is to concentrate on matters that concern each individual voter and make each one feel that he or she has the candidate's complete attention and interest. The candidate introduces him or herself, and lets the voter know about the canvass of the neighbourhood, asks if there are any concerns, and closes by asking for support. It is surprising how many politicians will do everything right except ask for support. They stay away from it as though there was something sleazy in the simple act of asking someone to vote for them. For some it may be the fear of rejection, but voters need to know that they matter, and asking them for their votes is an important way of showing that.

If support is indicated, candidates also ask if they can have a campaign sign put up, and if the voter has some time for volunteer work. The candidate must ensure that the campaign is notified of any additional information requested by the voter so that it can be sent out immediately. Sometimes the voter may need help for a particular problem with a government department or program. These problems are also given to someone on the campaign team so that action can be taken on behalf of the constituent.

Many suggestions can be offered to new candidates, but if asked, most veterans would offer advice much like the following:

- Be a good listener; don't pretend to have all the answers;
- Never argue, always explain, and leave some facts to be considered, keeping the lines of communication open;
- Apologize if you've interrupted a meal or a nap;
- Dress in a fashion that is appropriate to the district being visited;
- Always leave a calling card or a piece of literature;
- Don't canvass after dark;
- Be friendly and say hello to passers-by;

- Make no promises; the only one you can be sure to keep is to work hard on the voters' behalf, look into their problems and try to improve the overall condition;
- Never take notes about your visit while the voter can see you;
- Know the voters' schedules and be familiar with major events, i.e. you won't be welcome in too many homes during a World Series or Stanley Cup Playoff game;
- Not everyone will vote for you, so don't take rejection personally.

Some encounters between voter and candidate can get a bit nasty. PC candidate Martin Bidzinski in Dauphin, Manitoba got a punch in the mouth for his troubles when calling on a household during an election campaign. One local resident explained his neighbour's behaviour this way: "It wasn't that he was a Tory; they just don't like politicians."

Door to door canvassing is not the only way for candidates to meet the voting public. One method that has become less important in recent years is plantgating where the candidate greets workers as they go in to work and passes out literature. In Sudbury, Bud Germa's message was a simple one liner, "Vote the bastards out." Plantgating is less effective now because the workers can come from a number of different constituencies; more often, in the past, workers lived close to their workplaces and commuted very little.

Candidates might stop to talk to people at bus stops in the morning while voters are on their way to work, introduce themselves while voters are shopping in a local mall or supermarket, or visit with potential voters in a queue for a movie or sporting event. As long as the approach is warm and personal, and not artificial or opportunistic, talking to voters in any setting will reap some benefit for the candidate.

In the dual member provincial constituency of Vancouver Centre, Emery Barnes and Gary Lauk used to have a refreshing approach. They would station themselves outside downtown high rise apartments and offer orange juice and friendly "good mornings" to residents as they left for work. They made quite a pair and were hard to miss: Barnes was black, 6'4", and a former football player, and Lauk was a short and energetic lawyer.

Any place people gather during an election makes an excellent target for politicians. The best events are usually informal and community oriented. It is easier for candidates to mingle when there is less pressure on them and they can come and go as they please. Some candidates feel very awkward and uneasy at these kinds of events. They need to take people with them who are familiar with the crowd and can help introduce them to people.

Even old pros can learn new tricks. I recall Allan Blakeney's jubilance at discovering how receptive people were to him when he worked the line-up at a rural pancake breakfast. He found that by walking up and down the line-up he was able to discuss issues and do a little joking and entertaining; this was a lot better than interrupting voters after they had gotten their food and were sitting and chatting with friends, eating, scolding the children, or whatever.

Former Prime Minister Lester Pearson offered this account of his first day out meeting voters when he had decided to become a politician after a distinguished career as a diplomat. He was accompanied by Senator Farquhar, who was very well known in the Algoma constituency which had been chosen for Pearson to gain a seat in the House of Commons. Pearson wrote in his memoirs, "We would greet everyone we met, or if we were driving by, we waved. By the end of the day I had become relaxed talking to voters and a vigorous waver. Then, at the end of the day, I saw a farmer close to the road. So, naturally, I waved; the Senator's arms, however, remained still. He approved of my enthusiasm but said: 'You can stop waving now, we're out of the constituency.' It was another lesson in politics-selectivity and conservation of effort."

Sometimes, candidates stand on the edge of the road and wave at traffic while people are heading to work. I always think this is a good idea, but if the candidate doesn't like it, the potential for positive influence is diminished. Once I sent Les Benjamin, MP for Regina Lumsden, out to do this. He said he would "look like a dork," and he went only after extensive cajoling. He was right, he did look like a dork. The expression on his face didn't convey an upbeat message to the motorists; I should have listened to him in the first place. Les's strength is one-on-one, and his time is always better spent on the doorstep.

If that incident didn't show that roadside campaigning was a poor idea, then Alberta Tory Ralph Klein's excursion into curbside politics should throw a wet towel over the idea permanently. Klein, a group of supporters, and several media people were all gathered at the road's edge during the morning rush hour in Calgary, waving at the motorists. There for all to see on television was a two car accident which seemed to be caused in part by this political distraction. The entourage moved across the street, but as soon as they were re-established, again on television, another accident ensued.

Politicians who know how to work a room of voters are a joy to watch. They move effortlessly from person to person, showing great charm and wit, and leave a lasting impression on everyone they meet.

Here are some ideas, gathered from talking with successful candidates, that I pass on to new candidates about how to work a crowd.

The candidate should have a plan of action before entering the room. This can be done in two ways. Someone can check out the room in advance, make note of important people who are present and get a reading on the mood of the crowd and the kinds of things that are being discussed. It's also useful to know in advance if any opposing candidates or high-profile members of the opponents' teams are also present. An important part of this initial briefing is to plan what route will be taken through the crowd.

Other candidates do not need this advance work and are perfectly comfortable making a mental plan after an initial observation of the lay of the land from the entrance. Candidates want to stay away from people who may ask embarrassing questions or who want to monopolize valuable time. This makes prior planning of how to approach a crowded room even more important.

Some simple do's and don'ts for making a positive impression:

- Grin and bear hard handshakes that hurt. Try not to wear a ring on the shaking hand.

- Always have a firm handshake.
- Maintain eye contact. Don't look around the room or at another person while talking to a voter. (I have always found this habit most annoying. It says that there must be somebody more important in the room someplace.)
- Make each person feel that he or she is the only person in the room.
- Be energetic; pull yourself up straight with good posture.
- Don't be overbearing or bombastic.
- Don't wear dark glasses.
- Don't ignore anyone, particularly youngsters.
- Be honest and consistent in talking about issues.
- Be yourself.

There are other things such as the use of humour and touching that a candidate should be mindful of when meeting people. People like to share a joke or a light-hearted moment, but unless the candidate is using self-deprecating humour, then he has to be sure that his jokes are not insensitive or offensive. Jean Chrétien can tell a joke about French Canadian stereotypes, but it would be difficult for Bill Van Der Zalm to do the same without censure.

Many people shy away from any physical contact beyond a simple handshake, so candidates also have to be certain they are not getting a negative reaction from backslapping or touching arms or shoulders when speaking to people. John Turner might have given this a bit more thought before patting women's bottoms.

A candidate has to make connections between names and faces. This is where a helper is invaluable. Helpers can ask voters their names and introduce them to the candidate. Although there are a host of systems that can be used as an aid to remembering names, the best possible advice is to listen and if necessary ask to have the name repeated. Then, by using the name often throughout the conversation, there is a better chance that it will be remembered for future use. Some candidates put a lot of stake in courses in memory development and word association, but it is not that important in my view as long as a candidate who might have a difficulty in this area recognizes shortcomings and works at overcoming them. Besides, most voters will remind a candidate or elected official of who they are and on what previous occasions they may have met.

Candidates need to know their limitations or come to grips with any fears they may have when among people. During the Manitoba campaign in 1990, Sharon Carstairs told a Winnipeg *Free Press* reporter that her greatest fear was that she might accidentally walk into the men's washroom. She felt as though this fear had come true when, preparing for the leader's debate, she encountered a man in the washroom. It turned out that *he* was in the wrong place and not her.

Finally, encountering hostile voters can be the most discouraging part of working a room. The best strategy in these circumstances is to break off the conversation as quickly as possible and keep moving. It will do no good to get angry or become embroiled in an argument. People expect more from candidates than that. If it becomes difficult to move on, and the voter is clearly trying to bait a candidate, the best advice is for them to listen patiently and then make a graceful exit. The candidate will more than likely gain sympathy and respect from those who witness such a scene.

During an election, candidates often find themselves dealing with people who want to see them about some issue or another. I have had to deal with people wanting to see the candidate about issues as diverse as securing a ride on the next shuttle to Mars so that there will be artists in space, to homeowners concerned about local sewers.

Generally, the motives of those who want to talk to the candidate are genuine and sensible, but not all of them require the candidate's time. For instance, those who want to offer advice about how the campaign should be run or want to help the candidate should be referred to the campaign manager. Others on the campaign team can help those who require assistance with problems, or can at least make initial inquiries about the nature of the problem so that the candidate has as much information as possible and crank matters do not slip through the cracks. In most campaigns, all these requests for the candidate's time are screened by the campaign manager in advance, and usually, the most required of the candidate is a quick follow-up phone call or a signature on a letter.

The candidates finally presented to us in pictures, in person, or on television, have probably spent as many sleepless hours deciding what to wear as they have devoted to considering platform or strategy.

The general rule followed by most candidates is to stick to the styles that are prevalent in the community: they shouldn't dress any better than the local high school principal or bank manager. Yet, candidates will insist on being overdressed and arrive at a rodeo in a three piece suit. The trick for the candidate is to maintain an authoritative air, without being pretentious. The ability of individual candidates to do this varies and it really can't be taught. Roy Romanow can look as relaxed and informal at a picnic in a shirt and tie with his suit jacket slung over his shoulder as someone else might in blue jeans and a tank top. He can preserve the authority of his position and yet seems to fit right into the crowd.

If a candidate's manner of dress is noticed, then there is likely something wrong with it. A candidate's wardrobe should not detract from the effectiveness of the message.

I couldn't help thinking of this while watching Gary Doer in the 1990 leaders' debate during the Manitoba election. He took off his jacket and wore his shirt and tie. I am sure he was trying to convey a down-to-earth, no nonsense image, but his dress was distracting since it was so different from what we expect at such formal events. Most felt Doer was the most effective of the three leaders, but he might have been even more effective if he had been more conventional in his attire.

Here is the kind of advice many candidates receive about dress habits, and are offered by James Gray, who is a wardrobe consultant.

Tall candidates need to tone down their size and avoid being overbearing. Men should wear dark pinstriped suits when addressing large crowds or appearing on TV. They should wear a white shirt with striped tie, unless appearing on TV, when the shirt should be pale blue. Shoes should be dark with black socks that extend above the calf. When trying to tone down the authority conveyed by their size, they should wear medium to dark grey suits.

Tall women should wear suits or dresses with solid dark colours. Blazers should be dark blue or gray flannel to complement the dress or skirt. Blouses should always be long-sleeved and white, medium blue or cream coloured.

Short to medium men will likely select navy blue or gray flannel solid suits or black pinstripes. Shirts should be long-sleeved and solid white for highest authority or blue for TV. Ties should have subtle stripes in navy and red, while shoes are best when black or dark brown with laces. Women of the same height will wear suits and dresses that are navy, muted pinstriped, black, camel or gray flannel. Blouses should be solid white or blue pinstriped. Small women should always wear a blazer or jacket in situations demanding authority.

Presumably candidates do not heed Thoreau's advice, "Beware of all enterprises that require new clothes."

Some people say that voters are hesitant to support candidates who have names that are difficult to pronounce. In one American TV commercial I have seen, a candidate with a very difficult Slavic name produced commercials where people were shown having a very hard time getting the name straight. The result led to instant name recognition, even if voters couldn't actually repeat it out loud!

Ed Tchorzewski had a unique approach to the same problem. His campaign manager, Linda Sarafinchan, came up with two buttons. One had his first name above the first five letters of his last name. The second button contained the last six letters of the last name. This led to Ed being identified as "Eddy two-buttons," although the less reverent among us simply mangled the name by calling him "Ed Shot-of-Whiskey." People eventually got to know him as Eddy T. and had no doubt as to who they were going to vote for.

Many campaign managers, and the general public for that matter, overlook the fact that a candidate is not a neat and simple package. The stress and trial of the campaign trail are as much a burden to a candidate's family as to the candidate. No matter how thorough and intense the preliminary discussions have been between spouses and among family members about the campaign, and no matter how deep the commitment and support from family, nothing prepares freshman candidates and their families for what is bound to happen during the campaign.

Simply put, a campaign will alter the way in which the family is organized. The campaign, in the form of the campaign manager, imposes a new authority figure. Family finances are threatened. There is a dramatic change in the amount of time the candidate can allocate to family activities, and the family loses its privacy.

Candidates and their families quickly learn that the campaign manager has influence over many decisions which were previously the domain of the family alone. These include simple matters such as what to say, who to see, and what to wear. Or, they may be far more important items, including whether to attend events that are family oriented such as school concerts, or buying a new car.

The campaign sets even personal priorities, and family activities are regulated on the basis of the needs of the overall image of the candidate and the time required to meet as many voters as possible.

Many veteran political families will be used to these problems, but even some of them endure worse stress in later years in politics, when children are sixteen or seventeen and have different needs that are harder to meet than when they were six or seven. Often, some extra time from grandparents or other family members easily takes up the slack for political parents when their children are small.

Many of my organizational colleagues often question the true motives of politicians who retire or refuse extra responsibilities because they say they want to devote more time to their families; especially if they were not known as the greatest family people in the first place. However, the more I meet men and women in public life who have deep regrets that they did not spend more time with their families during their careers, the more I give credence to this excuse.

It is not only family routine that gets interrupted by politics; family finances also become more uncertain. The candidate's income, or at least a large part of it, may be removed from the household budget for a month or more, and at a time when money may be even tighter because of the necessity of covering additional clothing, travel, and family expenses.

The unknown can be even more disconcerting. Those who have

not been elected before may not know what the financial future will look like. Those who are in office have to face the possibility of loss of income if they are defeated, and may not have the security of a professional background or business to return to if they lose. The candidate may have lost enough objectivity to be oblivious to these problems, but the family at home will certainly give it a lot of thought.

If it's not bad enough to be concerned about financial prospects, most candidates have to decide where they are going to live when the legislative body they are running for is in session.

The spouses of candidates end up having to do even more work to keep house and home together. More chores and responsibilities are left behind when the candidate hits the campaign trail. The spouse has to cope with an enormously enlarged workload, not to mention the additional pressure to take an active role in the campaign.

The spouse may be the only person who is concerned about the candidate's well-being and health, and this can sometimes lead to the spouse interfering with the scheduling of the candidate's time and the day-to-day operations of the campaign.

Given the traditional role of women in the Canadian family, it is no wonder that there are few women in politics with young, growing families. Women need a great deal more support in their bid for political office than men, and it would be a special husband indeed who provided the same level of support to a woman that most women provide to their political husbands.

Families are hurt most by the loss of privacy. The whole family is part of the candidate's package, and people want to know as much about the rest of the family as they do about the candidate. Some candidates have long since worked out techniques for keeping the family removed from politics by treating family life as something outside the public arena. Regardless, you can be certain that the day will come when the politician returns home, only to find that the spouse has been hounded by the press for an interview.

Children can be confused and bewildered when they learn that the parents of their best friends do not support their own fathers or mothers, and they can become the target of cruel playground

catcalls and prejudices that other kids have picked up at home.
Candidates who are insensitive to the feelings of their children can
end up making the situation worse if they do not spend extra time
dealing with these problems.

Rumour and gossip become commonplace during election campaigns and can cause great damage to any relationships that are
already shaky at best. Researcher Janet Taliaferro notes that suf-
fering can be intensified by public knowledge of what were once
private and personal difficulties. If the candidate or spouse has an
infidelity, drug, or drinking problem, it often becomes the subject
of casual conversation, or can be brought up in the press; reputations can be destroyed.

The job of helping the family cope with these added pressures
falls on the shoulders of the campaign manager. The family will
want to fight back against the encroachment on their routine and
privacy. The campaign manager keeps the family informed and
makes them as much a part of the campaign as they want to be,
and at the same time, makes sure that the priorities of the campaign remain paramount. The campaign manager also provides
the support the candidate needs to maintain his or her position in
the family, and often has to take the blame for the inability of the
candidate to address common family responsibilities.

The best course for a candidate's family is to treat the whole
thing as a kind of adventure, one that has an end point to it.

At the beginning of this chapter I pointed out that next to the
candidate, the family was the best way of contacting the voter with
warmth and effectiveness. Not only should family members take
part in activities with the candidate if they can; they should also be
out campaigning in their own right. The wife or husband of the
candidate makes a terrific surrogate, and when he or she appears
at a voter's door, serves almost as well as the candidate. In fact, I
doubt there are many experienced campaign managers who
haven't said at least once, "We'd be a lot better off if Joe's wife were
the candidate."

Even the youngest family members can take a role in distributing leaflets, putting up signs, or helping around the office. Teen-
aged family members can help recruit that precious political
commodity, the young volunteer. Even babes in arms can make

wonderful soldiers by being conversation pieces who can induce even hard-nosed opposition voters to take a kinder view of a candidate.

One way a campaign manager works to soothe family members and remind them of their special status is to bestow a little extra attention on them. They will show as much interest in the canvass results turned in by the spouse as they do the candidate's. They might go as far as to provide additional organizational time for the spouse's activities if they are particularly effective. Too often, campaign managers treat spouses as a necessary nuisance, and do not take the time to keep spouses fully informed and learn what their needs might be. This is a fatal mistake, and almost always leads to deteriorating relationships between the campaign manager and candidate.

The wife of one Saskatchewan MLA told me how frustrating she found campaigning; everyone treated her as though she knew everything about elections, when she hadn't the slightest clue what it was all about or why things had to be done the way they were. People around her always assumed her level of knowledge was superior, since her husband was so successful. A quick primer on electoral politics and some reassuring words and she was an even more intense campaigner than before.

The most exasperating experiences with candidates' spouses happen at the other end of the spectrum; the husband or wife who knows it all and is sure that no one on the campaign team knows a thing. Such spouses try to run the campaign and the candidate and give directions to volunteers. The only way out of this situation is to take the lead of a good boxer who punches his way out of the clinches. The campaign manager has to organize his or her way out of the problem, by directing the energy and enthusiasm in a positive direction, always working toward advancing the candidate's cause. This means finding a role for the spouse that will promote the progress and harmony of the campaign.

As if candidates didn't have enough to worry about, what with being concerned about what to say and being sure they are saying it to the right people; being concerned about their attire and manners; and ensuring that all is well at home candidates need to pay close attention to their health.

Grant Notley always had to have a supply of oranges when he travelled during a campaign. High on the list of the wagonmaster would be a bag of Valencias, because everyone knew that Grant was subject to campaign colds induced by hard work and long hours. The oranges never prevented the inevitable cold, but they did serve as a temporary placebo and likely made Grant less cranky.

Candidates with medical problems, particularly if these are stress-induced, are courting trouble. The campaign period magnifies these problems, and if there is any way to reduce or eliminate stressful conditions such as over-indulgence in alcohol, or excessive smoking and eating it will help a lot in coping with the real stress caused by the campaign.

One way candidates can alleviate stress is to prepare a written campaign plan well in advance of the election. Regular reference to this plan will put candidates' minds at ease when they start to wonder if everything possible is being done to win and whether those things being done are right.

Candidates handle stress in different ways. Most who participate in some kind of sport find some time during the campaign to remain active; it gives a break from concentrating on politics and provides the body a workout. I like motor sports, and when I am racing, the last thing on my mind is politics. Political friends of mine who enjoy golf, racquet ball, or similar pursuits also share the old adage, "A change is as good as a rest."

I advise candidates that I work for to carve out time in their schedule that cannot be touched, that is theirs alone, to spend with family and to participate in activities that are important to them. And, as a rule, I like candidates to take a full day off shortly before election day, so they are prepared to give 100% in the final stretch.

As a campaign manager, it is my responsibility to see that the candidate is healthy. The candidate is the spiritual leader of the campaign, and it is an important part of motivating volunteers to be able to point to the hard work of the candidate. If he or she is irritable, late, anxious or depressed because of too much stress, he or she is no longer an effective part of the campaign, and I have lost my greatest weapon.

The thrill of success, the agony of defeat, the pressures of meeting the demands of a complex electorate, and the need to perform well and succeed, are all part of a campaign; all are stress-producing. Candidates can't always control what happens outside their bodies, but they can control what happens inside. The choice is theirs, and the difference just might win an election for them.

Taking proper care of their personal lives during a campaign means that candidates are more at ease when pressing the flesh, and in meeting that one voter who might make the difference in the results on election day.

8. The Candidate: Getting the Message Out

"Oh Lord, teach us to utter
words that are gentle and
tender, because tomorrow
we may have to eat them."
A politician's prayer
"The mind will absorb only
as much as the seat can
endure." *Tommy Douglas*

The candidate is the campaign's best vehicle for getting its message out to the public. Whether it's making a speech, debating opponents at an all-candidates' meeting, or taking advantage of free media coverage, the candidate has to apply time honoured and proven techniques to this campaign priority. In this chapter we will explore the ways Canadian candidates deliver the message personally.

When asked what qualities make a good candidate, the public will often consider good public speaking the most important. This is really a throw-back to a previous day in politics, when campaigning was more public and personal and did not rely so much on the media. Today, a candidate can go through an entire campaign and never be called on to make a speech in public.

Occasions requiring candidates to give full-blown political speeches are much fewer than in the days before the use of electronic, print, and mail media became so extensive. Public meetings were once the only way most voters got to learn about the issues, and a candidate had to be an orator in the classic sense in order to attract votes.

Candidates may be called on to deliver speeches to organizations, or to party and campaign meetings. It varies, but politicians' speeches are mainly given to the converted; they seldom speak to the general public during an election campaign. This means that political speeches take on less importance in voter choices between local candidates.

There are still occasions in modern campaigns, however, which do require good speaking and communication skills. These include all-candidates' meetings, debates, and media interviews.

Less emphasis on public speaking as a vehicle for political messages, though, does not mean that candidates shouldn't learn all they can about handling themselves in front of a crowd. Knowing that they can perform if they have to builds self-assurance and makes them more capable of carrying out other aspects of the job.

Before candidates begin preparing a campaign speech, whether it is to be given to a group of supporters or to the general public, they need some advance information. The campaign manager should find out all the pertinent details. How much time is being allowed for the speech, on what topic should it be? What kinds of people will be in attendance, and how many are expected? It is important to find out what else is on the agenda; who will be introducing the candidate; who will be at the head table if there is one; and whether there will be a question period following the speech. The answers to all these questions form an important part of planning what to say and how to deliver that message.

Candidates take a number of different approaches to planning a speech. Some make no notes at all, and are proud of their ability to "wing it," but only a very special speaker can speak without any reference, because the speaker's job is to present ordinary information in a way that makes sense and inspires passion and commitment from the listeners. It is pretty hard for a speaker to get from the beginning to the end of a speech without running off the road without a plan.

The plan needn't be elaborate because candidates are dealing with ideas and concepts with which they should be familiar. The most difficult part in delivering any speech is getting started and finished. To avoid running around in circles, politicians often write out the opening and concluding paragraph or two of a speech; the remainder is recalled through simple point form notes.

Grant Notley was a master at speaking from the simplest of notes, which were never more than three or four points written on a scrap of paper; this was all he needed to stay on track and make his points.

Often, politicians speak from scripted speeches written by them-selves or others. This can be time-consuming; revisions and amend-ments have to be made to suit individual styles and understandings of the issues. One Edmonton MLA I knew always wrote his own speeches and spent a lot of time refining them and bouncing ideas off campaign workers. This was his way of avoiding going door to door. He lost his seat, but he gave some great speeches.

Candidates who rely on written speeches must be sure they are thoroughly familiar with the contents. If they don't know what they are actually saying, they can put an audience to sleep, and do very poorly at answering questions. The best situation for someone who uses a written text is to make sure it is always authored by the same person; that way there is consistency in the style and presentation of ideas from one speech to the next.

Politicians should avoid a false sense of security that might creep in just because they are packing a hot speech in their pocket or purse. Delivering a speech from a written text requires as much thought about pace and timing as any other speech.

The needs of the campaign plan must be served every time a candidate speaks in public. Contents and direction of speeches need to be consistent with the overall theme of the campaign because, in order for voters to understand and accept a political message, it needs to be repeated over and over, whether it is delivered in leaflets, ads or in speeches.

The need for repetition is the most offered advice to candidates concerning speech content. They must tell the audience what they are planning to tell them, tell them, and then tell them again what has just been told them.

I usually accompany the candidate I am working with to a speech so that I can offer an assessment afterwards, and assist with interviews with the media. I hate attending these events because I worry about the candidate slipping up, even though this rarely happens. I'm strictly a white-knuckled listener.

Here are some notes on public speaking offered by Tommy Douglas to CCF candidates. I have seen the same list in various forms in campaign manuals of the Conservatives and Liberals as well, proving that common sense knows no partisan bounds.

- Look your audience in the eye.
- Do not talk about your opponent.
- Be positive; do not spread gloom.
- Be brief.
- Do not dawdle into a speech.
- Do not waste the time of the audience by making up your speech as you go along.
- It is not what you say that counts, but what the audience hears. If they are not listening, you are only talking to yourself.
- Avoid distracting mannerisms.
- Avoid lengthy quoting of statistics. Know the numbers, but only give the conclusions to be drawn from them.
- Three rules of public speaking: 1. Stand up to be seen, 2. Speak up to be heard and, 3. Shut up to be appreciated.

Two of the most common mistakes made by professional and novice politicians alike, is failing to show a positive attitude and not knowing when to end a speech.

Too often, politicians will be negative in attitude and outlook. The greatest crime is to lament the size of the crowd or admit the strength of an opponent. For example, candidates seem obliged to apologize if there is a small turnout for a public meeting they have sponsored. If the crowd is sparse, it will be noticed. If excuses are necessary, that's a damage control problem best left to the campaign manager. The candidate needs to thank those who did take the time to turn out.

Tommy Douglas's final rule: "Shut up to be appreciated," is shattered far too often by well-meaning candidates. They make really fine speeches, touch on all the important themes, and use dramatic examples to drive each point home; then they ruin all the impact of an otherwise excellent speech by not knowing when to quit. I suppose they are enraptured with their own voices and stunning logic and wisdom, but the point comes when it should be turned off. Allan Blakeney has a wonderful sense of when he has passed the audience's ability to absorb any more of his speech. He bridges the gap between the body of his speech and the closing with a line like, "I have probably missed two or three excellent opportunities to get out of this speech..." This regains the attention of his listeners, and he can hit them with a tough closing that repeats everything the audience may have missed earlier.

Part of the preparation for candidates is familiarizing themselves with the answers to anticipated questions. Even if there isn't a formal question and answer period, there are always people who will come up after a speech to ask questions or make points, and if there are media representatives covering the event, they will want some quotes to help in preparing their stories.

Question periods following a speech can turn into free-for-alls, particularly if there are people in attendance who hold specific views very firmly. The uncontrolled nature of a question period can lead to situations that produce major errors, and they are usually too long or dominated by a "know it all." Some questioners may also be there to cause trouble for candidates by baiting them with difficult or embarrassing questions. And if those are not enough reasons to be leery of question periods, candidates can make matters even worse by spending too much time answering simple questions or by forgetting what message they should be delivering, leaving conflicting or inconsistent ideas in the minds of the listeners. Candidates should try to relate a question to a specific principle or theme. That way, if they haven't all the necessary information on the topic, they can still provide a cogent and satisfactory reply.

My preference is to allow no more than a very brief question period and then schedule a lot of time for the candidate to be available to mix and mingle following the meeting. This satisfies those who have points they want to make and provides some accessibility to others who are reluctant to ask a question in front of the whole crowd.

When I first moved to B.C., I had to get used to a phenomenon with which I had little experience, being a gentle Prairie-boy. This was the heckler. Yes, I had attended meetings where someone grumbled a little from the back of the room, or where others shouted spontaneous words of encouragement, but that was nothing compared to B.C. political audiences. There, heckling is entertainment in itself.

Great campaigners learn to turn the heckler's words into positive statements to help them make their points. Above all, candidates should face this challenge with humour, remaining cool and in charge at all times. Heckling can be harder to handle when it comes from supporters who urge candidates on by imploring them to make some negative comment about the opposition which has been overlooked, usually on purpose. It's hard for speakers to maintain their composure when all this is going on, but if they keep their balance, they endear themselves to the crowd.

I have always thought that hecklers were frustrated politicians, their heckling reminds me so much of the background during the proceedings in the House of Commons or provincial legislatures. The phrases that get thrown back and forth in a particularly lively audience would be right at home in those political fora.

My first experience with hecklers was in 1975, during the B.C. provincial election. Alex MacDonald, who has a terrific wit, was speaking to a rally in support of MLA Gerry Anderson in Kamloops. Everything went well until the heckling began. The first volley was fired by our own people, who offered Alex a variety of colourful phrases to describe Social Credit. This must have inspired a couple of Socreds, because they started in with some of the problems of the Barrett government. That was all MacDonald needed. He cranked up the Scottish brogue and destroyed his detractors, to the delight of everyone. I began to look forward to public meetings so I could catch more of this theatre.

It is unfortunate that the trend today seems to be toward calling the cops or sicking a goon squad on hecklers and protesters to drag them a safe distance away. That kind of action seems to diminish democracy.

Some candidates take themselves and their topics far too seriously and don't see that politics is the place for the odd well-placed joke. Humour has an important role to play in a political speech. Jokes that have a flavour of real life coming from candidates' own experiences have the most effect. These jokes can offend no one and add a personal touch to an impersonal situation. Candidates can also make positive points with an audience by making fun of themselves. Statements like, "I am concerned about what is happening in government— it has caused me a lot of sleepless afternoons," helps build a solid rapport with an audience.

Bob Orben writes jokes for politicians as a living. He has written for the Red Skelton TV show and for personalities as diverse as Barry Goldwater and Dick Gregory. He suggests that humour in politics should be relevant to the content of the speech in which it is used. Jokes should be funny (which can be difficult if the audience is not led up to the laugh), should emphasize commonality, and should show an understanding of the audience's situation.

A common public speaking problem for many candidates is being caught short when asked to say grace at a public meal. If they are not in the habit of doing it at home, they may end up speechless and lose some face if they cannot deliver. I know many politicians who carry a suitable grace in their wallets and pull out a tattered scrap of paper to serve on these occasions.

You might think candidates would welcome every opportunity to present their views to the public, but, in fact, there are many occasions when such invitations are ignored or turned down flat.

Candidates are sometimes invited to speak to groups in front of which they do not wish to appear. Usually this is because the group might support another candidate or is in favour of policy positions not supported by the candidate. In these cases, it is likely a waste of time for the candidate to attend; there is no political advantage to be gained. Candidates know their own supporters in the group will understand the political realities of the situation. There are always exceptions to this rule, and each candidate has his or her own preference as to how to approach these situations. He or she may feel that the chance to gain a handful of converts is well worth the effort.

Debates and all-candidates' meetings are two other kinds of public campaign events in which candidates may elect not to participate. The theory is that if you are ahead, you should not expose yourself to potential disaster. Candidates who are ahead have everything to lose with a poor performance; those who are behind or are challengers have everything to gain. You never see a ten-year incumbent politician challenging a political newcomer to debate.

Candidates who wish to avoid these encounters instruct their campaign managers to drag out negotiations for a date as long as possible, resulting in a situation where, "time constraints make the debate impossible." The other favourite tactic is to announce that the candidate does not have time to debate since he must see every voter possible and is just too busy to waste time in a debate.

When an organization holds an all-candidates' meeting and one of the candidates is not in attendance, there is usually some mention of it in the media. Certainly those candidates who do appear raise the fact in their addresses. In spite of this, truant candidates rarely suffer much political damage if they are in a comfortable position.

This is not always the case, as Alberta's Premier Don Getty can attest. He refused to debate with the Liberal candidate in his own constituency, citing a busy schedule as party leader. The Liberal, Percy Wickman, showed up with a large stuffed chicken, which he placed in the premier's chair. The resulting press attention went a long way in building Wickman's campaign, and resulted in Getty losing personal credibility and his Edmonton seat.

Candidates who do take part in these events make sure they have as much control over the conditions as possible. This includes being clear about all the ground rules, such as the length of time for opening statements, what manner or form of questions will be posed, and how much time will be allowed for opening and closing statements from the candidates. Campaigns also take special measures to ensure that at least some of the crowd is friendly. They work hard to turn out supporters, complete with placards, and prime them with a supply of questions to ask the candidate and his opponents.

Although I would never counsel a candidate of mine to avoid a debate, debates are, more often than not, a nuisance. The crowds are almost completely made up of supporters of the various candidates, which means valuable time has to be spent organizing a group of supporters to attend a meeting where little can be gained.

Candidates are more willing to attend debates if there is evidence that the sponsors will spend some money promoting and advertising the event, which might help to bring some real voters through the doors. Far more debates and all-candidates' sessions are proposed than are actually staged. The reluctance of a front-runner to attend, or the mutual agreement between candidates that a particular format is unacceptable, leads to the scuttling of many of these events before they get off the drawing board.

Candidates use three prime means of making their points in these meetings. First, they attack their opponents and their positions on the issues, or on their records of representation. Second, they sell their own position on important issues, or their own credentials. Finally, they ignore questions or attacks, and continue to restate their own positions and underline the themes of their own campaigns.

All in all, if you are a campaign manager, it's a matter of praying for the best and putting your campaign in the hands of the debate gods, hoping that there isn't a disaster such as this example from the federal election of 1978. When asked at an all-candidates' meeting held at a high school his opinion about the legalization of marijuana, a candidate I had recruited said he thought it should be de-criminalized. However, not wanting to leave it at that, he added that he used pot all the time and saw no harm in it. In spite of his assertions that pot was harmless, there seemed evidence that he had lost some brain cells, at least from the area of the brain that controls political self-preservation.

Nothing creates more pressure for new candidates or provides more opportunity for mistakes by old pros than media interviews and press conferences. Most candidates know that these can be the most valuable public appearances for their campaigns. News coverage has two wonderful benefits for a politician: it is free and it is credible. Thirty seconds on the evening TV news with the right message is worth a lot of money. Not only can the amount of time be measured in terms of dollars, but the extra emphasis that news coverage provides gives more credence to that candidate's advertising.

Campaign news coverage on TV and radio, or in the newspaper, is more effective than paid advertising in the same media as a means of getting across more about issues and the candidate. *Maclean's* magazine published results of a poll they conducted with Decima Research following the 1988 federal election, which showed 26% of the respondents found TV commercials helpful in deciding how to vote, but 51% found media coverage of the election an aid in deciding how to vote.

Candidates know how much credibility the news carries. Copying TV news formats has always been a favourite means of increasing the impact of free-time television broadcasts. For the same reason, many candidates will copy the style of neighbourhood newspapers to produce hand-out materials. Former Ontario MP Max Saltzman even produced a leaflet which was a dead ringer for *Time* magazine with a big picture of himself on the cover, of course.

Most candidates receive some coaching from their parties on how to handle themselves with media representatives. This advice usually takes the form of explaining what to say and how to say it.

What to say is simple; they continue repeating the central themes of the campaign. Candidates who understand the theme can answer almost any question or handle most policy explanations by reference to the main theme of their campaigns.

How to say it is a little more difficult to teach. Delivery of ideas and messages in a media news situation requires candidates to understand the mechanics of what is happening between them and interviewers. The interviewer's job is to come up with some news or an article that will be interesting. Media people need to be provided with some interesting and provocative material before they can produce a news story that is attractive to their audiences. Candidates have to use language and images that appeal to those who consume the news.

Candidates are trained by using video cameras to provide pointers on technique and constructive criticism of mannerisms and delivery. The trainer asks the candidate difficult questions in the same style that can be expected from a reporter. The tape is then used as the basis for providing critique on style, content, and mannerisms.

To keep a candidate prepared for any eventuality in an interview, I like to use the definition that I once saw in a "B.C." cartoon strip as my model when I role play a media interviewer. The definition is for the word "bushwacker": a reporter who can read lips.

It used to be that candidates needed to reply to interview and news conference questions in thirty-second clips that would be suitable for news editors, but this is much less true in today's political world than it was a few short years ago. TV cameras now use inexpensive video tape, and lots of it, not film. The TV camera is left on for much longer periods of time. In fact, news crews are often on electronic fishing trips. They can pick up a lot more that would have gone unnoticed when tape was first used, or expensive film was the medium and required processing before it was useable.

The same holds true for print and radio reporters, who can back up their notes with word for word audio tape of everything that is said during an interview or press conference; these tapes are kept on file for a long time. Under these circumstances, interviewees needs to be mindful of what they are saying and doing all the time reporters are present. Every response needs to be punchy; there is no certainty about which items will actually show up in a news item.

It was this unfamiliarity with technological changes in news gathering that tripped up John Turner at the beginning of his return to politics. He didn't realize that the media were recording everything he said and did, rather than waiting for the punchline of his speech to turn on their cameras. Hence, a pat on the bum became the news, rather than the verbal political message he might have wanted to deliver.

Many candidates make the mistake of believing they are speaking to reporters "off the record." The media generally treat everything said by a candidate in an interview as on the record. Reporters have been burned too often by candidates who tell them something "off the record" and then watch as the same information is given to another reporter, so that they lose a scoop. Therefore, the important rule for candidates is not to say anything they wouldn't want reported.

MP Simon de Jong received a dramatic lesson in this axiom. He granted an interview to a freelance reporter who was a former member of his parliamentary staff, on the subject of his rumoured decision to contest the NDP national leadership. de Jong recounted a number of details in the interview that he did not want published, but it all came out very soon afterwards in an exclusive story. Simon missed the opportunity to enter the leadership race with a bang; he had made it hard for most people to notice that he had entered the race. Other reporters were reluctant to deal with the story afterwards, because it was old news, and they were not given the same courtesy as the first freelancer.

Few will forget Simon's second media problem in that leadership campaign, which occurred when he was wearing a hidden microphone for the CBC's *Journal*. The resulting story about his private meeting with Dave Barrett between ballots has inspired quite a few political jokes.

Candidates sometimes argue with reporters or charge them with being unfair in their coverage. This is always a no win situation. While some reporters do have trouble understanding some complex issues, getting on the wrong side of any reporter will only cause more problems for a candidate. If anyone needs to question the style or content of a news story, it should be someone other than the candidate. Given the amount of backup audio and visual material available to reporters these days, a challenge is not likely to fall on fertile ground.

Ray Martin found this out during his first run for a seat in Edmonton. He had been quoted by an Edmonton *Journal* reporter as calling on the Lougheed government to provide "compulsory" daycare in a speech to daycare workers. He meant to use the words "universal, accessible and affordable," but unfortunately, that is not what came out.

After the story was printed, Ray got into an argument with the reporter over her story. Rather than the clarification or retraction he had hoped for, the reporter decided to make Martin's original statement the issue rather than his real beliefs. She even had photos of her written notes reproduced alongside an article repeating the original story. This incident taught Ray to choose his words with care and not to get into a fight with reporters.

The care and feeding of journalists requires a good deal of common sense, patience, and tact. Any candidate has to take as much advantage as possible of media contacts, without falling into some of the traps awaiting the unsuspecting politician.

One of those traps is taking a personal relationship with a reporter for granted. A reporter is always a reporter, and will almost always use any information received, regardless of its source. Few reporters consider anything "off the record."

I also tell candidates that they should realize that they will almost never win an argument with a reporter about whether or not they were misquoted.

Candidates have to be wary of reporters who seem harmless and quiet. Candidates may try to fill quiet periods in interviews with verbiage, with the result, on some occasions, that they contradict themselves, or qualify other of their announcements. The wise candidate never says anything he or she wouldn't want to see or read in the news.

Candidates also have to deal with the natural cynicism of reporters. Many of them feel it is necessary to wear it on their sleeves. One New York *Times* article noted that the relationship between the media and politicians is a strange one, because by editing the words and pictures of politicians, a favour of concision and focus is done them that makes them look decisive and powerful, when in reality, up close, many politicians seem and act like fools.

Photo opportunities are another way politicians try to get the most impact out of free news coverage. A picture is worth a thousand words and a thousand words in politics costs a lot of money. Whenever there are TV cameras or newspaper photographers around, candidates want them to be able to get interesting material that can be used to complement stories and help focus the attention of the public.

Watching the party leaders in an election campaign illustrates what a good "photo op" is meant to be. They will talk about jobs at a factory, education in a school, fishing on a dock, consumer prices in a grocery store and so on. This gives some visual backdrop to the message and helps draw attention to what is being said by the leaders.

The best guidance I have been able to give candidates about getting a picture on the front page of a newspaper or on the television news is: "never wear a dead chicken on your head." In other words, don't look like a jerk, because looking like a jerk does not build confidence in the electorate. I still keep a picture of Joe Clark in a "Sou'Wester" in the Maritimes as an example of this principle. He was a very unlikely-looking fisherman.

Photo opportunities do not always serve to make a candidate's point. Two examples involving a member of the Alberta Liberal Party follow. Every party has had countless similar experiences.

One such shot was taken when this candidate was making some points about the environment and the need to promote recycling to relieve the pressure on landfill sites. He held his news conference at a garbage dump on top of a pile of garbage. The garbage received most of the attention in the news stories, and became the butt of political cartoonists. This issue would have been better illustrated at a recycling depot or at a plant that manufactured products from recycled materials. These venues leave a positive impression that something can be done, rather than emphasizing the negative side of the issue.

The second example came from the political custom that calls on leaders to be seen talking to farmers. The candidate's foray to the farm left a comic image. As he walked through the farmyard talking to the farmer, his eyes were always on the ground. It was clear he was more interested in watching for what he might be stepping in than in what the farmer was telling him about how tough things were down on the farm.

Radio and TV talk shows are another way that candidates use free media to influence public opinion. The "hotline," or "open-mouth" programs are very popular in some media markets and are probably at their best on radio, although they are tried with mixed success on television as well. Candidates go to a great deal of trouble to get invited to appear on these programs. If the host of the show thinks that the candidate has sufficient profile or can be made controversial enough to help the ratings, that person will be invited.

If the candidate is going to appear on one of these shows, the campaign team has to line up enough "impartial and spontaneous" callers to jam the phone lines and pose questions that are slow pitch softballs that can be hit out of the park, rather than the bean balls likely to be thrown by supporters of the opponent. This is the time that the automatic redial on modern telephones gets a genuine work out. If they fail at this exercise, they can expect to hear about it from the candidate. Nothing unnerves a candidate more than being beaten up in public.

There are a variety of reasons for candidates to be in the news during an election, including announcing their candidacy, saying something positive about themselves and their policies, or saying something negative about their opponents and opposing policies. The one circumstance for which we rarely see a candidate in front of the cameras is to make an apology.

I believe that politicians miss the opportunity to endear themselves to the public when they refuse to admit their mistakes from time to time. When an apology *is* offered, it is usually under extreme circumstances when no other choice is available.

This reluctance to admit personal error is probably born from the natural arrogance of politicians. Even the most unassuming people have most of their humility kicked out of them by politics. It isn't that there is somehow a nasty part of the personality coming to the surface; it's more a function of an ego on the psychic equivalent of steroids. Whenever candidates have been successful, either in a previous election, or in just gaining the nomination, this inability to recognize personal fault occurs. It is caused by the reaction to putting reputation, ideas, and financial well-being on the line a number of times, and being accepted by the voters. This leads to an increased opinion of self. As a result, it becomes quite inconceivable that errors could be committed; it is only possible that the media or public have misinterpreted statements or actions.

Saskatchewan NDP Leader, Roy Romanow, has a favourite story about one of the most arrogant of politicians, Pierre Trudeau. He tells of sitting with Jean Chrétien during the constitutional negotiations and asking him, "Chrétien, why does Trudeau act so goddamn arrogant?" Putting on his best imitation of the famous Chrétien accent, he continues, "Romanow, you know Trudeau acts goddamn arrogant because he IS goddamn arrogant."

Apologies might be useful for politicians after they have made an about-face on some issue, or better yet, when an explanation is required for not being able to change a decision. An interesting example of this happened to the Regina City Council. They had passed a motion proclaiming "Gay and Lesbian Pride Week." When Council members began getting a negative reaction, they decided to call a special council meeting to rescind the previous motion, even though the proclamation and newspaper ad declaring the week had gone to print. Several members of council changed their votes, but one of them would not allow unanimous consent, and the original decision stood. The resulting image was of a council that made hasty decisions without seeming to think them through. Their real strategy should have been something like regretting that some people were not happy about the decision and apologizing to those who felt offended and promising to review the rules under which these proclamations are granted.

Endorsement by the media is one thing most candidates crave and few receive. The electronic media rarely offer endorsements of candidates or parties. When an endorsement is offered, it takes the form of a station editorial, often delivered by an identifiable individual. This is not as powerful as the impersonal endorsement of a newspaper, which appears to be offered as a consensus from a broader base. Rather than making endorsements, electronic media are more inclined to alter their news coverage in reaction to how they perceive the election is developing; they may enhance or detract from the images they present, depending on how news editors and staff feel about the direction of the election.

Newspapers were once considered to be the organ for one party or another and were expected to endorse the candidates and policies of that party regardless of what was happening in the real world. This is rarely the case any more. The newspaper industry is big business; managing editors cannot afford to offend too many readers or advertisers by taking strident views on political issues, unless it is clear that these views are held by a majority of the public. It is becoming more common, however, for newspapers to endorse a group of candidates, usually some from each of the parties.

Politicians gain endorsements by asking for them. They visit the editorial boards of newspapers or meet with influential television and newspaper public affairs and news directors with the hope of influencing their opinion. If candidates present their cases in a way that reflects the established tone of the news outlet, they have some chance of being received favourably. I have sat in on some of these meetings, and editors often make it clear what answers they prefer; it takes strong-willed politicians to remain consistent to their own views.

The media often act with a "pack" mentality. They all climb on the same wagon, whether with positive or negative stories about a party or the politicians. It is almost as predictable that after a while, they reverse their approach, as if to say, "we have been a little harsh;

now we'll practise a little reverse discrimination." The first time this registered with me was during an Alberta provincial election. During the first two weeks of the campaign, Social Credit Leader Bob Clark was shown as a lonely and forgotten man leading a forlorn party that was a pale image of its former self. Then, almost by magic, the media reversed their tone and reported about a party that could do a lot of damage to the Lougheed Tories and was on its way back in Alberta politics. Neither scenario was true.

The plight of John Turner in the 1988 federal election is another case in point. The media was on him like "rust on a muffler" from the opening of the campaign, ready to report any unhappy comments from fellow Liberals, to the point where they had him mortally wounded during the campaign with questions on his ability to lead and his grasp on important policy matters such as child care. After Turner provided a decent debate performance, he could do no wrong; the media virtually tripped over themselves to help his campaign along.

The debate rages around whether or not there is manipulation of the media by the candidates, or whether the political process is influenced by the media, or both, or neither. It is certain that manipulation is happening, but it probably depends on the perspective of the observer not unlike Dave Barrett's description of the relationship between big business and the B.C. Socred government. He delights audiences by saying, "They are both under the covers. We don't know who is doing what to whom, but we know who is getting screwed." People who consume the news and make political decisions based only on what they see and hear through news outlets will be the losers in the game of political news manipulation.

There is no question that politicians do everything they can to communicate their message to the public through the news media in the most positive light, and do it in a way that best meets the goals of the media: to inform and entertain audiences. If there is a crime in this, it is likely victimless.

The argument about who is doing the manipulating in Canadian politics continues. Politicians try to influence news coverage and news directors and editors try to provide what they consider unbiased and balanced news coverage. There isn't much individual voters can do to be sure the news they receive is unbiased and accurate. They simply have to trust their instincts and judgement and remain as informed as they can.

We certainly cannot blame politicians for taking every opportunity they can to influence public opinion through the media. In the political business, if you don't blow your own horn, there's no music.

Speeches, debates, interviews, media coverage and endorsements are all among the free ways that candidates deliver their messages. In order to make sure that every target voter gets the message, candidates have to fill up the warchest in order to be able to afford to buy the space and time necessary to mount a media blitz.

9. Money: The Stuff of Politics

"A candidate with money has
a campaign; one without it
has a cause."
Dr. Murray Fishel, Kent State University

Will Rogers once said that politics has become so expensive that it even takes a lot of money to be beaten. That is no less true today.

Money is the real stuff of politics. Without money, there is no campaign, no way of spreading the message and convincing voters to support a particular candidate or set of ideas.

"In the political lexicon there is no substitute for money," one American senator is reported to have said. "Money is the principal prop of propaganda. It's what you need to sell the merchandise. Just as it takes a jack to lift up a car, so it takes a lot of jack to lift up a party."

Money is an often misunderstood cog in the Canadian election machine. In this chapter, we will explore why the money is needed and where it comes from.

Candidates spend a great deal of money getting elected. In the United States, candidates for relatively low-level races regularly spend five hundred thousand to a million dollars. Those who seek a state-wide office, such as a U.S. senatorship or governorship, may spend two, three or more million.

Money has a direct relationship to a candidate's chances of election in the U.S. In the 1990 elections for the House of Representatives, of the 405 people running for re-election, 296 either had no major party challenger, or had challenger who had raised less than $25,000. Eighty-six challengers were financially uncompetitive in that they had less than half the funds of the incumbent; in only 23 races did the challenging candidate have more than half the funds of the incumbent. In 1988, not one House challenger who spent less than $300,000 was elected.

Fortunately, in Canada, it doesn't take this much for an individual to be elected. In fact, we have spending limits in most jurisdictions which effectively control the amount of money a candidate can spend to be elected to represent us.

These spending limits are usually calculated on a formula which is based in some way on the number of eligible voters in a constituency and the costs of communicating with them. A large urban constituency in a federal election might have a spending limit in the range of $60,000. Limits in provincial elections vary from province to province, but they range from $25,000-$40,000 on average.

These limits apply to the election campaign only; they do not ordinarily include expenditures made to build the recognition of the candidate before an election is called, unless the material is actually consumed during the election period. For instance, signs purchased before the election would be included, because they are not ordinarily used until the election is called. On the other hand, a billboard that is up for three months, two months before and one month during the election, is valued differently. Only the one month rental during the election and one-third of the cost of putting it up fall under the limits. This provides a distinct advantage for the candidate who has the resources to begin a campaign early.

Even without spending limits, as is the case in Alberta, it is difficult for a candidate for provincial office to spend much more than $30,000-$35,000. They could spend more; there is nothing stopping them except good sense. But there comes a point when there are diminishing returns for each dollar spent. The campaign can buy more buttons or balloons, but there is only so much that can be done on the most important job: getting out the message. For this reason, experienced campaigners say that the first dollar spent on a campaign will have as much impact as the last five.

As international political consultant Joe Napolitan puts it, how much money you have to spend is not as important as how and when you spend it. It is comforting to have all the money needed to conduct a campaign, but it is not always the candidate with the most access to ready cash who wins. If too much is allocated to offices, travel, and equipment, for instance, there will not be enough to buy ads and leaflets, which are the things that get the message out. In addition, if money for spreading the word is not available in the first days of the campaign, when people are making up their minds, then no amount spent in the last days can make up for the lost ground.

Money can be squandered in an election campaign and many candidates have done so. But in most campaigns, where each of the candidates has an equal base and similar amounts of money, it is the one who manages money the best who wins— the one who gets the best bang for the buck.

Well, what makes up the usual campaign budget?

The first thing that comes to mind when you think about elections is the endless number of television commercials. Most candidates do not spend much money on the visual electronic media advertising their cause. It takes so much exposure to make any impact in major media markets that the costs are prohibitive for an individual candidate. There are wiser ways of spending money. In most political parties, individual candidates provide funds to their parties' central campaigns to have generic ads placed on the local media which highlight central campaign themes and leadership. Candidates might get their names and constituencies mentioned at the end of the ad.

While a 30 second TV ad on a big city station can cost a thousand dollars or more, plus production costs, rural candidates with a small station nearby may be able to afford some TV in their budgets.

In the 1986 Saskatchewan provincial election, several Conservative candidates in an area around Yorkton known as the "Red Square" produced their own TV ads. These ads ran along with the slick NDP and Conservative central campaign ads, and there were a lot of those, since this was a target region for both parties. The local PC ads had terrible production values compared to the big city produced party ones. However, they were much more effective, since they were produced with slides and talking heads, as were most other local business ads in the Yorkton area. They reflected the values and the usual image of local TV advertising, and so had a positive impact. Since all these PC candidates won, some of them by only a handful of votes, they can probably credit this to using some of their budgets on TV advertisements.

Even if candidates spend very little or no money on television, they may have modest radio budgets. Radio is a good medium for political campaigns because messages can be much more targeted to specific audiences. Each radio station has a format aimed at specific kinds of listeners. If a candidate has targeted young people, then a rock station would make a good media buy. Of course, the message needs to be tailored to the audience. The same advertising copy that would be used on a middle of the road station would have no appeal to those between 18 and 25 years of age who like to get cranked up on hard rock.

Radio expenditures are also useful on ethnic and special interest radio stations. These can be excellent vehicles for reaching potential voters among whom there might be a language barrier for a candidate and his workers.

In rural Canada, radio takes on more importance than it does in the city. People depend on the radio for timely information on crop prices, current events and local news. Rural radio time, like rural television time is quite inexpensive; rural radio offers a captive audience that spends a lot of time travelling by car from community to community or sitting in the cab of a tractor listening to the local radio station. Rural listeners are also very loyal to their local radio stations.

The value of newspaper advertising varies from campaign to campaign. Ads in daily newspapers ads large enough to capture the attention of voters from among the variety of department store and supermarket ads cost as much as $500 or more. Meanwhile, rural weeklies and dailies in smaller communities can be a vital way of building name recognition and advancing policy positions. These newspapers are more likely to be read because of their local content. In fact, some voters will search the paper during an election to see if their favourite candidate has an ad and will want to know what is wrong if it is not there.

Some people say that smaller newspapers will not run much news about a candidate unless they purchase ad space. This may or may not be true, but I always counsel rural candidates to attach ads to their press releases; the free news usually seems to appear in an unaltered form. This is not the case with the large dailies. Some parties run little or no campaign advertising, yet still receive as much print coverage as parties that buy several full page ads.

In Alberta, for instance, the New Democrats buy absolutely no newspaper ads with funds from their central campaign budget, while the Tories buy several full-page and many other large ads, in addition to the hundreds of thousands spent annually on government advertising. Yet, both parties are treated more or less equally in the amount of coverage they receive.

The amount a candidate spends on paid advertising varies depending on the costs and the effectiveness of the particular media to reach target voters. An individual candidate in a large metropolitan region will no doubt be seen or heard by a number of his or her own constituents, but will also be spending money on being seen or heard by many thousands of people who can not vote for the candidate, because they don't live in that candidate's constituency. In such cases, candidates are better off turning over a portion of their budgets for central ad placements by their parties or co-operating with other candidates to increase the impact.

Any kind of advertising can be a waste of money if it does not aid in targeting the message. The same problem is associated with outdoor advertising such as bus signs and billboards.

Print shops love political candidates. Candidates have an insatiable appetite for printed material. On average, each serious campaign produces three leaflets during the campaign period alone; and, often, one or more in the period before the election. Even more literature is used in a nomination contest. These leaflets serve a variety of needs: they introduce the candidate to the electorate and extol her or his virtues and abilities; they tie the candidate to the larger issues and themes of the campaign; they tie the candidate to the local issues of the campaign; and they attack opponents.

Printing is often the major part of a candidate's budget. You can't buy much of a leaflet for under six or seven cents per copy, and it's not hard to spend twice that for better quality paper, colour, and lots of pictures. Candidates' egos often come into play in leaflet production and they want their pictures gracing only the best quality pieces available. Predictably, leaflets printed on 8 1/2" x 11" bond paper are not good enough. Only 14" glossy paper will do. And, of course, there are never enough pictures of the candidate.

In addition to leaflets, local printers can expect orders for calling cards for the candidate to hand out, buttons, possibly bumper stickers, cards to tell people where the polling stations will be, and a supply of letterhead and envelopes.

Outdoor advertising is a common budget item, and may take the form of billboards, signs on buses, and on bus stop benches. Almost always, some money is allocated to purchase lawn signs and related material, such as lumber and hardware to put them up. Lawn signs come in a variety of sizes, with the common size costing about $1.50 each including materials; a 4' x 8' sign can be worth as much as $40 each depending on the quality of material and the method of constructing the supporting frame.

Signs do not have a lot of value in helping to identify new support, but they do have a terrific effect in motivating volunteers and potential donors and, if they are deployed according to a careful strategy, they can also affect voter opinion about the candidate and the extent of public support and the strength of the campaign.

In the last Ontario election, one sign in particular fulfilled these requirements. John Ruffolo, who lived in Kitchener, but was a Tory candidate in an east end Toronto riding, announced that he was voting for the Kitchener NDP candidate and even put one of his signs on his lawn.

Candidates usually have some paid campaign staff. Payment may consist of a small honorarium for an office manager/receptionist, but it may also include salary and expenses for a professional organizer and experienced organizational team. Almost every campaign has some costs associated with people helping on the campaign, including monies to help defray expenses such as gas and other out of pocket items.

Campaigns have to provide for the expenses of the candidate as well. This can include salary, travel, and items such as child care and even assistance in upgrading wardrobes. Depending on the federal or provincial election laws in effect, these expense items may not form part of the spending limits, but usually they have to be reported. Regardless, the funds often have to be raised, although many candidates do undertake to pay for these items themselves.

One of the scariest things a campaign manager can hear from a candidate is, "around here you can't get elected without one of these." Then the candidate pulls out a ballpoint pen, a book of matches, or a refrigerator magnet. A Canadian candidate is usually not as much a slave to trinkets as his American cousin, who may show off emery boards, fly swatters, fans, or goofy sunglasses before you can blink an eye. In Canadian campaigns, these giveaway items are considered too expensive and to have almost no positive value, but salesmen for novelty companies look forward to elections almost as much as printers.

A wall card with the candidate's name and some useful information such as phone numbers for various emergency services might help. One Conservative candidate in the Windsor area tried to help his constituency by providing metric conversion charts; the trouble was, they conversions were wrong! This mistake probably resulted in some poorly baked pies and tough biscuits.

A Saskatchewan provincial candidate in the 1986 election proved he was behind the times about appropriate handout material. The matches he passed around had his name printed boldly on one side; on the other was a picture of a bare breasted woman.

Some candidates sell T-shirts or baseball caps with their names on them as a way of raising funds, or at least breaking even, on an advertising display item. A Social Credit candidate in B.C. sold adult T-shirts, but gave away one free child's shirt with each purchase.

Candidates need somewhere to call home base. Office space can be very expensive and hard to find, although commercial space can often be rented at the last moment. A building owner will not want to commit the space to a candidate too far in advance of the election, but once the election is called, a month's or two months' rent in advance is welcome; permanent tenants can't usually move in that quickly. It can be a little eery to work in an office that is openly on the market. That was the case in a recent Saskatoon Eastview by-election, where the landlord often showed up with prospective renters in the middle of a strategy meeting.

Sometimes construction site office trailers are used, and, in extreme circumstances, even private homes have been used. Candidates for different constituencies from the same party might share office space, even though this means the office of one of the candidates will be outside his or her riding boundaries. My first experience with shared office accommodation was in Brandon, in 1969, where two candidates worked out of the former "Fuzzy Whale," Brandon's first and only experiment in the world of coffee houses. You had to walk quietly in the Fuzzy Whale; if you made too much noise close to one wall, it set off the burglar alarm in McGavin's Bakery next door.

Campaign budgets need to allow for utilities and telephones as well as insurance for liability, fire, and theft. Furniture arrives by magic from basements and home offices, so very little should have to be rented.

Campaign offices are as well equipped as any modern business office. Electronic typewriters, computer equipment, photocopiers, fax machines, cellular phones, and so on are no strangers to a political campaign. Much of this equipment will be rented for a short term or borrowed from friends.

The final touches to well-rounded offices are those things that make living easier for campaign volunteers and full-time workers, such as coffee pots, fridges, microwaves, TVs, maybe stereos, and lounge areas.

A host of other expenses are considered; funds are allocated on the basis of how they serve the overall campaign plan. For instance, postage may be only a minor budget item, just enough to pay for miscellaneous mail, but it might be a major expense if the campaign plan calls for a concentrated direct mail attack. Other expense items might include hall rentals, meeting notices, and parties for workers, in addition to the final victory party on election night.

The following is a budget for Simon de Jong, MP from Regina Qu'Appelle, for the 1988 federal election. Simon's constituency is 55% rural; the balance consists of the northeastern portion of Regina. This constituency has about 60% as many voters as a typical Toronto federal riding.

Election Expenses Within Limits

Salaries and Expenses	$11,000
Headquarters	
Urban	3,000
Rural	1,000
Headquarters Signage	300
Furniture and Equipment Rental	1,000
Utilities	500
Insurance	300
Urban Phones	420
Rural Phones	110
Phone Bank Phones	530
Long Distance	2,000
Telephone Installation	500
Postage— Rural	750
Pamphlets (Three)	5,500
Issue and Fact Sheets	500
Candidate's Canvass Material	500
Letterhead and Envelopes	1,000
Posters	500
Misc. Printed Material	300
Advertising (Rural Papers Only)	4,000
Signs, Material and Expenses	4,500
Hall Rentals	1,000
Contingency	3,000
TOTAL	**$42,210**

Expenses Outside Limits
(allowable expenses under law which fall outside limits but which must be reported)

Quotas Paid to Party Headquarters for Central Advertising Campaign	$13,000
Candidate Expenses	
Motor Home	1,500
Travel Meals	1,000
Audit	450
Nomination Deposit	200
TOTAL	**$16,150**
GRAND TOTAL	**$58,360**

Well, it's pretty clear that candidates need money to run a competitive campaign. Where does it all come from? Very few politicians risk that much of their own money on an uncertain prospect.

Most campaign contributions come from three sources— individuals, businesses, and organizations, such as trade unions.

The financial reports from the three major national parties tell a lot about their circumstances and outlook on Canadian affairs. By and large, the Conservatives receive most of their money from large corporations; very little of their income comes from individual contributions. The Liberals, now out of grace in national politics, receive a lot of their money from the same corporations as the Conservatives, but there are currently fewer zeros on the cheques. New Democrats raise most of their money through individual contributions; some is in lump sum donations from trade unions.

All campaign funds originate with individuals, in one form or another. Most business or corporate contributions are the result of an individual's decision or, at best, one person's recommendation to a board of directors. Even trade union contributions, which come from revenues generated from all members, are made based on the decision of an executive. The trade union contribution is more democratic, in the sense that it usually flows from a convention resolution indicating support for a particular party, candidate, or those candidates who support issues that the union members feel are important.

It would be a rare circumstance indeed if a vote of the shareholders of the Bank of Montreal determined who would receive how much money from that institution; certainly, bank customers are never consulted. It's ironic that a person pays fees to a company like the Bank of Montreal, a portion of which ends up as contributions to political parties that largely support notions of finance and business that are often contrary to that person's sense of economic fairness or well-being. It will ever be thus.

There are, however, notable but rare exceptions. During the Alberta Provincial Election in 1978, the NDP central campaign received a contribution of around $1800 from a large Edmonton development company. The surprise was that one of our platform items was a healthy development tax on companies like this one. I was tempted to return the contribution for a variety of reasons, not the least of which was that I thought it possible that the donation might have been a set-up to discredit our land development policy. But, after reading the accompanying letter, we decided to keep it. The letter explained that a sum of money had been set aside for political contributions, and based on a vote by the employees of the company, the funds were allocated to the parties, an example of workplace democracy other corporations would do well to emulate!

Why do individuals give up so much of their disposable income to support political candidates in an age of growing cynicism about politicians and their motives? Or, why would the directors of a company take a chunk of their profits and hurl it down the sinkhole of campaign budgets?

One simple reason is that campaign donations can be used as tax credits. Contributions to national parties and candidates lower income tax payable. The same is true in some provinces; others are examining the idea of implementing similar legislation. True, many citizens made sizeable contributions long before these tax breaks came into being, but overall, tax breaks have made it possible for a greater percentage of the electorate to become involved in the political process. In so doing, the influence of large corporations and special interests on public affairs has been reduced.

People may contribute because they are close friends or relatives of the candidate or because they have an emotional tie to the issues and themes of the candidate. These kinds of contributors are the most valuable to any campaign; such contributors can usually be counted on for large sums and can be solicited from many times.

A donor may feel that the election of a candidate or support for a party will lead to significant improvements in the services or future prospects of the local community. Indeed, this can be argued to be the prime motivation for political partisanship in Canada. Political parties or candidates which seem to have little or no chance of winning a particular election still may attract considerable amounts of money.

On the other hand, contributions may be made for the opposite reason. The funds may be provided to defeat another party, or a candidate who advances a policy that might be harmful to the individual or the community at large.

Some make contributions in the hope of personal gain. Businesses contribute so that they will come to the attention of political leaders and, by so doing, have an inside track on government contracts or influencing appointments to government boards and commissions. This greed motive is not limited to business either. Many large individual contributors will know that one of the leading guidelines used by politicians when making political appointments is the relative generosity shown towards the party by the respective candidates.

There has been some publicity lately about special clubs of high dollar contributors to particular parties. These "investors" are given special access to leading cabinet ministers and government decision makers. They believe this gives them added leverage when doing business with government departments.

This greed principle can also have a different spin. The donor may believe that support of a party might lead to the donor saving substantial sums in the form of tax relief, reduced pressure on public debt, or cash grants. Contributors may support ideas like free university tuition and inexpensive quality health care or special transfer payments because such programs would provide a direct improvement in their own financial status. It has long been a practice to buy votes with programs that provide significant interest rate relief for homeowners and small business or direct cash payments to farmers, for example. Standing in favour of such programs attracts dollars as well as votes for politicians.

There can be no denying the role of ego in campaign contributions. In my experience there is a group of contributors who like to feel they are part of the in crowd. Their money allows them to say they are close to the campaign and that they have a personal involvement. They usually try to impart some advice as the price of their contribution; they can then tell their friends and associates that they are part of the team. This attitude lingers as long as the candidate is on top, but as soon as the candidate trips up, they disavow any links with the campaign. These kinds of people who provide a bit of a bellwether for a campaign. If there are a lot of

opportunists hopping onside to help out financially, it becomes a
good indication of the possible future success of the campaign. I
have often seen big money contributors come forward in a campaign when things seem to be going right, but as soon as the
political winds shift, they are gone. A finance chairperson should
cash their cheques as soon as they are offered.

People who like to show off their largesse will more than likely
go straight to the candidate to make their offerings, rather than
giving it to a bagman. By delivering the money personally, they feel
they will be able to call on the candidate in the future and exact
some kind of favour, such as attendance at a business or family
event so the donor can put "his" politician on display.

This kind of contributor always wants to be on the side of the
winner. His or her contribution and its resulting value is lost on a
loser. During my years with the New Democratic Party, these kinds
of people have been few and far between, except in places where
the NDP has been in power or has a decent chance of gaining office.
These people will be hardly heard from between elections, but
when the campaign hype starts they come out of the woodwork,
hoping to be noticed and remembered on the strength of their
dollars.

It has always been my suspicion that many people make contributions so they won't be pressed to volunteer time for an election
campaign. Their minds are put at ease; they have done something
useful without giving up any of their own precious time. They have
done their part.

Some people are motivated to give simply out of fear. They may
feel that their position in society will be jeopardized if a particular
party or candidate is defeated or elected. It may be as simple as
realizing that their jobs may end if the wrong party is elected.
Political folklore is full of stories about Maritime province Post-
masters or highway equipment operators who simply throw their
keys over to a representative of the opposition if their party loses
an election. Although these examples are extreme, senior civil
servants have a lot to fear when government changes, given the
savaging the civil service has suffered in recent years when governments have changed hands.

People also contribute to election campaigns out of anger.

These people are genuinely opposed to something a candidate or party has done or is proposing to do in the future. Angry people may contribute as a result of a reaction to the negative messages they have heard about certain ideas, in which case they contribute to those who are more positive. Businesses may feel that one party will impede their ability to make profits; individuals may think that rights or benefits which have accrued to them in the past may be eroded.

But these are simple analyses of why people contribute to political parties and candidates. In most cases, there is a mixture of motives for writing a cheque or throwing money into the hat when it is passed at a meeting, not the least of which is tradition. They may simply support "their party," regardless of the candidate or the issues, and always give money. The amount of the contribution may vary according to the presence of some or all of these differing motives, but there is always money available whatever the electoral chances of the candidate.

However, no money will likely be found in the campaign bank account if there isn't an effective finance chairperson. Talented fundraisers are in great demand by politicians and they are hard to find. Not many people like to ask others for money; to come across someone who not only doesn't mind asking, but relishes it, is like discovering the motherlode.

Finding such a person does not necessarily mean that they will serve; I have seen as much arm-twisting to recruit a financial chairperson as occurs when trying to convince a particularly good person to be a candidate.

Ideal finance chairpersons are well known and respected in the community. They are usually, professional or business persons; or, in rural ridings, respected farmers. If this person is known to handle money well, this helps make donors feel more at ease. Donors need to know that money is a healthy, vital part of the election system. A campaign has as much need and right to ask for dollars as to ask for votes.

The fundraiser has to raise the money when it is needed the most. In almost every case, that is as early in the campaign as possible. Early expenditures have the most influence on voters. If the cash isn't in place at the beginning of the election, then one of the fundraiser's tasks is to find people who will co-sign a note at a bank or credit union, in order to provide operating capital and satisfy those suppliers who insist on their payments up front.

The ideal fundraiser hands the money over to the campaign committee without comment, and does not get involved in the day to day operation of the campaign. This is easier said than done. A lot of what happens during the course of a campaign has an effect on the fundraiser's success, and if the campaign begins to go sour, so do the chances of raising money; the fundraiser will want people to know what the problems are and why they are occurring. Certainly, a fundraiser who is doing his or her job will be listened to a lot more than someone who is only along for the ride and fulfilling the position in name only.

As I mentioned earlier, cash flow has always been one of my gauges for determining the success of a campaign. If it keeps coming in throughout the course of the election, I can usually feel assured that our message is getting through to the right people. A campaign feels ominous and dark if money suddenly dries up ten days before the election. I knew we had no chance in Alberta during the 1978 election, when the money came to a dead stop about fourteen days before election day. In 1982, we did better electorally and contributions didn't stop coming in until a week before the vote. In the last election, when the NDP became the undisputed second party, the money kept coming in, even after election day.

There are a lot of ways to spend money on an election, but there are only a few ways of raising it.

The most effective way of putting bucks in the bank is personal contact. Visiting potential donors at home or in their offices, making a case for the cause at hand, expressing the need, and asking for a contribution.

At the top of the list of potential donors are family members and close friends and associates of the candidate. These are the easiest to convince and often yield the largest amounts. This is known as the FRANK principle of fundraising. The FRANK list of potential contributors is made of: Friends, Relatives, Acquaintances, Neighbours, and anyone else you Know.

Following closely behind are those people who have contributed before and members of the candidate's political party. Voters who indicate support for the campaign to canvassers and volunteers during the election also make natural contributors.

Campaigns that are concerned about raising enough funds make sure that all the activists are kept up to date on financial affairs. When people know the situation they are more mindful about wasting money, and help by offering names of people who should be contacted for donations or going after money themselves.

Canadian candidates differ from those in the U.S. in that they rarely ask for money personally. They keep lists of possible contributors and see that every offer of money is followed up by the finance team. Americans devote a significant portion of their time strictly to raising money.

The first rule in soliciting funds is never to ask for a contribution in a way that "no" can be given for an answer. The only point of debate should be how much and what form the contribution will take. Fundraisers get whatever they can, whether it is cash now or a post-dated cheque or a signed pledge for some specific date in the future. This helps to keep the fundraiser's disposition sunny.

The second rule is not to ask for too little. Contributors never tell you that you have set your sights too low and offer $100 when you ask for $50. Flattery will get you someplace most of the time, and most people feel flattered to be considered capable of making a significant contribution. Fundraisers need to be prepared to ask for a large sum and let the donors set their levels. The trick comes in determining what amount to ask for, and that's where experience and knowledge become definite assets.

The last important rule is to ask often. A campaign should never settle on one contribution from a donor, but keep going back on a regular basis. Once someone is comfortable with making contributions, he or she will help out many more times if asked. This doesn't mean they will dig deep every time they are approached, but they will certainly make more contributions than they would if left alone.

A frequent mistake for fundraisers is to overlook small contributors. In an effort to raise large amounts quickly, several $20 contributions can be passed over in search of one $100 donation.

Everyone possible should be involved in financing campaigns. The small investor has as much a stake in the outcome of an election as the large donor. Effective fundraising strategies include obtaining every kind of contribution possible, even if it means going door to door in a "cold canvass" for money from the general public. The smaller donors can also be contacted on a more regular basis.

This brings to mind the story of Mae West and her friend Maude. When Mae asked Maude where she got her beautiful new fur coat, Maude replied that she had got herself a $10,000 man. When Maude asked Mae West where she had gotten her coat, Mae said she had 10,000 one dollar men. Mae West knew that your batting average is less important than making the most of your number of at bats.

The coat of arms for candidates should be a knife and fork on a field of mashed potatoes, flanked by a chicken leg and a piece of stringy roast beef. Not because a political army marches on its stomach, but because dinners and luncheons are a key to building a warchest. There's probably nothing that hasn't been tried when it comes to food. Dinners are a great way to raise money, since the givers are also getting something: they are seen at an event by their peers and get to hobnob with the candidate and other personalities.

Many different philosophies go into the planning of such fundraising events. Some like to organize low-ball events where the price of admission is reasonable, say $10-$25 per person, and then have a financial appeal for further funds. Others eschew begging the public for money as tasteless and opt for a high ticket price which might range from $100 to $1,000 each.

The key to attracting people to any of these kinds of events is to offer something different that people might not get elsewhere. This can include some feature entertainer or an unusual guest speaker. The format might be intriguing and inviting. A good example of this was a "Jazz Brunch" sponsored by MP Ian Waddell. The event had great eggs benedict, champagne, and a delightful crew of New Orleans style jazz musicians all set off in a trendy Vancouver harbourfront restaurant. An event like this attracts people who do not ordinarily attend political meetings or dull rubber chicken banquets, and appeals to a sense of adventure. The people buying the ticket are getting something for their money.

Another memorable event was organized by Dave Barrett's constituency organization: a "continuous" spaghetti dinner. It lasted all day. Each hour, an authentic spaghetti dinner was served with all the trimmings and atmosphere; in between sittings there was a lot of great Italian entertainment.

Those who are trying to raise money for a candidate should try every fundraising idea that has already worked for other organizations in the community, as long as they are legal. In some provinces it is illegal for political parties to hold raffles, for instance. They should avoid conflict with the timing of other similar events for fear of angering important organizations, but whatever has worked for others is worth a try.

Third party endorsement is also used by candidates to raise money. Here, a large contributor hosts a small dinner party or reception for the candidate, attended by a group of the host's personal friends and associates. Part of the agenda calls for the host to endorse the candidate and call on the guests to match his contribution.

The only limitation to the possibilities for fundraising events is the extent of the planners' imaginations. It never failed to anger me, when advising constituency associations on possible activities, to hear the predictable, plaintive whine, "We tried that ten years ago and it didn't work." No idea should be dismissed without careful study of the economics and impact of an event, and if committee members are not sure, they should be running the ideas past others to determine their merits.

While the main purpose of these kinds of events is to raise money, they also have political impact. A rousing dinner of 500 who paid $10 each to attend can be a lot more positive and newsworthy than one which has attracted 50 $100 patrons. Both events raise equal amounts of money, but the values and image are dramatically different.

Candidates usually shy away from functions that impart the wrong image. While bingos might be great moneymakers, few candidates want to be associated with a method of gambling that often takes money from those least able to afford it.

I have admired the Parti Quebecois for their door to door

fundraising drives. News reports have carried stories of the huge sums they raised in their version of doorstep democracy. It has always been my contention that if you can get someone to contribute any amount, even two or five dollars, they follow that billfold commitment all the way to the ballot box.

Grace McCarthy of the B.C. Socreds also proved the efficacy of this theory. When the Socreds were out of office in the early 70's, she towed a little trailer all over B.C., stopping in mall parking lots and at roadside sites. She was selling $2 memberships in the Social Credit Party and spreading information, some might call it misinformation, about the NDP government. Voters remembered those two dollar bills when the next election came.

These small contributors take a lot of effort to develop, but once people have made the first contribution they can be quickly graduated to higher levels. The political impact of this sort of popular fundraising is undeniable.

A popular fundraising tool for all kinds of organizations is direct mail. Few Canadians have been spared pleas for funds in the mailbox from deserving groups, not to mention some with questionable credentials and motives. Frequently, this pile of mail includes appeals from political parties and candidates.

Many ask, how did they get my name? Don't they know I don't vote for them? Well, the answer is that you are simply part of the numbers game.

Direct mail strategy assumes that most people will not contribute. A 3% return is considered good from a prospect list. This makes direct mail the most inefficient way to raise political funds, but at the same time, it can be the most productive from the view of cost-efficiency. A 3% return from a mailing to 100,000 households means 3,000 replies that might average a minimum of $50 each, yielding an income of $150,000. Even if the mailing was a very expensive package that cost as much as 60 cents per piece, the profit is around $100,000 and, more importantly, names are being built into a list of contributors for future contact, or what is known in the trade as a "house list." These are attractive numbers for any political fundraiser.

Direct mailers abandon all barriers of grace and good taste. Their letters are tough and direct. Ambiguity does not generate dollars. If you read the first few sentences of a direct mail piece, then you will likely read every word. Otherwise, a liberal use of underlining draws your eye to the nastier bits about the other parties and to stir your emotion and take you through to the end.

A classic example of a tough and specific appeal was this short letter mailed by the Democrats in the United States:

> Dear Friend:
> There are two reasons why I need your money and need it now— Nixon and Agnew.
> Sincerely,

Well, how did they get your name? Almost always, your name was purchased. Political parties buy subscription lists from magazines whose readership closely typifies the demographics of those most likely to give to their party. Some direct mail sales houses sell the names of people who buy goods through the mail; sometimes direct mail houses arrange for clients to exchange lists. Once you have made a contribution, you end up on the house list, and you can expect to get a lot more mail!

Direct mail works well for the parties, but is a dismal failure when tried by individual candidates. The problem is simple— the numbers aren't there. There is rarely a large enough base of likely contributors to make mail prospecting for money a reasonable expenditure. Some candidates use it as a way of softening up prospective contributors, particularly party members, close friends or family and supporters, the FRANK group. A letter becomes the sales pitch and the closing is done later by telephone or in person. Some contributions are generated by such mailings, but their real value comes in preparing people for the eventual personal hit.

As inevitable as winning or losing is the sure knowledge that political campaigns usually wind up in the red. This happens to victors and losers alike. Clearly it is easier for an elected official to clean the slate. A financial appeal at the victory party will often offer up sufficient cash and pledges to balance the ledger, and if not, banks and creditors are going to look more kindly on the plight of an MLA or MP.

Losing candidates have a more difficult road to follow. Money is usually harder to raise and suppliers are more nervous than they are about the winner. The local party organization is a big help in offsetting a deficit. The local constituency association usually undertakes to raise the necessary funds since the candidate was their nominee.

The American system differs in these matters in that there is not much of a party organization at the grass roots level and campaign debts are considered the responsibility of the candidate. Mind you, so are the surpluses, which explains why American candidates take such a great deal more personal interest in their campaigns' financial progress than their Canadian counterparts.

A credible campaign cannot be mounted without money. It's as simple as that. At the same time, the temptation to subvert natural principles or advance platform ideas designed only to attract money or help must be avoided.

Some say an example of this is happening today. During the 1988 federal election, most observers agreed that the Tories were in a lot of trouble over the free trade issue— this for a party that had always opposed free trade with the U.S. It was not until groups like the Canadian Manufacturer's Associations, the banks, and other assorted wealthy and powerful individuals and institutions weighed in with their parallel ad campaigns and election money that the tide began to shift in Mulroney's favour.

In 1990, the PC government hit the lowest point in the polls of any government in Canadian history, and they barely finished ahead of spoiled ballots in two August by-elections. Even in England, at the time of wholesale civil unrest over the Poll Tax, the Thatcher government was still 10 points more popular than Mulroney in Canada. Instead of scrapping the Goods and Services Tax, Mulroney is likely to pay the ultimate political price in the next election.

Why? In my opinion, he is paying back those who helped him win in 1988. These are the only people in favour of the GST, which lowers the corporate tax burden and shifts it to consumers. If his government is defeated in the next election, it will be a result of short term political expediency.

There are strong arguments in favour of citizen-based funding of political activity. There is no democracy in a large corporate political contribution. And though I do not agree with it, some will argue the same is true for a trade union contribution. It is true unions and corporations do not vote; it would enhance our democracy if funding were left only to those who do vote.

François Gerin, MP for Megantic-Compton-Stanstead, wrote:

"Does the worker in my riding, who barely makes $15,000 a year, seriously believe that an engineering firm, a major bank, or an entrepreneur gives $50,000 to a political party without hoping for a return on his investment? Does this same worker think that he counts as much in the political process as this engineer? To ask the question is to answer it."

He continues:

"Political party fundraising, which is limited to individual citizens, would be a very clear endorsement of morality by political figures. It would be an unequivocal statement that big contributors no longer have disproportionate influence in our political decision-making system."

10. The Campaign Roadmap

"Strategy: The science and
art of conducting a campaign
by combination and employment
of means on a broad scale for
gaining advantage."
Funk and Wagnalls

Designing strategy and tactics in a modern election campaign can be a confusing process for new candidates. Even seasoned political professionals have a great deal of difficulty drawing a line between strategy and tactics.

In simple terms, strategy is a campaign plan. It is the foundation for proper organization. A strategic plan answers some very simple questions: who will receive what message, where, by what means, at what cost; why will the message convince voters and what will be the final result of this strategy?

The execution of the strategy is the tactical part of the campaign; how will the campaign plan be actualized? It has been put best by top campaign managers that, "the strategy is the forest and the tactics are the trees."

Political campaigns have often been likened to military operations. Here is a quote from Sun Tzu's "The Art of War," a book on military strategy: "All warfare is based on deception. When near, make it appear you are far away; when far away, that you are near. Anger his general and confuse him. Keep him under a strain and wear him down. Attack where he is unprepared; sally out when he does not expect you. These are the strategist's keys to victory. With many calculations, one can win; with few, one cannot."

In politics, the end is definite. The political battle is won or lost in a specific period of time. In war, a combatant can always come back to fight again as long as there are enough troops and territory remaining.

A casual political observer might feel that this is pretty basic stuff: of course a lot of planning goes into mounting a high dollar political campaign. But the fact is that readers will take more time to read this chapter than most campaigns will spend devising a detailed plan of operation for an election.

Effective strategy starts with solid research. This research need not be highly complicated in order to be of value to the planning process. Previous election results provide some of the most useful and necessary information. A careful analysis of individual poll results helps determine where the campaign's attack should be focused and who should receive the message. Campaigners will concentrate on those areas of a constituency where a particular candidate or party has achieved reasonable success in the past, or can expect a good return on effort in the future. Campaign strategists concentrate their tactics in a way that will maximize the available vote potential.

Any vote which has taken place within the boundaries of a particular constituency supplies some information campaign planners can use. In partisan contests, recent federal and provincial election results have the most relevance. But municipal and school board elections and ballot referenda also tell much about local voting behaviour, by showing what kinds of people were elected and what issues were important as well as how likely it is that people will actually vote.

When reviewing this information, a healthy amount of subjectivity needs to be added. Inconsistent voting patterns may have occurred when, for example, a poor candidate ran for one of the parties in the past, or, in a particular election, a very unpopular government was turned out of office. It may not be wise to pay too much attention to unique historical blips.

Other important research material for election planning is gained by conducting a thorough examination of the known strengths and weaknesses of each candidate in the field. This includes determining what assets, such as speaking ability, community profile, good looks, or public record, exist. When making personal assessments, equal attention has to be paid to considering apparent weaknesses. Self-deception is a big enemy here. Campaigns have to be as brutal and frank in assessing their own candidates as they are in examining their rivals.

Candidates need to be up front with the campaign manager, if no one else, about what things in their background might be revealed during the election. This ensures that appropriate means of responding to any allegations have been developed beforehand. The kinds of matters that need to be explored include bad business deals, drunk driving charges, academic records and a host of possible personal and family problems. Some of these matters may have been beyond the control of the candidate, but they will reflect on him or her anyway.

Candidates sometimes hold back on good things about themselves as well. In one campaign I was involved in in Ontario, my candidate was quite nervous about visiting seniors' retirement homes and we had targeted older voters as an important audience. It wasn't until the election night celebration that I found out he was a tremendous piano player and a terrific singer. This would have been a perfect way for him to meet retired people and win them over to his side, if only I had known sooner. At the same time he would have overcome his nervousness with seniors much more quickly.

The public records of candidates are an important source of campaign strategy research often overlooked by campaign teams. Even if a candidate has not held elected office before, he or she may have some kind of public record through speeches that have been reported by the media, activities in various kinds of associations and groups or general reputation at work and in the community.

Campaign teams should research available records for peculiar or conflicting statements by the opponent and have them ready for use in debates, on the doorstep or in campaign literature. There are even special computer programs to store this information and make it available in a variety of forms very quickly.

The trouble is that most campaigns fail to take the same amount of time to research their own candidate as thoroughly as they might their opposition, which can result in embarrassing silence when a similar charge is levelled against them. They don't know how to respond because they haven't a clue what it is all about. I always advise campaign managers to know more about their own candidates than the opposition does.

Data on every constituency in Canada are readily available at the local library. StatsCan Census data details who lives in any area of the country, including information on age, sex, ethnic background, income levels, type of housing and so on. While a lot of this information is also familiar to people with experience in any constituency, having it confirmed by reliable data is important.

It doesn't hurt campaign managers to drive around the constituency and have a look first-hand at local conditions. Short conversations with storekeepers, teachers, or other people who come into contact with residents on a regular basis are helpful in providing important information on local attitudes and opinions.

A key method of answering most of the questions critical to building an effective campaign plan can be found in polling data. In every election there is a good deal of cynicism about polls. Politicians are accused of offering programs based on the polls, and after elections, they seem to govern as though they have fresh polls in their hip pockets at all times.

Actually, even though the parties themselves spend a great deal of their campaign budgets on survey research, individual candidates rarely make use of this research device in planning election strategy. It is ironic that a campaign will commit thousands of dollars towards getting the message out without being absolutely certain what the message should be or precisely who should receive that message. Those are some the things that polling can inform campaigns about.

Large companies spend significant sums of money on polling before they spend a dime on marketing, but candidates do not seem to want to spend money on polling. It is as though they have a deep suspicion of polling as some sort of black art and think they lose something of themselves if they rely on science rather than on their own gut instincts to help design a campaign, but no competent business manager would spend $50,000 on selling a new product without first spending $1500-$2000 on market research.

The availability of pollsters is quite narrow for candidates; not all pollsters will do political work, and nearly all of them who do political research have some partisan affiliation or other.

One other reason for a lack of reliance on polling research may simply be the cost. I don't blame candidates for being shy about paying some of the prices demanded by many pollsters for their work, which can be really outrageous for what they are actually doing. They get away with it because they cloud the process in mystery and magic. Since I make my living at polling for candidates, I feel I know what I'm talking about.

There is no reason for the high cost of polling other than the fact that polling companies seem determined to keep the prices that way. They also tend to obscure the process, which is really quite simple and straightforward. They are something like the CEO of Federal Express who once told an audience that if people knew that in order to get parcels from San Diego to San Francisco overnight they had to be flown to Nashville first, they wouldn't use the service. Well, if polling consumers knew how simple polling really was, they would do it themselves.

That is exactly what the Saskatchewan NDP decided to do after contracting an American pollster who ended up charging over $50,000 U.S. to conduct a poll among 800 voters. I reckoned, for that amount of money, you could take those 800 people out to dinner, ask all the questions you could possibly think of, and still have a fair chunk of change left over. After that experience, I was given the task of developing the NDP's own in-house polling operation, which proved to be extremely reliable, cost effective and easy to administer.

It would be useful to take this opportunity to examine just what are the steps in polling. A little more understanding about this research tool can help us relate it a little more closely to campaign strategy.

The main elements of good polling are really quite easy to understand. Accurate and useful polling by telephone requires careful attention to five basic steps. First, the sample, or the group of telephone numbers from which the interviews are going to be conducted, needs to be drawn in a way that ensures that everyone within the polling universe, in this case let us assume it is a federal constituency, has an equal opportunity of being interviewed. In a rural constituency, the quantity of telephone numbers needed will be about four times the number of completions desired; in an urban riding it might be as high as 5 1/2 to 1, depending on how transient the population is. This ratio takes into account the fact that not everyone is home when an interviewer calls; some refuse to be interviewed; some numbers are busy or are not in service.

These telephone numbers can be generated by computer programs that randomly make up a variety of phone numbers, by a system of increasing or decreasing the digits on phone numbers already selected, or by going to the phone book and selecting residential numbers on an interval that satisfies the requirement of having enough numbers available throughout the constituency. Each system has its advantages and disadvantages, but the latter provides the most consistent results.

The second requirement for accurate polling is to ensure that the questionnaire or survey instrument is as unbiased as possible. A question like, "Would you vote Liberal or like a sharp stick in the eye?" will likely draw out a lot of Liberal support that really doesn't exist. After I design a questionnaire, I try to determine who I might think was calling if I was asked to answer the questions I have set. Ideally, the questions will seem neutral or even like a survey from another party.

The next step is conducting the interviews themselves. Telephone volunteers can do the job as long as they are properly supervised and the supervisor ensures that the interviewers are not influencing the responses by the way they ask the questions. Professional interview services or "bucket shops" are also available for those who don't have their own telephone staff.

The one step that might require outside assistance is processing the data from the survey. There are lots of data processing companies around that can handle this kind of work; sometimes campaigns might get a friendly university professor to "crunch the numbers" for them.

Finally, the analysis of the results provides the research information that campaigns require for the planning process. From these data, campaigns will determine what issues need to be emphasized and which need to be ignored or avoided. Depending on the questions asked, campaigns can have a handle on the opinion held by voters of the candidates, leaders, issues, performance of the government and how they feel about the kinds of arguments that are advanced by each of the parties. And, of course, they will have the bottom line, the vote preference, which, when cross-tabulated with all the other questions including the demographic data on age, sex, occupation, etc., will give the campaign the answers to the important questions of who should receive what message.

Meticulous and systematic application of each of these steps provides any campaign with survey research as good as that provided by the country's top names in polling.

To be sure, this is a simplistic overview of what polling research is about, but it really is not much more complicated than that. If campaigns decide to do their own polling, they are money ahead in the long run and will be armed with a lot of meaningful and up-to-date information. They have to be careful about when they conduct their surveys and who receives the information, though. Ideally, a poll will be conducted before an election is called to be an aid to the planning process, and again a couple of weeks before election day to track important issues and make some last minute adjustments to the plan.

Poll results need to be kept among a small group of people. The flavour of a poll can be communicated to many if this serves a motivational purpose by telling workers that the campaign is on the right track or within striking distance of the opponent. One organizer, who is now a Saskatchewan MLA, conducted his own poll in a constituency three or four days before election day, when it was of no use. It showed the candidate would lose. and the word got out among the workers. They were debilitated and deflated and all the energy left an otherwise vital campaign.

Though this discussion hasn't examined all the factors that affect the eventual reliability and utility of surveys, it is important to know they have value at all levels of political campaigning, not just at the top. The technology is available to anyone who wants to take the time to learn more about it and apply it.

Everyone has an opinion as to whether polls have any effect on an election's outcome. I think the available research on the topic indicates that they do not. Polls do have an effect if candidates use them as part of the process of developing a winning campaign plan. It's an old political saying that polls never win an election, but you can win an election with what you do with them.

Once all the research is completed, campaigners begin to form the strategic plan. The most important elements of a campaign plan are that it should be simple, and it should be written down. The questions that need to be answered by a campaign plan are not hard to understand, so neither should be the solution. If the campaign plan is hard to understand or represents a complex answer to simple questions, it likely won't stand much of a chance during the heat of battle. If it's not written down, then it will be open to interpretation, and will surely become a matter of agitation between candidate, campaign manager and the rest of the campaign team. If the plan is written down, there can be no confusion.

Too often, I have seen an academic left alone to come up with the campaign plan, and as often as not, it comes out in a form that no one can comprehend. The only solace is that, if such a plan fell into enemy hands, they wouldn't know what the campaign was really up to.

A political campaign strategy should always be win-oriented. While many candidates know well in advance that their chances are between slim and none, many recent elections have demonstrated that sometimes you simply have to be in the right place at the right time. There have been few provincial or federal elections in the last ten years where there haven't been upsets in some constituencies. Therefore, a campaign strategy must be prepared to take advantage of shifts in public opinion when they occur, by making the best use of the available resources and employing all the tactics at hand. Each candidate has to approach campaign planning with a "never say die" attitude. Many of the successful NDP candidates in the 1990 Ontario election would not have won had they not prepared a plan that allowed them to take advantage of the changing public mood during the course of the campaign.

Sometimes campaigns adopt what might be described as a "modified" winning strategy. This is one that sets goals that are more likely to be attained, such as achieving a certain percentage of the vote, winning a particular number of polls or even using one campaign as the base on which to build a winning campaign next time out.

Winning campaigns make sure that their campaign plan is dependent on their own efforts, and that it can be achieved with their own resources. If campaigners can only assume success in the event that their opponents trip up, then they have no control over their own destiny and they really have no plan, only a dream.

An effective campaign plan must also be realistic. The plan contains consideration of all of the available research, the financial budget, and a knowledge of how many volunteers will be available to put the plan into action. Still, many campaigns make plans that require more volunteers than are available or require more funds than can be expected to be raised or that the law allows to be spent.

Those campaigns which do take enough time to develop an effective campaign plan can fall into the trap of not building enough flexibility into their plans to allow them to react to changing opinions and attitudes as an election unfolds. We will discuss marketing at length later, but sometimes too much of an election campaign is already "in the can" and candidates are reluctant to scrap this material to accommodate new conditions. This can make the material quite irrelevant by the time election day rolls around because they haven't been able to make changes that address conditions that were not initially anticipated.

The final stage in preparing the campaign plan is to choose a theme. This is the general image or impression that campaigns want voters to associate with them. These themes need to be consistent with the philosophy of the candidate and party, and not one developed out of polling information alone. Too often, relying on the polls to assist in designing a theme will result in future inconsistencies between the theme and a candidate's position on many of the issues, resulting in a loss of credibility.

The main test of an effective theme is that it should unify the various messages in an election campaign; it really becomes the rationale. For candidates, it answers the question "Why me now?" At the same time, this theme should state or imply the answer to the other question, "Why not the other candidate now?"

Campaign planners become profoundly confused between themes and slogans. Countless hours of valuable time and brain cells are devoured during late night sessions trying to come up with a slogan. It's quite a useless exercise in my estimation. Slogans rarely serve any positive purpose, but political neophytes feel it is something they need to have. It's something they always see and hear throughout every election campaign, therefore they feel that in order to win, they have to have a slogan as well. They act as though it is the magic button, that, once pushed, somehow turns voters into automatons who will joyfully march to the polls and support the candidate come hell or high water. A slogan for an individual candidate rarely captivates the mood of voters in that way and has shown only marginal utility for any party's central campaign other than to fill in the blank space on buttons and bumper stickers.

Candidates often get so hung up on a slogan that they lose their focus on the campaign plan itself. Candidates dream up slogans such as "Working for You," "On Your Side," "Effective Representation" and so on. The most imagination goes into symbolic slogans such as, "I Dig Clay," "Conquer with Koenker," or "de Jong and the Restless."

This is not to say that slogans are bad in themselves. They can help develop fundraising materials for candidates and can go a long way in motivating the troops; they just don't win a lot of votes.

It is the theme that can affect people's attitudes and opinions, not the slogan. The theme flows from the campaign plan and should be the question campaigners want the voters to be asking when they finally enter the voting booth. The question varies from campaign to campaign and might be as simple as "Who will represent me best?" or, "Which candidate understands the issues that concern me the most?" or, "Which candidate has the best leader?"

Jeffrey Simpson in his book, *Discipline of Power*, discusses this aspect of campaigns, and suggests that incredible energy during election campaigns, in all the different political camps, goes toward encouraging the greatest number of voters, on their way to vote, to have the correct theme in mind. He notes that the battle between the parties comes down to the posing and answering of questions by the parties, and their abilities to convince the voters of the correctness of those questions and answers.

Probably the most important function of the campaign plan is to unify the various aspects of the election, such as the budget, volunteers, candidate, research, campaign issues and marketing. The plan should be the glue that binds all the parts. Put another way, these are the parts of the formula that make up the campaign plan or overall solution.

One of the best examples of developing a solid campaign plan and sticking to a consistent theme occurred in Regina in the civic election in 1988. Mayor Larry Schneider had stepped down to be a Conservative candidate in the 1988 Federal Election, so there was an open race for the Mayor's chair. There were six candidates in the field, three of them "serious." They were in the race early and had good community profile as well as fairly large campaign organizations. The main campaign issue was whether business and property taxes should be cut by 10%. This seemed like an idea that would be pretty popular with most voters and two of the three major candidates embraced this position.

The one candidate who did not support the tax cuts was Councillor Doug Archer. After all the research had been conducted, it was determined that while tax cuts were attractive, they lost their appeal if the cuts also meant a reduction in services and the loss of jobs. Archer's theme was simple. Tax cuts mean service cuts, and whenever the 10% tax reduction came up in any form during the campaign, he simply referred to them as service cuts and never wavered from that position.

As the campaign unfolded, the other two candidates modified their position on tax cuts, often only on the basis of who they were talking to at the time. They began to look inconsistent on the main issue. They felt that an appeal to basic greed would be sufficient to attract votes. They were wrong. They underestimated the intelligence of the voter.

Archer's campaign manager, Heather Padfield, developed an operational plan that made as much use of available volunteers as possible and saw to it that all the tactical activities continued to emphasize this one theme and did not allow the campaign to get sidetracked on any of a host of other issues that come up during the course of a normal municipal election campaign.

Even though the Archer campaign had less than half the money of its two main opponents, he won handily in the biggest turnout in any Regina municipal election. The reason he won was that his campaign developed a theme and a winning plan to sell that theme. They were successful in making voters define their voting decision by asking the question, "Which candidate will make sure that my city services are not cut back?", rather than "Which candidate will save me the most money?", which was the test the other candidates wanted the voters to apply to the contest.

Finally, before hitting the streets, a campaign requires a determination of what issues will form the backdrop of the campaign messages. Issues are the fighting ground for the campaign. Polling research will be the main means of selecting the appropriate issues for campaigns.

Using polling research to determine issues is often confused with the idea that politicians are governed only by the polls and haven't an original thought of their own. In most cases, this is not true. It wouldn't do any candidate much good to talk about road repair, for example, if the number one issue in everyone's minds was job creation. The candidate's position on road repair may be the finest ever advanced, but it is not what voters want to hear if they are more interested in how the politicians intend to create jobs. This candidate can talk about how road repair can be a part of a job creation plan, but not about the condition of roads alone.

If candidates are not talking to people about things that the voters are concerned about, they might as well be talking to the wall.

The federal election of 1988 is an example of this. When all the polls showed that the electorate was most interested in the Free Trade deal between Canada and the U.S., national NDP strategists ignored the issue as much as possible, hell-bent to proceed with their campaign plan that had been assembled well ahead of the actual election. The widespread concern about Free Trade would have been a good reason to adjust their campaign plan and concentrate on that issue, but, it seemed they did not feel the issue would have the legs or the continued intensity that it eventually displayed. As a result, the NDP continued their plan of highlighting a different issue every day with only casual reference to Free Trade. It was left to local campaigns to carry the freight on Free Trade. The result for the NDP was not disastrous, since they did better than ever before, but the real shame of it was in the opportunity to become the number two party that may have been lost for some years to come.

A common mistake for many candidates is to decide to feature too many issues. Even six platform items might be too many in some election campaigns. For instance, one Progressive Conservative campaign manual cautions candidates not to be overly issue-oriented. It says the principle issue is to form government. They go on to counsel their candidates to look for the one "gut issue" that can be battered home to almost every voter and concentrate on no more than three issues at the most in an attempt to avoid confusion and the alienation of too many voters.

Candidates select too many issues because of the mistaken belief that their position on every issue needs to be delivered to everyone, or because they want to leave the impression that they are clever and opinionated. To be sure, there are people and groups who want to know candidates' views on a variety of issues, and the answers should be prepared and available when requested, but the largest number of votes will swing on the main campaign issues or concerns. Sticking to two or three issues allows for a consistent image.

Sometimes campaigns have little choice about defining the issues by themselves. Their parties will tell them what issues they want the candidates to use and the only decision for local campaigns is to decide which ones are more relevant and need more emphasis, or what local spin can be put on the thrust of the central campaign.

Incumbent politicians have a distinct advantage when it comes to developing issues. They are in a position of strength and should never relinquish the opportunity to set the campaign dialogue and timing. Challengers always have to be trying to change that agenda in an attempt to make the incumbent lose his or her stride.

Put in the simplest of terms, there are three kinds of issues. These have been described best by American campaign managers Baus and Ross as "heart," "belly," and "power" issues.

"Heart" issues are those which appeal to ideology and philosophy. They embrace concepts that might be described as motherhood issues, and are advanced by candidates saying they agree that the main issue might be job creation, the same as their opponents, except that they are more capable of solving the problem than the opposition. Appeals to loyalty and patriotism are central to heart issues. These kinds of issues are the ones that might form the backbone of a speech at a partisan rally.

There are really two kinds of "belly" issues: money issues and what are called "soft-side" issues. The money issues include those perennial campaign favourites such as deficits, taxation, pensions, inflation, interest rates and the like. In short, they are issues that appeal to the pocketbook. A variation on money issues might include pork-barrelling, spending money from the public treasury on local improvements such as parks or highways. But not all people are motivated by money alone. For some voters, issues like child care, education, housing and health care are just as critical when deciding who will receive their vote. It is a rare election campaign where there is no mention of belly issues; they are usually selected by candidates because they feel that if all else fails, people will vote in their own self-interest.

"Power" issues concentrate on who will use power and on whose behalf it will be exercised. Issues like women's rights, civil rights and constitutional affairs take precedence here. In fact, one of the major debates in Canadian politics at all levels for several years now has been the power issue centred around the role and responsibilities of all political jurisdictions towards each another. The main focus of this debate has been how much power should be centralized in Ottawa as opposed to the provincial capitals, but even municipal governments enter the debate with some valid claims for a change in their relationship with provincial and federal governments. The controversy over an elected Senate is another current power issue. (However, that issue has not been around as long as Don Getty was quoted as saying by the Edmonton *Sun*— "Canadians have talked about Senate reform for hundreds(?!) of years.")

Some issues can be used in all three ways as different people express them with different emphasis. Free Trade in the 1988 election was a good example of this.

The Liberals appealed to the Canadian electorate largely by making the debate a heart issue for them. They wrapped themselves in the flag and asked voters to consider the issue with an appeal to their patriotism. They were saying this agreement would affect the unique nature of Canada and would lead us quickly down the path of Americanization. The Conservatives made Free Trade a belly issue by using the promise of future prosperity as their main selling point. New Democrats, on the other hand, used a scattered approach making arguments on all three levels but focused on power issues. They talked about how Free Trade would affect women, workers, and programmes which were unique to Canada such as regional development, Unemployment Insurance and Medicare. Their message was that the FTA would dilute Canada's ability to control its economic and social future.

Candidates don't always select positive issues on which to base their campaigns. The general public often is subjected to a barrage of negative attacks among candidates and parties. We often refer to this as "dirty" politics and people will tell you they don't like to see or hear too much of it. The truth is, however, that it is used because it works.

In recent years, a common campaign strategy for the parties has been to spend the first part of an election attacking its opponents and then in the last days, presenting itself as a positive alternative. This worked for a while during the late 60s and the 70s and was used in one form or another by every party in different parts of the country. The problem with this tactic is that it violates a basic rule of campaign strategy which requires campaigns to establish their own credibility before an attack can be credible. Put in another way, a campaign needs to offer something to vote for before people will vote against an opponent of that campaign, not the other way around.

In fact, speaking of those campaigns that have used the negative-positive phases successfully in election strategy, one could offer the argument that the governments and candidates who were defeated were already on their way out anyway. All that may have been needed on the victor's part was to show up.

The important point that candidates and their campaigns need to remember when they get into a war of words is that the campaign that controls the issues will likely get the majority of the votes.

The trick is to know when to answer and when not to answer negative attacks. Trying to respond to charges from the opposition may simply add more credibility to the attack. On the other hand, an attack that is allowed to stand without challenge may be considered true by the voters regardless of how untrue it might be.

When the attacks are personal, candidates have three main options for response. First, they can ignore the charge. This is probably the most dangerous of all. Silence may be seen as an admission of guilt. I remember one candidate from northern Saskatchewan who told me his opponents were spreading rumours that he and his sons were selling drugs. This was a stupid charge that was certainly not true and the candidate did not want to dignify these negative tactics by responding, but his strategy was wrong. He should have gone public with the issue and used it to ridicule his opponents and point out how desperate their campaign was. The burden of proof lies with the attackers and if they go unchallenged, they do not have to prove anything. If they are not forced to put up, they won't shut up. Also, I think voters expect politicians to stand up for their own honour.

The second common response of candidates is to simply answer the charge. This is fine as long as that is the end of it, but candidates need to consider all the angles. One case that comes to mind to help illustrate this point was the situation of an Ontario candidate who was attacked for not supporting French language education in a part of the province where there was a large francophone population demanding more French educational facilities. This candidate denied the charge and said she was always in favour of expanded rights for francophones. Two days later the opposition held a news conference and produced a press story from another province where the candidate had made statements that indicated the opposite was true.

The third typical response is a kind of "so's your mother" reply. It involves candidates stepping aside and firing a volley or two of their own on an unrelated topic.

In most cases, candidates are the wrong people to be making negative statements unless the policies of the opponents are in question. Even then, it should never be done through paid media. Any attacks that are personal in nature should come from a third party. For instance, getting an opponent embroiled in a battle with the campaign manager is an excellent tactic. It allows the candidate who is providing the attack the opportunity to take the high road while the opponent is stuck in the mud with a subordinate.

I believe that negative campaigning has an important role in

Canadian elections. I don't like the role it plays now, where it becomes the basis of rumour and innuendo; those who use it do not stand behind their remarks. That's a cowardly approach. However, I have some admiration for the American approach in this respect, even though it might be a little too pervasive. There, if a candidate has something to say about another he will say it and try to stand behind it. After all, if one of the things campaigns are asking voters to do is to choose which person from a group of candidates will best represent them, why shouldn't they know as much as possible about the candidates before they make their decisions?

One thing that does disturb me is the need for those candidates and parties that are in opposition to be persistently critical. Yes, I know it is their role, but as the saying goes, "Even a stopped clock is right twice a day." There needs to be a place in politics to admit from time to time that the opponent has a good idea that is worthy of support. I can't help but believe this wouldn't go unnoticed by most citizens and be good for building a positive image. I wouldn't recommend that it be done twice a day mind you that would be carrying a good thing too far but now and then on minor issues it can help catch the opposition off guard and retain voter respect.

One final point on issues and their selection; there is a controversy over whether or not voters can be converted during a campaign. One school of thought claims that if only voters hear the right message or see the right advertisement, they will certainly vote "the right way." There is a second opinion that maintains that you cannot change anyone's mind during an election: the time for that is between elections, and all you can do during an election campaign is find as many people as possible who support you and get them out on election day. The truth probably lies somewhere in between these two opinions.

If the latter were true, then why would we bother having elections at all? The only sensible course would be to call an election one day and compel all eligible voters to cast their ballots the following day. It would save a lot of money and time.

The fact is, people do change their minds during an election. There have been times when a party or candidate has entered an election and are seen as having a lock on it, yet in the end they have lost or barely won. Some voters must have changed their minds. A dramatic illustration of this occurred in Saskatchewan in 1982. Many workers in that election told me they thought that people lied to them on the doorstep. They had said they were going to support the re-election of the NDP, and yet the NDP was slaughtered. Well, people didn't lie, they simply changed their minds. The Conservatives selected issues and presented them in a way that appealed to a majority of voters, even many of those voters who considered themselves closest to the NDP in the early days of the election. A more recent and equally obvious example occurred in Ontario in the 1990 massacre of the Liberals by Premier Bob Rae.

True conversion, on the other hand, is a myth. It simply cannot happen during an election. There is no place for political education during an election because there isn't enough time. But that doesn't mean voters can't learn things about candidates that they did not know before or that they can't find out that things they thought were true really aren't, resulting in a change of mind.

Effective campaign planning sets as its objectives to find a prospective voter, create a message to make that prospect an advocate, and then convert that advocacy into activism.

Of course, you can run an election campaign solely on luck and superstition. During the 1986 Alberta general election I travelled with NDP Leader Ray Martin. Marilyn Burnett was the press officer on that tour. When we learned that Ray Martin's son-in-law Barrett and his wife Etta were going to have twins, we made sure that we got a picture of Ray with the newborns at the hospital. This wasn't only because it was a prime photo opportunity, but also because Etta and Barrett's first child was born during the by-election to replace the late Grant Notley. The NDP won the by-election and preserved their official opposition status in the Alberta Legislature. We felt that being twice-blessed during the general election could only be a positive omen of the outcome and it turned out we were right. Fortunately, though, that campaign was not based only on good omens and crossed fingers.

When all is said and done, most campaign organizers will say that at least four components of Murphy's Law are bound to come into play. They are: "in any field of endeavour, anything that can go wrong will go wrong at the worst possible moment; left to themselves, things will always go from bad to worse; if there is a possibility of several things going wrong, the one that will go wrong is the one that will do the most damage; and, if everything seems to be going well, you have obviously overlooked something." Fortunately, with a good election plan, the application of Murphy's Law can be held to a bare minimum.

Research, strategic planning and issue selection provide campaigns with the ammunition they need to fight an election. However, they are truly useless unless there is someone to pass that ammunition. That is where the armies of volunteers enter the picture. These are the people who put the tactics to the plan. They design the leaflets and ads that deliver the message. They identify how voters intend to cast their ballots. They get people to the polls. All of these activities are organized and prioritized on the basis of the strategic plan.

11. The Volunteer Army

"A strong political party
cannot be built from the
top down. It must be built
from the bottom up."
Richard Nixon

American campaign managers Baus and Ross correctly point out in their book, *Politics Battle Plan,* that the blood and guts of an election campaign is the volunteer. A campaign might be won on the creative and concentrated use of mass media propaganda, but in most cases that alone is not enough.

Politics is people in action, and among the more vital factors in any campaign is the number, the dedication and the productive utilization of volunteers. A campaign without volunteers can be flat and listless, without substance and without prospect of victory.

Estimates vary, but most campaign managers agree that campaign organization is worth at least 5% of the vote and, in tight races, it can be worth a lot more. The only way an effective campaign organization can be built to help gain this advantage is by forging a volunteer army to execute all of the tedious tasks of an election. While volunteers give a campaign visibility and can save the campaign budget substantial sums of money, their true value is in showing voters that the candidate is worthy of commitment from other citizens. Volunteers not only deliver messages by distributing leaflets, phoning and canvassing, they are a message in themselves.

Campaigns have an enormous, intense need for smart people to do stupid work for free. The labour is simple; the labourers are not. Equating volunteers with the level of work they do will offend them and cause them to be under-utilized. It is a special campaign organizer who understands this fact.

Political campaigns are a matter of communication, identification and transportation: delivering the message, determining who will vote for the candidate and getting those voters out to the polling station on election day. Volunteers are given these most important campaign jobs to do under difficult circumstances and under the strictest of deadlines. To top it off, volunteers perform their work on an election campaign often after having put in full days at their own jobs.

But after saying all this, volunteers are a pain in the neck for any campaign manager. They always want to perform a task differently than the way they have been shown. They can be counted on not to show up when they have been asked to arrive at the campaign headquarters and, when they do arrive, have some excuse to leave early. Each volunteer will be convinced that some other person has been given a better job to do under better conditions such as a sharper pencil or better light or a more favourable poll to canvass.

Even so, you can't fire a volunteer because they are free, and that's the reason why volunteer recruitment and keeping volunteers happy is an important part of the job of any person who has a management role in a campaign.

Campaign volunteers come from a variety of sources. Some of the most likely prospects are those people who are closest to the candidate, such as the candidate's friends and family along with people they are associated with in business and community organizations. These people know better than anyone that the candidate is worthy to be elected and usually want to volunteer some time if it is at all possible.

Party membership lists are an obvious source of volunteers. The candidate is now their standard-bearer and their position in the community is affected to some extent by the success or failure of the candidate. Many party members have volunteered in numerous previous elections and already know what job they want to take. In my experience, many of the party faithful will be the first ones in the doors of the campaign headquarters looking for some work. Others, even those with lots of experience, would sooner give the cat a bath than work on a campaign. Still other party members take a perverse delight in playing hard to get by volunteering eagerly and then being hard to nail down to a specific task or time. Campaign organizers have to deal with all kinds of people.

Not all party members want to work on election campaigns. Some feel the act of buying a party card is support enough; some may not like the candidate or may hold some personal grudge against someone on the campaign team. It's also not uncommon to find former volunteers from the membership who are unhappy with the way they were treated in a previous election. They have to be assured that the same thing will not happen again.

Most volunteer recruiters make the mistake of believing that party members have a duty to perform some task on the election. Nothing could be farther from the truth in the mind of the party member. An appeal to party loyalty will not motivate every member.

Once the two sources of potential workers, family and friends, and party members, have been exhausted, campaigns might have no more than half of the people they really need. Successful volunteer recruitment takes a great deal of innovation.

Some volunteers come from organizations and groups which share the same point of view as candidates or parties on a particular issue. These are excellent sources for workers as long as the volunteers continue to believe the commitment for that single issue remains an important part of the campaign's agenda. Should the campaign start to waffle on the issue, however, these volunteers can be the first to walk out the door.

Anyone who had a sign on their lawn in the past or made a financial contribution to a campaign may be approached to help in the election. These people have already shown some desire to help. The idea of volunteering time may never occur to them if they are not asked. After all, most people have no concept of how much work goes into building a strong campaign since they rarely see more than the advertising and news broadcasts, neither of which seem to require any volunteer input. In my opinion, this is why recruiting volunteers has become more difficult in recent years. The emphasis on media as a the prime method of getting the message to voters fosters a "couch potato" attitude among potential volunteers.

Technical volunteers are as important as foot soldiers. A political campaign has a real need for a huge variety of technical skills that would cost money to obtain on the open market. These volunteers might be people who perform that kind of work in every day life, but this is also a way to involve young people, particularly students. A graphic artist is an important addition to the work of a publicity committee; a student with expertise in computers can perform valuable work keeping lists and producing direct mail pieces. An election campaign is an excellent learning tool for a political science student. The student gets an opportunity for a little practical application in an area of specialty, and campaigns get important work done.

Volunteers themselves can become recruiters. I always ask them if any of their family or friends might lend a hand on the campaign. If they understand the need, and feel they have been treated fairly and have enjoyed their work, they will often want to share their experiences with others.

People who express support to the candidate or other campaign workers during canvassing and at public events are also recruitment targets as is any person who innocently wanders into the campaign headquarters looking for more information or who just wants to see what is going on. Candidates are instructed to turn in the names of prospective volunteers so that they can be contacted immediately while the commitment is fresh. Some candidates walk around with offers of help scribbled on notes in their shirt pockets for days without telling anyone, and by the time the information is turned in the recruit's fire has gone out. When anyone walks into a campaign headquarters, they are asked if they want to help with the election campaign after they have been invited to have a cup of coffee and have been chatted up.

Not many of today's campaign managers are very realistic when it comes to expectations of how many volunteers they can expect in a campaign. There is too much competition for every individual's spare time. TV has made politics a spectator sport. With more disposable income available, well-meaning people can satisfy their latent political activism with a cheque. And with partisan politics sliding into disrepute in some circles, it is not always a fashionable activity. All of these factors make it more difficult to get people enthusiastic about taking an active role in politics and means that under normal circumstances a campaign will always be swimming uphill in its fight for volunteers.

Once a campaign accepts the fact that there will never be enough campaign workers, and that most of those that are available won't want to do the most critical jobs in the campaign, such as canvassing door to door and on the telephone, the main priority for the campaign manager and organizers is to keep the volunteers that they do have happy, enthusiastic and productive. Their people resources have to be budgeted in a way that ensures that critical strategic priorities are all covered.

Keeping volunteers is as difficult and demanding as finding them in the first place. Campaign managers and organizers have to be very skilful at managing human resources. Those who do not have this talent will not last long in the campaign business. They will not be able to handle the frustration and disappointment that is part of the turf when working with large numbers of volunteers.

Volunteers cannot be fired since they really hired themselves. So what might be threatening enough to motivate a regular employee in any other kind of organization just won't work with political volunteers. There isn't much you can hang out as incentive other than the satisfaction of doing a good job and advancing a cause they feel is important. There is almost no patronage to pass around so the only carrot that can be offered is the pride of being part of the winning team. The only sure way of keeping a volunteer is to work hard at making them want to come back, over and over again.

The very first error that campaigns make in dealing with volunteers is not telling them enough about what they are doing and why they are doing it. If I sit someone down in front of a box of 15,000 leaflets with a stack of rubber bands and ask the volunteer to bundle them in 100's, how does he know I won't rip the bands off as soon as he is gone and get someone else to do the same thing? The volunteer needs to know clearly why this job has to be done. The answer might be that 40 people will be in the office at 6:00 p.m. to pick up leaflets to distribute door to door and if they are bundled in 100's it will be a lot easier to get them out on the street doing their job. Then what seemed a pretty mindless job takes on new meaning and importance.

The other lesson from this example of bundling leaflets is that the volunteer is learning a bit more about the campaign and how his job fits into the overall scheme of things. Many volunteers are unable to do those jobs that they feel are the most important like canvassing, so they need to know that others are counting on them to perform their job well, no matter how unimportant it might seem.

Another great campaign crime is to give people too much to do. If a job appears to have no end, it has little appeal to a worker. I try to give someone a job that will take an hour to do but give them an hour and a half. That way they will feel a sense of accomplishment, and when they get promoted to new jobs they will know they are of real worth to the campaign. This also allows the opportunity to compliment the volunteers on a job well done and show real appreciation for their efforts.

I like to encourage volunteers to make suggestions about how their job can be done better. They should feel they have some control over their own working conditions without jeopardizing the final result of the task.

It is a difficult job to challenge volunteers with new and interesting work because it is all so tedious. Yet, by giving a volunteer new jobs on a regular basis, campaigns can avoid ending up with bored volunteers who are reluctant to return to the campaign office.

Campaign organizers should never waste a volunteer's time. It is important to be sure the work that the volunteers are expected to perform is properly organized before their arrival at the campaign headquarters. If they are going canvassing, then their kits, complete with maps, leaflets and supporting material should be assembled and ready. The more time it takes to prepare the work, the less time the volunteer will have to do it. This lack of preparation will leave the wrong impression in the volunteer's mind about the state of the campaign's readiness and sensitivity to helpers.

There is something warm and appealing to walking into a busy campaign headquarters where everything is humming along smoothly. It fosters confidence. It makes you want to be part of it all. Not all campaign offices can be palaces, but they shouldn't lack creature comforts either. There should be coffee available and facilities to make tea and other beverages that workers may want. A fridge is useful so that volunteers can bring their own lunches and a microwave will mean that everyone can have a hot meal from time to time. It's not a difficult matter to organize some supporters to prepare cookies and cake on a regular basis for the workers. Clean and well-appointed washrooms and a comfortable lounge area for relaxation add the finishing touches to an attractive workplace for volunteers.

Music always seems to help the time pass more pleasantly when performing tedious tasks. Edmonton MP Ross Harvey always plays music ranging from classical music to 50's rock and roll in the background while he is working on an election. I'm a CBC audiophile and my personal radio is tuned into the "Mother Corp" morning, noon and night during a campaign.

I have found that it is important to avoid competitive situations among volunteers. It doesn't serve any useful purpose to compare output or set up situations where they feel they are racing against others to meet some deadline. Co-operation is more powerful a tool than competition in a volunteer organization.

Campaigns are a wonderful place to bring people together. New friendships help to make coming back to work on a campaign easier for the volunteer and adds warmth to the whole scene. Romance is not a complete stranger to a political campaign either. It doesn't really matter why people keep coming back to work, as long as they do.

One way to be sure of keeping volunteers is to pay them. Well, you really can't do that, that's not volunteerism any more. What campaigns can do for volunteers though, is hold an appreciation evening. The 'workers' party is a standard mid-campaign, social event designed to thank everyone for what they have done to that point and exhort them to greater sacrifice in the last few days of the election.

Campaigns also have to show some interest in a volunteer's personal life. If a worker said she could not come in the next night because her daughter had a ball game, I would not try and leave the impression that her family had somehow damaged the election effort. Some campaign managers will resort to pleading and even suggesting that the game isn't as important as electing the candidate, which is nonsense. I would also make a point of asking the volunteer how the game went when she next returned to the headquarters to help out.

As in love, an immutable rule in dealing with election volunteers is to never take this object of affection for granted. Volunteers have to be thanked and thanked often for their help. This display of appreciation is the only real thing that can be offered without reservation. This is the only way that volunteers can gauge their effectiveness and worth to the campaign. Although the direct supervisor of a volunteer's activities should offer thanks often, the most effective person to do this is the candidate. This may seem obvious but it is surprising how many candidates feel that volunteers are their due, that they deserve to have them and as a result, take little or no interest in them and what they are doing to get the candidate elected.

Candidates need to take time out regularly, daily is best, to talk to volunteers working in the headquarters, canvassers when they come off the streets and telephoners when they are finished their shifts, and to thank them all. Sometimes candidates may never see all the volunteers, members of the sign crew for instance. In these cases, I put the candidate on the phone to call them and say hello and find out how it is going. Saskatoon Eastview MLA Bob Pringle was extremely effective in doing this during his by-election victory. He always took time to stop and talk with campaign workers. He took a genuine interest in them personally and their views about how things were going on the campaign and it showed in the renewed enthusiasm of the workers afterward. They were always easier to re-recruit after they had spoken with Bob.

A good example of how important leadership from the candidate is in motivating the troops was given by Alberta Premier Don Getty in reverse. His campaign team left the impression that everything was fine in his riding and that volunteers were not really necessary. He spent no time in the constituency and by the time they realized they had need of workers, they were all working in an adjacent riding for Doug Main. Getty was the first Alberta premier to lose his seat since the 1930's.

It is a common political saying that politics is the art of vote harvesting and the political machine is the reaper. And while the term "political machine" conjures up images of Chicago ward bosses, Tammany Hall or other visions of the darker side of politics, "political machine" is really the most appropriate term to describe a volunteer army and the jobs that it performs during the course of an election campaign.

Before this machine can be put to work harvesting those votes, the campaign strategists have to determine what jobs need to be done and how many people it will require to complete the work within the time allowed. This is decided by determining how many polls will be foot canvassed and how many will be telephone canvassed, how many pieces of literature will be distributed, how many signs put up or how many letters will likely be mailed. This may seem a simple and obvious notion to the layman, but few campaigns ever do this.

If an election team took the time to prepare a volunteer budget as carefully as they determined their financial budget, it would cause a great deal less stress for the campaign manager, who ends up worrying whether everything will get done on time. It would also mean less competition among organizers for valuable workers within each of their own functional responsibilities. Knowing the overall volunteer needs of the campaign allows recruiters and supervisors the chance to offer a volunteer other activities and challenges in the campaign that will keep their interest up while getting more labour out of each volunteer. Campaigns always seem to put their heads in the sand when it comes to a realistic assessment of the potential to recruit volunteers and the end result is always frustration, frayed tempers and anxiety over a situation that could have been controlled with some forethought and a minimum amount of planning.

Issues, strategies and advertising are vital to a good campaign, but they have no effect if the people who are moved to vote for a party are not identified and taken to the polls on election day. These are the two critical jobs of a political machine... identification and transportation.

The main tool for identifying people who will vote for candidates is through canvassing, both on foot and on the telephone.

The great strength of door to door canvassing is that it is personal. It is one-on-one voter contact. Voters are impressed that volunteers will take the time to visit voters and talk about the candidate and the issues. This advantage is enhanced if the particular poll the voter lives in is targeted for more than one canvass. After a second and even a third trip to the voter's home, the canvasser and voter build a temporary relationship. During the provincial election of 1969 in Manitoba, the campaign of Len Evans in Brandon East actually did five door to door canvasses! Four of them were during the election and another immediately after the election to say thank you for the victory.

Even if a poll is not slated for more than one canvass, the first trip to the elector's home becomes the foundation for more voter contact. Depending on his or her response, the voter may receive a telephone call, a letter or another visit from the canvasser. There are three general responses that canvassers are looking for: an expression of support, non-support or indecision. Canvassers determine the feelings of voters by introducing themselves, telling the voter why they are there and inviting the voter's opinion on the issues. In the early days of an election, canvassers are usually instructed not to ask for support outright; instead, they will say something like, "I hope you'll join us in supporting Jill Smith."

If voters come right out with something indicating they will vote for the candidate such as, "That's our candidate (or party)," or "I always vote for your party," they are recorded as being a positive supporter. Voters are asked if they will put signs on their lawns, whether they will help in the campaign and whether or not they will make a financial contribution. As well, they will be notified of any political events that might be coming up during the campaign.

Sometimes the support is not as clear, and voter say they are leaning that way, or that they won't be voting for the opponent. These voters are classified as positive and leaning towards the candidate and will receive a great deal more attention as the campaign goes on.

Early in an election it is difficult to get any reading at all on many voters. They become part of the mass of undecided voters. Sometimes they are not really undecided, they haven't said that they are, but the canvasser is undecided on how to classify them. Again, these people will receive more attention during the campaign.

It's fascinating to watch the movement of these "markings," as they are known to organizers. The undecideds will eventually begin to break in one direction or another. Some will become definite supporters or lean towards the candidate, while others will go the other way. Although you always hope they will start to come your way, the movement in the electorate is important in itself because then some basic assumptions can be made about the effectiveness of the strategy and techniques that are being used in the campaign.

Of course, there are always contrary-minded voters, and you only hope there are not too many. They are identified in the same way as positive voters. They are usually a bit more blunt in their response to the canvasser's patter. These voters will not be visited again and will likely not receive any more literature. However, there are many stubborn canvassers and organizers who will take the belief to their grave that if they continue to visit these "hostile" voters they will somehow influence them to vote for their candidate rather than the opposition. This is wishful thinking. Once a voter declares for one candidate or another conversion becomes highly unlikely. All that is accomplished by visiting an opposition voter is to succeed in getting them angry enough to work or give money to the opposition while wasting your valuable time and material. It's best to let sleeping dogs lie if at all possible.

An important advantage in canvassing door to door is that canvassers can speak to all members of the household who are eligible to vote. This is important because there are increasing numbers of families who exhibit a gender or age gap in political preferences, and it is important to know whether children have a different preference than parents. Spouses also may differ on the candidates they prefer. Campaigns need to know these differences so they do not end up pulling opposition votes on election day. It is an indication of growing political maturity to see election signs of different candidates on the same lawn.

Foot canvassing allows a sophisticated campaign to deliver highly targeted messages. For example, when canvassers visit a household and the voters are retired people, they can deliver an entirely different message about the candidate and the issues than they would to a young family. Competent research will tell the campaign what messages carry the most weight with different demographic groups, and if used properly, provides the volunteer foot soldier with powerful ammunition.

Canvassing also becomes research in itself. It provides terrific feedback to the campaign management on what people are thinking and feeling about the election. This information is gleaned during the process known as "debriefing." This is when canvass organizers go over the canvassers' results. The organizers want to know what people say when they express support for the candidate or for the opposition. Is it the candidate or the party leader or the party platform that is the most attractive feature of the campaign? Or, is it outright opposition to one of the other candidates or parties that is driving voters this way? All this information can affect future strategic decisions.

Another benefit of door to door canvassing is that it is possible to determine if there are people in the household who have yet to get on the voters' list, and, if they are supporters, this information will be relayed to the campaign headquarters to make sure the voter is put on the list of electors.

Door to door canvassing has its pitfalls as well. It's time consuming and uses up a lot of the volunteer budget. It is definitely not weather-proof and many people are reluctant to open their doors in cold weather or on dark nights. Some polls are just not canvassable because of security apartments and long distances between homes, or they simply aren't in safe neighbourhoods. It is not an effective tactic if the canvassers are not trained properly, because an organizer has absolutely no control over what canvassers say on the doorstep.

Canvassers hate to have their time wasted. In one Ontario election, I had some time on my hands while visiting in Toronto and offered to do some canvassing in a poll for a local campaign. During my debriefing, I was berated by a young organizer for marking one household as hostile. "Why, they're party members," she said. These people told me they didn't want any of the literature and that I was wasting my time with them. My automatic conclusion was that they were not sympathetic.

After that incident, I always insisted that strong supporters and party members be made known to canvassers in advance. This is not so the load is lightened, but so they know they needn't spend a lot of time trying to reach those voters if they are not home; or, if the voters are home, the canvasser can concentrate on helping to reinforce their support and perhaps get some volunteer help or a contribution. I can see the voter being annoyed at the thought that I didn't know that he and his family were rock-rib supporters.

Telephone canvassing is used more with every election campaign. It takes special talent to design and execute this technique effectively. When it was first employed in election campaigns, it was used to shore up holes in the foot canvass. Organizers simply tried to duplicate the doorstep approach on the telephone with disappointing results. Telephone canvassing has its own distinct advantages and disadvantages.

One of the major disadvantages is that telephone solicitation is pretty unpopular in some areas of the country. People don't like being bothered and a ringing telephone is an imposition. Therefore, a telephone script has to be written with care to separate it from all the other kinds of calls that go into the average household. The best way to ensure this is to make sure that telephone canvassers speak naturally and use words that make them comfortable. The first thing that will set off many voters receiving telephone solicitation is to hear a person at the other end of the phone reading their lines without feeling or emotion.

The big disadvantage to the telephone is that face to face contact is lost. Inflections and facial expressions can tell a lot about what a voter is thinking. This is lost on the telephone, and for that reason the script has to be quite direct in asking a potential voter for support. This is the element that was missing from the earliest telephone canvassing efforts.

But, telephone canvassing is weather-proof. It is far less time-consuming than doing the same work on foot. You can keep calling until you finally get the voter at home. When telephone canvassing is combined with direct mail follow-up on issues in which the voter is interested, highly targeted messages are possible. And, this form of voter contact and identification can make great use of people such as handicapped volunteers, older people and those who cannot or will not let themselves be seen doing political work in public.

The greatest heartbreak in telephone canvassing is the difficulty in volunteer recruitment. People will agree to telephone, but it is quite another problem to actually get them to show up. Where the volunteer fallout in foot canvassing might be around 10%, the no shows in telephone canvassing are often as high as 50%. This is partly due to the newness of the technique and workers do not view it as being as important as door to door canvassing.

The other cause of this problem is the fact that the best phoners are women. They are less threatening and more conversational on the phone than men. Unfortunately, many women do not have total control over their agendas. They may commit to a phone shift and learn later that there is some family event that they were not told about previously, or that they are expected to do some other task around the home with little notice.

Foot and telephone canvassing are the most important forms of voter identification performed by volunteers, but not the only ones. Candidates can be good canvassers, though few have the objectivity to make a fair assessment of their own support. It is not entirely their own fault. Voters wish them luck and are open and friendly and candidates mistake this friendliness for support. This friendliness can be among the paving stones to disappointment for all but those candidates who have learned to specifically ask for support from voters and know when it is being genuinely offered.

Campaigns may try to identify support by sending out leaflets with a mail-back portion asking for ideas on issues and support, but this is hit and miss at best and not a legitimate way to build a viable list of potential votes.

Some campaigns resort to calling people on the voters' list, posing as a polling company; they use those responses as the basis for vote identification. This does allow some objectivity from the voter since the caller isn't identified as representing a particular candidate as would be the case in a true telephone canvass. But using this back-handed route denies campaigns the use of direct mail and home visits for follow-up and removes the possibility of being able to ask to put up a lawn sign or ask for some volunteer time. Besides, in my own experience at least, many telephone volunteers are reluctant to misrepresent themselves and their purpose on the telephone.

Human nature being what it is, campaigners are always looking for shortcuts to solve difficult logistical problems, particularly when they are volunteer poor. Some people resort to a technique affectionately known as "kitchen table canvassing." Here, one or two people who know a district or poll and the people in it well, sit down with the voters' list and mark off all those whose politics are known. All those whose preference is not known are then visited. This is used extensively in rural ridings where there are great distances to cover. It loses its accuracy when too much is taken for granted about voting patterns. The volatility of the Canadian electorate means that people can't be expected to vote the same way all their lives any more.

Maritimers are well known for their familiarity with the voting behaviour of everyone in the neighbourhood, which is demonstrated by this story told by journalist Jeffrey Simpson. A new Roman Catholic priest had just moved into a rural parish. He had the only TV set. Just before the election, a few staunch Liberals asked this newly-instated priest if they could come by his house on election night to watch the results on his TV. They arrived at the priest's house, and mostly spoke among themselves until the local results came on. The numbers were 87, Liberal, 46 for the Conservative. You might have thought they would be simply pleased at the the positive Liberal outcome, but instead, they all turned to stare at the priest. When he asked them what was wrong, one of the men told him that they knew there were 87 Liberals in the community; but they also knew that there were only 45 Conservatives.

To be sure, there are more volunteers in an election campaign than just canvassers and election day workers. There is always something that has to be done in the headquarters. This is where the most tedious chores are performed, such as the classic envelope stuffing, letter folding, and the like. These workers give an important visual impact to the campaign. Passers-by are usually impressed with a busy office. It says something about the vitality of the campaign and can make people interested in investigating for themselves.

A lot of volunteers are required to put up signs and drop literature in mail boxes. Teams of young people are usually used for the latter job, but there are all kinds of people who thrive on this activity. Irene Dyck of Calgary, whose commitment to the NDP is legendary, will walk miles a day delivering leaflets and it doesn't matter whether there is an election or not. In Calgary there is no such thing as overkill for the NDP.

The second part of the winning formula that is dependent on

volunteer work forces is the election day organization. Really, an election is divided into two campaigns. A twenty-eight day election is comprised of twenty-seven days of delivering the message and identifying those who will vote for the candidate, and one day of getting supporters to the polls. Since canvassers cannot take the ballot box with them and have the supporters they find cast their ballots right on the doorstep, an idea that appeals to me, each campaign has to spend a lot of energy getting out the vote.

The election day machine is the most labour-intensive part of the campaign, requiring literally hundreds of workers in some constituencies.

The theory is pretty simple. One group of workers sits in the polling station as scrutineers for their candidates. They have a copy of the voters' list. As people vote, the scrutineers mark them off the list. An outside scrutineer comes into the polling station periodically, gets a list of those who have voted, and compares that to his or her list of supporters who have been previously identified through canvassing and other activities. Those who haven't yet voted are visited and urged to get to the polls. This is usually referred to as "pulling the vote."

The watchword for these activities is friendly persistence. Support is of no use on election day unless it is in the ballot box. These outside scrutineers are often the same persons who have been canvassing that poll, so the voters are familiar with them and will feel more obligation to follow through on their promises of support. The outside scrutineer does anything to make it possible for the voter to get to the polls.

Shortly after the 1975 election loss for the B.C. NDP, I was travelling through the B.C. Interior helping constituency associations get back on their feet. At a meeting in the Yale-Lillooet constituency, a group of workers from the election campaign was complaining to me about Socred dirty tricks on election day. This aroused my curiosity and I asked them to tell me more. Instead of getting a description of some kind of vote fraud or dark deed, the tale they recounted was exactly our system of getting out the vote! It seems the technique hadn't yet penetrated the Rocky Mountain interior, at least in NDP ranks.

Supporting the scrutineers is a fleet of drivers to give rides to the polls for those who need them, and a full complement of office staff at the headquarters to field all the calls from people who want to know where they vote. During election day, campaigns begin preparing for the victory party later that night and set up a mechanism to record and display the vote for each poll when the results are phoned in by the inside scrutineers after the votes have been counted.

One other volunteer who is indispensable on election day is a lawyer. I prefer to have one at headquarters during the day, but even if they agree to take calls on a priority basis from their office, that is a big help. There are always problems interpreting the Election Act on polling day, and I find a lawyer cuts more weight with the returning officer when dealing with the law. Lawyers can speak with authority and they can often intimidate a returning office into making a ruling that will be positive for my campaign's efforts if that is necessary.

On election day, the only way to treat candidates is as another volunteer. There isn't much left for them to do except pace the floor. Except in a genuinely close race, they will already know what is going to happen. A ritual during the preparations for election day is to count the number of supporters identified during the canvass. This is not a precise reflection of the outcome, but it does give a pretty accurate picture of the potential. This is one time in the election that candidates are particularly useless and usually get in the way. I try to get the candidate to help pull the vote, but many will not do it. I suspect they feel it is too self-serving, but I can't imagine why. They can usually be persuaded to visit polling stations and say hello to the workers and deliver them lunches and coffee, but beyond that, they are of little value to the task at hand.

I have said it elsewhere, but the prince among candidates I have known was Bud Germa. His enthusiasm and energy was boundless. When I asked him what he wanted to do on election day, he wanted to pull the vote. But he didn't want to cover one poll like most volunteers, he wanted three and didn't want any help.

Not only do volunteers perform the important jobs in an election campaign, they can also be counted on to provide public visibility for the campaign. Whenever an instant crowd is required at headquarters to meet the party leader or stack a public meeting, the volunteers are called off the street.

Volunteers can be used to develop publicity stunts such as ganging together to deliver the campaign's 10,000th leaflet, greeting the candidate when they have just driven the 20,000th mile or knocked on the 2,000th door.

Above all else, volunteers are voters. They influence other people to vote for their candidate through the simple act of volunteering. Many people feel that if a candidate is good enough for a friend of theirs to work for, then they must be worth voting for. Volunteers do vital work and they do it for free. They breathe life into a campaign by bringing enthusiasm, commitment and ideas and campaign managers need to treat them well and show each one how much their time is valued.

Every managerial technique must be brought to bear on the volunteer situation. It takes charismatic leadership, charm and an appeal to loyalty to get the most from everyone. And in the final days, most managers will also resort to healthy doses of guilt and rage to get every ounce of work possible on the phone and at the door. It's just liable to make the difference.

It is said that the prime purpose of volunteer association is for people to achieve collectively what they cannot achieve alone. A political campaign is a perfect example of this theory in action.

12. Getting the Word Out

"I fear three newspapers more
than a hundred thousand
bayonets." *Napoleon*
"Believe me, publicity isn't
what it's made out to be."
Pete Rose

The political campaign's one goal is to elect the candidate. In no more than four or five weeks, the publicity team has to transform a sometimes obscure name into a household word. Putting aside noble thoughts about democracy, the campaign committee is a marketing organization. The product is the candidate— his or her physical image, family, party affiliation, position on the issues and community profile are all parts of the basic product. The consumer is the voter who supports one candidate or the other, or no candidate. The strength of each consumer's support can range from a single vote, to convincing others to support the candidate and even to working on behalf of the candidate or making a financial contribution. The extent of the consumer's involvement in the product will depend on the effectiveness of the marketing.

This is not to say that candidates are little more than boxes of soap and can be sold in the same way. Voters are more sophisticated than that. However, it was not long ago that that was the prevalent attitude in the political advertising world.

When paid campaign ads were first introduced in the 1952 presidential campaign by Dwight Eisenhower, many stations flatly refused to run the ads because they felt the Presidency was not a tube of toothpaste. Self-serving campaign communication experts tried hard to promote the idea that candidates could be marketed in the same way as consumer goods so they could expand their client base. But campaign marketing or propaganda has advanced well beyond the level of selling detergent or deodorant. Selling politicians is a far more complex job.

Research has shown that consumers' acceptance of a product

can be influenced as much by emotional reactions as by rational ones. In fact, the user's ability to identify positively with a product or image can even outweigh some degree of weakness in the product's performance. Therefore, the marketer's job becomes more than the presention of plain facts about candidates, more than just comparing one kind of soap to another; marketers have to make the voters want the product.

Marketing political candidates requires careful attention to some pretty straightforward principles— clarity, simplicity, honesty and careful execution. But above all, campaigns are rigorous in making certain that the theme conveyed in all publicity, paid and unpaid, is completely consistent with the campaign's strategy.

In the simplest terms, campaigns adopt a three-stage marketing plan. The first stage (which is executed in the early days of the election and should even begin in the pre-election period) is designed to position the candidate in the field. This is done by building name recognition for candidates and then clarifying their positions on the important campaign issues and comparing their positions with those of their opponents. The second stage occurs in mid-campaign when candidates attack their opponents' positions and build their own credibility. Finally, in the last days of the campaign, candidates try to build momentum by conveying the impression that they can win.

Political propaganda is distributed by four main methods: news coverage, paid advertising, campaign literature and special events. At the same time that individual candidates are pursuing publicity using these vehicles, the political parties are also creating a great demand on news and advertising time and space, as each competes for the attention of the voter. No two candidates will place the same emphasis on these propaganda vehicles, whose use is determined by the relative cost effectiveness of each.

News coverage is more effective than paid advertising, which is more effective than leaflets or staged events. However, each has its place in an election marketing strategy and each serves a particular purpose in helping to meet the different goals of a campaign. Let's look at news coverage and other forms of free publicity first.

News coverage doesn't come automatically, it has to be earned.

Candidates will usually feel that if they have something to say on a subject, that alone makes it newsworthy, but they often have a poor idea of what makes good news. A few gratuitous words about education, for example, are not news. News outlets are becoming more reluctant to be a source of free advertising for candidates.

These days a lot of candidates are holding press conferences in rooms where only half or less of the local news outlets are represented. This is because of a lack of adequate staffing, and because local candidates are rarely that interesting. Also, newsrooms are not running press releases sent to them by individual candidates as editorial copy any more. News departments are leery of being manipulated by politicians and tend to reflect this by paying less attention to local races and reporting more on the central campaigns and activities of the parties and leaders. Besides, it is easier for them to cover national or provincial central organizations rather than hundreds of individual candidates.

Why is this? Aren't radio, TV and newspaper news staffs always looking for good stories? Of course they are, but they are less interested in simple policy statements. Many news directors have told me they won't run a candidate's release on education, for example, because they don't want to give an advantage to one candidate over another who may not issue as many press releases. The exception to this is if the releases they do receive contain attacks on political opponents. That way they have an opportunity to go to the other candidates to seek a reply to the statement, thereby providing some balance to their stories.

Unstated in this preference for critical press releases is the desire to stir up the pot a little. Controversy makes a news story more interesting and more attractive to readers or listeners. Using our education example, a candidate challenging a sitting provincial member might attack that member for local school closures and accuse him of being asleep at the switch while classrooms and jobs were being lost. This not only implies that the incumbent does not care much about education, but that he is also an ineffectual member and a poor local representative. The challenger can still present a positive position on his education policy, but this would be the last part of the release, or would be attached as a background paper to add substance to the main points of the release.

The other factor that increases the chances of a candidate's news releases being reported is the presence of local content. Strong references to local problems add an attractive feature for news outlets. In addition, innovation, style and controversy will catch a news editor's eye, and consequently, increase the chance of free publicity.

Party leaders do not need to add a negative note to their press statements to be reported. Representatives of major news outlets travel with the party leaders, or will have a representative available at any planned news events involving the leaders. As long as they are getting newsworthy stuff, outlets provide fairly equal coverage to each of the leaders in a campaign. This assurance makes it possible for the leaders to be more positive in what they say about the issues or in presenting their party's platform.

One of the first problems candidates experience when dealing with the media is getting them angry by not treating all the outlets fairly. If certain media feel they are not getting the stories as quickly as others, they will be reluctant to run any story, particularly if they have been "scooped" by a rival. Fax machines make it much easier to ensure that everyone gets the same information at the same time. Candidates need not worry too much about the publishing deadlines of newspapers being a handicap for them against electronic media who can broadcast a story immediately if they want. Newspapers make up for this by being able to provide a good deal more background on a story than can the electronic media. If candidates feel their story will have major impact, they may put a release time on their press releases to give newspapers an equal opportunity to carry the story.

Besides their own press releases and news conferences, the main opportunities for free news coverage for candidates are predictable. On the day the election is called, candidates are contacted to make some comments about the campaign. They get another opportunity when they hold the official opening of their campaign headquarters and again later in the campaign when most media run an impartial profile of each local constituency and the candidates. Every time candidates speak in public, there is an opportunity for publicity managers to inform all the local outlets of these events, and provide news releases based on the remarks that will be made. Sometimes the whole speech is released, if it has been prepared in advance. Media also provide coverage of other events like all-candidates' forums and debates.

Candidates shouldn't feel compelled to respond to every question about the campaign. There are times that some questions, particularly those related to the organization or progress of the campaign, should be referred to the campaign manager. If things are not going well, candidates shouldn't try to put a brave face on a bad situation. That should be left to their managers who can do it more convincingly.

The same holds true about comments on poll results. Candidates have to be consistent in their policy about answering questions about what pollsters are saying. If a candidate comments once, he or she will have no choice but to offer comments, whether the results are good or bad. This is even more difficult if the methodology is suspect.

I remember one Calgary *Sun* report on a "poll" released by a PC candidate. Actually, the "poll" consisted of results from the candidate's personal canvassing one evening in a strong area of his riding. Of course, the results were completely lop-sided; yet the media asked opposing candidates and leaders to comment on this story. Those who had a consistent policy of not responding to polling stories had a much better chance of responding properly than those who saw a chance to make points every time a microphone was thrust into their faces.

Publicity managers get pretty wily about the timing of news releases. A good story released on Friday will likely run all weekend on smaller radio and television stations because there usually isn't a lot happening and fewer reporters are on duty. Mondays are also a good day, as newsrooms are just getting up to speed after the weekend. At the same time, there may well be days to avoid. A newspaper story on the same day that all the grocery store ads come out will be lost for sure.

Getting effective free publicity in weekly newspapers is no easier than in dailies. Writing press releases for these papers takes special skill to make the information topical and timely since it will be printed several days after it is written. New printing technologies are compressing weekly newspaper deadlines, though. Where, in the past, a deadline for a Tuesday publication may have been the previous Friday, it may now be as late as noon the day before.

There are lots of other sources of free campaign publicity for candidates. Friends and supporters can be encouraged to write letters to the editors of local papers. Campaigns may go as far as to provide a draft of the letter they would like to appear. Weekly newspapers may allow candidates to submit regular columns to their publications. The op-ed pages in major newspapers present a good opportunity for candidates to publish in-depth articles on important topics, building their credibility and enhancing their stature in the community.

The electronic media have a variety of talk shows and public affairs programming which welcomes candidates during an election. Imaginative publicity managers may try to get their candidates on celebrity programs such as cooking shows, or participating in telethons to provide exposure for more human sides of their candidates.

Even leaks to the media are a way of getting free publicity. Safire's *Political Dictionary* describes two kinds of leaks. One is an official leak which is often attributed to a campaign spokesperson or an informed source. The other is a courtesy leak, designed to earn the favour of a particular reporter or pay back a favour made in the past. Leaks are often used in a creative fashion by candidates and parties to get a feeling for the public's opinion of some issue or policy initiative without really having to be directly identified with the idea. If it's not popular, nothing more will be heard about it, and if it is, then a more formal statement will be made very quickly. This is often referred to as a "trial balloon."

Leaks are sometimes used as a way of getting a nasty piece of information about an opponent into the public domain. Campaign managers or publicity managers for a candidate might give a media person a tasty tidbit about an opponent that is far too hot for their own candidate to handle in public personally. If the story can be backed up, then the reporter has a good piece and a step has been taken towards undermining an opponent's credibility. Even if the story can't be used, it becomes a source of rumour and works almost as well.

Some people argue that leaks are an important part of the

democratic process in that they invite public opinion and reaction without any risk, and thus help politicians formulate policies and programs that are more democratic. I suppose this may be true in government, but when it comes to political campaigns, leaks serve only one purpose, and that is to enhance the messages of candidates and increase the flow of propaganda coming from their campaigns.

While using news opportunities to get out the message is cheap for candidates, this does not allow the undisturbed control that paid advertising affords. When they pay for their time and space, candidates can say just about whatever they choose, and most do.

When we looked at the campaign budget process, we examined the types of advertising that most candidates use and the cost considerations that surround the selection of each of the advertising media. There are three central considerations candidates use when deciding whether TV, radio or newspapers will do the best job, and which outlets within that medium best meet their needs.

The first consideration is to know the audience of the outlet. To the novice, television and daily newspaper audiences may seem the same. Actually, some fairly sophisticated targeting is possible using these media. Certain sections of a newspaper appeal more to women than men, and vice versa. Other sections of a newspaper are read by business people, and others are aimed at young people or those concerned about current affairs.

The same holds true for television. While it is a medium for the masses and almost everyone watches some television, people do so at quite different times of the day and for varied reasons. Local television salespeople will provide a lot of useful demographic information for candidates, but often some of it can be determined from survey research. I often place questions on polls about viewing habits to determine when the target audience is most likely to be watching television. It might be that the undecided voters are watching later in the evening; it is a lot cheaper to buy time for that period than during prime time. Then it is only necessary to purchase the odd ad during prime time to keep the comfort level of supporters on an even keel, so that they can feel their candidate is still alive and in the fight.

Cable television is just coming into its own in Canada, but once it develops more, it will become an important and oft-used political advertising medium. Its potential for precise targeting of voters on a geographic and a demographic basis is a dream come true for ad agencies trying to sell individual candidates to the public. For candidates, the attraction is money. Cable ads are a fraction of the cost of regular broadcast station rates.

Radio is considered the best of the media for delivering a targeted message. In large markets, stations range from heavy metal FM to ethnic broadcasters. Each one has a very particular kind of audience and the trick for media managers is to chose the stations that will do the most to complement the campaign plan and reach those voters who will make the difference on election day.

Of course, the second consideration, after the make-up of the audience, is to know how many of these people can be reached at any particular time. Campaigns can get that information on electronic media from BBMs, the broadcast industry's measure of audience share for all of the outlets. Newspaper circulation is pretty constant, but campaigns do need to know if there are particular days when there might be a larger print run, like a Saturday or Sunday edition.

Audience size, or reach, as broadcasters call it, actually becomes one of the major downsides to paid advertising for individual candidates, because their message is being delivered to a lot of people who do not live in their particular constituencies, and cannot vote for them. This is the reason why many candidates from the same party in large urban markets are more likely to pool a portion of their media dollars for generic advertising.

The third limiting factor in making advertising decisions is the cost. Many campaigns make a common mistake. They will get the advertising rates for different media and decide how many placements they can make based on the budget that is allowed for advertising. Even if they take into account the size of the audience and select media that will reach the appropriate target audience in sufficient numbers, it is almost guaranteed that they will forget to calculate the costs to produce the ad. Production costs can be astronomical and no one should proceed unless the ads can look and sound acceptable.

Television ads are the most expensive to produce. They require people with special skills working in a studio or on a location. Their time and knowledge cost a lot of money. These costs can be reduced if the ads are being produced by a television station, but it still will not be cheap. Most radio stations will help with the production of their ads, using either a voice supplied by the candidate or a local announcer. The only time there is any significant production cost associated with radio is if candidates go to private studios because they want to hire a particular voice or use a lot of fancy sound effects, or music in their ads. Newspapers are usually equally helpful in helping candidates lay out campaign ads, and there is usually no cost associated with this assistance, unless some pictures need to be re-formatted for the size of the ad. Again, there are always professionals ready and willing to design and produce newspaper ads for candidates, but candidates can get along without the pros quite nicely with a little planning.

It is hard to know how many times these simple and sensible rules have been violated by candidates and their campaign teams. If if there were campaign advertising police, there could never be enough of them. It would be hard to remember the number of times I have seen a TV ad for some candidate at 3:00 a.m. during a late movie or stuck in among Saturday morning cartoons because someone saw that those were the cheapest times available. I have seen candidates advertise in a Jewish newspaper when the largest ethnic group in their riding was Italian, while others spend big money buying space on the third page of a huge daily newspaper that serves fifteen constituencies, while they do not bother with a community newspaper delivered to every door in their constituency, and where the advertising rates are a quarter that of the big paper. Stupid and ill-conceived advertising decisions are usually fuelled by the vanity of candidates, or through wrong-headed financial planning. There's no point in doing something well that shouldn't have been done in the first place.

The role of candidates in planning advertising is quite often misunderstood. They certainly should not be writing ads and should not have any final say in the content. I believe candidates need to be consulted about all the ads that are run on their behalf and should be invited to offer some opinions on content, but this is one area where candidates should leave it to the experts to do the work. Well-meaning amateurs have no place in designing and executing advertising plans. There are too many votes at stake and too much money.

Some say that campaign advertising is a matter of give and take. "The candidates keep giving until the voters can't take it any more." It is a rare campaign in which one doesn't eventually hear some grumbling from voters about the amount of advertising. The challenge for the candidates and parties is to make their advertising interesting and informative and, if appropriate, entertaining. If they can produce ads that meet these criteria, their advertising is more likely to be noticed and less likely to have a negative effect on the public. This becomes even more important for candidates who are facing tight multi-candidate races, or who are in a very large market where a lot of candidates are advertising. In these situations ads must use bold strokes to give campaigns some zip; they must stand out in the jungle of competing campaign messages.

An important consideration for campaigns when planning an advertising program is to make sure that everything remains consistent with the overall campaign plan. The content of their advertising must coincide with speeches their candidates are making, with the message in leaflets and letters, and with the message that telephoners and canvassers are delivering in their contacts. This integration is critical in getting a message to voters without confusing them. The more issues campaigns talk about during an election, the less impact they will have on voters. After all, the object of campaign marketing is to influence voters, not to impress them with the amount candidates know about issues. Most voters don't keep a scorecard to determine how smart candidates are.

Campaign advertising provides a vehicle in which candidates can react to changing situations. For this reason, wise campaigns do not commit all their advertising dollars too early in the election. They leave some money to produce ads at the last minute so they can react to changing issues or increase the frequency of existing ads. Leaving some contingency money in the advertising budget allows candidates to amplify their messages if it becomes apparent from other campaign activities, like canvassing, that the campaign plan is working.

The NDP campaigns in Saskatchewan and Alberta in 1986 provided an interesting example of contrast in this ability to react and adapt. The Saskatchewan NDP had anticipated a campaign for months, and in some ways, they over-planned. A great deal of the advertising had been produced so they wouldn't be caught short when an election was called. The problem was that polling data began to show that some of it wasn't working. Spending laws and budget limitations made it very difficult to alter the advertising plan to adjust to changing issues and attitudes once the campaign had started. In Alberta, on the other hand, almost no ads were "in the can". As the NDP campaign gained momentum they were able to design advertising that reflected public opinion and a growing mood for change.

Whether candidates have all the money in the world or are operating on the slimmest of shoestring budgets, every campaign will produce some kind of leaflet or hand-out material. Leaflets can perform three very important communication functions for candidates.

Leaflets are an excellent vehicle for introducing candidates, presenting their credentials and building credibility for them, by showing they have the background and ability to perform the duties the position demands.

Leaflets also give the candidates the opportunity to present their positions on the issues they believe are important. At the same time, candidates can contrast their positions with those of their opponents, an invitation to compare. Leaflets also allow candidates to associate themselves with popular issues being advanced by their central campaigns and through their party leaders, or to discuss solutions to pressing local problems that do not reach prominence on the larger election stage.

Finally, leaflets and campaign literature can set the mood for a campaign more easily than any other paid medium at the disposal of candidates. Through the proper use of pictures, text and design, a leaflet can convey concern, passion, commitment or winning momentum to voters. Leaflets should be treated as though they were TV ads delivered directly to households.

Naturally, for leaflets to be useful at all, they must be interesting and attractive enough to read. There is a graveyard somewhere that holds all the leaflets that have gone straight from the mailbox or canvasser's hand to the garbage bin. Some even had the "middle-man" cut out of the process because they were judged too ugly to distribute in the first place.

While the communication potential of leaflets is enormous, their effect is often blunted by poor design or execution. Leaflets need to be as simple as the campaign plan and provide no more information than is necessary to position candidates on the issues identified in the strategy of the campaign. If a campaign has decided there are four main issues in an election, then there shouldn't be six or ten issues in a leaflet. But, too often, this is the case. Some recent research has indicated that when faced with a list of issues, voters are more likely to extract the one or two they do not agree with rather than associate with those they do agree with.

Campaigns make a mistake by trying to present too many details about an issue in their leaflets. Presenting a reasoned solution to a problem rather than an emotional one will not motivate many voters.

Liberals adopt a technique known as the "Least Objectionable Theory" when selecting propaganda materials and assessing their potential worthiness. Those ideas or items that receive the least negative opinion from the planners are used for the campaign. It's probably as good a method of developing campaign material as any other. At least it keeps the candidates happy.

Voters are intimidated by too much text. Publicity managers who are trying to impress folks by how many scholarly words they can put on a sheet of paper are not producing material that will influence voters. The real challenge for leaflet writers is to reduce the campaign themes and issues to the simplest expressions possible. The goal should be to write to about a grade six level. Although the "KISS" technique (Keep It Simple, Stupid) applies to all campaign communications, it is most applicable to campaign literature.

Pictures are worth a thousand words, or so they say. Pictures are certainly powerful communication tools for candidates and photographs used in leaflets need to be chosen with great care. Each one can carry a message that re-emphasizes points made in the text of a leaflet. This is important, because campaigns want voters to look at the pictures as a minimum response to a leaflet. Even if voters will not spend time reading the words, campaigns will know the pictures have left a feeling about the nature of the candidate and the tone of the campaign.

Of course, this only happens if there are pictures available. Even if candidates have taken the time to get a nice portrait taken of themselves along with some family shots, you can be almost certain that very few others exist. Photos of the candidate with seniors, young people, working people, shopkeepers, meeting voters, and at work, are standard leaflet fare. There almost always seems to be valuable campaigning time lost trying to get the proper pictures for leaflets.

You could likely earn a tidy sum of money betting that campaigns will fail to ask permission of the people in the pictures before they use them in campaign literature. I have had the experience of having the strongest of supporters get extremely hostile because pictures of them had been used by the publicity people without permission.

A similar problem occurred for Sharon Carstairs in the last Manitoba election. She had called the media to a child care facility so that she could release her policy on the issue. The media were told they could not take any pictures of the children there, because permission from the parents was necessary and none had been given.

Leaflets are often used to present endorsements that have been collected by a candidate. Words of praise from prominent citizens, along with their pictures, are paraded through a leaflet to show the depth of support behind candidates. These are calculated to impress voters and usually do exactly that. These types of endorsements can form the backdrop for building a winning image, a bandwagon effect, that is so important in the final days of a campaign.

Some candidates also use press clippings about them arranged in a collage to show that their ideas are getting through. This can lead to trouble, though. Tory candidate Don Clarke was named Citizen of the Year in 1988 by the Edmonton *Journal*. That's a fine bit of information and is an impressive credential for any candidate. He hurt his cause by reprinting the entire *Journal* article in a campaign tabloid which left many with the impression that he was in some way being endorsed by the Edmonton *Journal*. Whether this impression was intentionally given or not, the *Journal* leapt to its own defence and called attention to this tactic; in so doing, they likely diminished a good deal of Clarke's credibility. As Alberta PC Executive Director, Bert Murray, told the *Alberta Report*, "We're working with volunteers here," he sighed, "sometimes they don't jump the proper hurdles."

Finally, leaflets are used by candidates to solicit help and ideas from voters. Leaflets often include a message that welcomes people to come to the campaign headquarters to talk about the issues or encourages them to join the hundreds of other volunteers helping to elect the candidate. The actual results from these invitations are negligible, but they create an image of politicians as being open and accessible. These are valuable traits in a politician.

Political communication takes two forms. One is broadcast. Examples of broadcast communication are newspapers and television, where there is some opportunity to target a message, but not as precisely as with other media. The other, and more effective method, is narrowcast. Here, messages are tailored to specific people in a highly targeted manner. Personalized direct mail is a hi-tech system of delivering the most narrowcast of messages.

Direct mail at its best takes the form of a follow-up to a previous contact with voters. A foot or telephone canvasser identifies an issue that concerns an undecided voter, for example, and that voter then receives a personalized letter from the candidate about the issue. The impression that is left with the voter is that the candidate is concerned about the same issues as the voter and that the candidate will take the time to let the voter know that he shares the voter's concern. It is a tremendously powerful means of communicating with voters.

A good deal has been made in recent elections about some apparent magic used by the Conservatives, federally and in some provincial contests. There is nothing special about it, only the careful application of voter contact and direct mail follow-up applying the best mailing techniques available.

Almost as effective as the personalized response to voters is direct mail that is sent by candidates to occupational groups, ethnic communities and similar sorts of lists. Candidates send letters to teachers, for example, about educational issues. This assumes, of course, that education is the most important issue in the minds of teachers. Likely it is not, but teachers will nonetheless be interested in the position of candidates on educational issues, and the letter becomes an excellent voter contact tool if a paragraph emphasizing the main campaign theme is included.

While generic mail to occupational groups or members of community organizations has some positive effect, the real trick is to see that the right person gets the right piece of mail. Everyone is made of many "special interests." As an example, a voter can be a teacher, homemaker, parent, athletics coach and member of the Sierra Club. The message the voter receives has to appeal to that part of his or her make-up that will be making the voting decision. So, while there may be many pressing issues in education, this voter may be more concerned about property taxes or preservation of wilderness areas. The campaign that targets its message in the most precise manner will be the one most likely to gain the support of this hypothetical voter.

The least effective kind of direct mail is the "Dear Friend" variety that is dropped in mail boxes. Unless these are extremely well done, they get no more consideration than any other piece of junk mail and certainly do little to provide a positive impression for the candidates who use this kind of voter contact.

Direct mail is only useful if it is designed in a way that makes people want to read it. A few tricks are used to make this possible. Things as simple as the way the postage is affixed or how the letter is addressed can influence the final inclination of the voter to read the message. An envelope with a postage stamp, particularly if the stamp is not put on quite straight, is more likely to be opened than one stamped by machine. The machine stamp is better than a printed postage number, which is better than an "occupant" delivery. A hand-addressed letter is far more personal and more likely to be opened than a typed address. Following these two ways of addressing a letter, campaigns find labels and window envelopes slightly less effective.

While the means of putting on the postage and addressing the envelope go a long way in making sure that a candidate's direct mail will get opened, that is only half the battle. The letter has to be read as well. The copy needs to be easy to understand and straightforward. Like a political leaflet, direct mail has to communicate its message in language that most people can understand, and the letter has to use emotional terms that help to bond the candidate and the voter. The first few lines are critical. It is the general opinion of direct mail experts that if the first twenty or thirty words are read, then so will the whole letter. Just in case, some system of highlighting the important points in the letter is used. This takes the form of underlining, or even using yellow highlighter to emphasize those parts of the letter which have the greatest emotional appeal to the reader.

The first use of direct mail in American politics is believed to have been during John Kennedy's campaign for Congress in 1946. During that election, his campaign mailed out thousands of stories about his WWII exploits as a PT boat captain to households and returning war veterans.

On the other hand, Canadian politicians are just starting to explore the possibilities of direct mail. Some of the earliest attempts were pretty crude. Candidates can produce an excellent message that explains an issue and their own position very well, but then forget to tell voters what they expect from them. If they don't ask for support, direct mail is an expensive and futile use of valuable resources.

Candidates also need to exercise their imagination when it comes to selecting possible targets for their direct mail attack. While groups like teachers, nurses and small business people are pretty obvious, there are other sources and authors who can have positive impact. A sports coach writing to the parents of team members about a candidate or a prominent teacher writing to other teachers probably leaves a more positive impression with voters than sterile letters from the candidates themselves.

We can expect to see much more direct mail during our election campaigns. Whether or not these will be as effective as direct mail from some of the great mail factories, like Jimmy Swaggart's and other old hand direct mail practitioners, is hard to know.

I don't want to foster a cynical attitude towards political communication, and direct mail in particular, but it's important to know that what mainly decides the content of these messages is: *what is true is not as important as what is believable.* Saskatchewan New Democrats were taught a hard lesson about this axiom. During a critical by-election in southern Saskatchewan, they produced a letter from Leader Roy Romanow aimed at exploiting the health care issue. The Conservative government had become very unpopular because of dramatic changes they had made to health services and the ways in which health services were delivered. The government had received a report on the future of health care that also indicated that a number of rural hospitals might be closed. Romanow's letter charged that all five hospitals in the riding were in danger of being closed. This was the truth, but it just was not believable to most of the voters. As a result, what should have been a narrow NDP win turned into a comfortable Tory victory.

Special events are also used by campaigns as a marketing tool. Rallies, parades, and banquets provide opportunities to get a message to voters through the news coverage they generate. When these events are planned properly, they can leave a lasting impression of vitality and excitement with voters that can pay dividends on election day. A big crowd crammed into a hall that is barely large enough can keep people talking for days afterward. More important for campaigns is the encouragement and regeneration of volunteers and supporters a successful event causes.

There is one special campaign event that probably causes the most anxiety for everyone involved at the local level. That's a visit by the Leader. I doubt that I have ever met a campaign manager who had kind words for the hassle and aggravation caused by these events.

The problems start with a visit from the advance man. Usually, two or three people advance each stop made by the Leader. They will come a week or ten days before the event and work out the details with the local campaign organization. Most advance people are pushy, arrogant, and demanding. Their job is to make sure every detail is planned and that the "locals" are doing everything they can to stage the event properly. They make no friends and it is rare for them to work in two successive elections in the same province. They would be lynched the next time through town.

During the days before the Leader's stop, all the work takes place to ensure a good crowd and positive media coverage. This always takes a lot of time from the local campaign. There are lots of calls from the tour's central "anchor" who wants to know how the arrangements are progressing and make last minute changes to the agenda and format. Then, on the day before or on the same day as the event, a final advance person comes to check everything out one last time.

Leaders surround themselves with a large entourage. There'll be a wagonmaster who is in charge of making sure everyone arrives on time, gets luggage moved around and ensures that the schedule is followed as well as taking care of any last minute details for the Leader. There is at least one press officer and a researcher in addition to support staff. Leaders even travel with their own sound and lighting technicians. Touring rock bands often have fewer "roadies" than a political leader!

The local candidate is usually frustrated at being given a minor role in the program and at being strictly limited in the amount of time available to speak, usually in introducing or thanking the leader. The campaign manager is usually stuck with coming up with a suitable explanation if there was a poor crowd, and even if the event was a huge success, the manager almost always has to deal with some form of damage control over a remark made by the Leader or people who felt snubbed because they weren't recognized, not to mention having to scramble to make up for time lost from the campaign plan.

A major reason for the problems between the Leader's tour and local campaigns results from their competing goals. The Leader's tour is looking for provincial and national coverage to enhance the central message. They argue that their job is to get the message out in a way that will help elect as many candidates as possible. Local candidates are only concerned about their chances of getting elected and want these stops from the tour to make them the star attractions.

I recall accompanying Ray Martin to a campaign stop in Athabasca, Alberta. Local hospital politics were a big local issue and we had decided to use the hospital there as a backdrop for an announcement on our health policy. The local candidate, Leo Piquette, was determined to get in front of the cameras with Ray and exploit the local issues for his own campaign, as opposed to giving Ray the exposure on the broader provincial health issues. I had to grab Piquette by his belt to hold him back until the cameras had been turned off.

A whole variety of special events can be turned into good marketing tools for candidates. Dinners, picnics and visits to local factories, institutions and schools are all occasions for a candidate to get the message out to the public.

Even the simple act of filing official nomination papers can be used to a candidate's advantage. If the local law requires 25 signatures, and the candidate shows up with a thousand, each person having also contributed a dollar to the campaign fund, then the candidate has created a news story that can say something positive about him or her and the chance of their campaign's success.

Marketing political candidates and their ideas is an important part of any election campaign. Those who can get their message out in a way that average people can understand and identify with have the best chance of winning. Selling soap is easy compared with the challenge facing would-be politicians and their publicity handlers.

13. The Dark Side of Politics

"Winning is not everything,
it's the only thing."
Vince Lombardi

I would like to be able to say that political campaigns are gentle
contests engaged in by honourable people with competing ideas,
but this is not always the case. The athletic metaphor of "winning
at any cost" finds its true meaning in many election scenarios.

There is a dark side to electoral politics that receives very little
publicity since much of it is kept behind the scenes, but these
practices can still affect the eventual outcome of any race. Much
of what the general public finds distasteful about present political
campaigns is variously called dirty tricks or hardball politics, and
best described as the practical application of strategy by Machia-
vellian campaigners. Dirty tricks may be manifested in mischievous
pranks, vandalism, harassment, law-breaking or verbal attacks.

Even though no candidate openly condones them, dirty tricks
are becoming a frequent tool of campaigns. In Canada, these
campaign practices rarely take the form they do in American
elections where Watergate is the most well-known and glaring
example. It's a common tactic south of the border to do things like
cancel a booking an opponent may have made for a banquet or
meeting room, or order fifty pizzas to be sent to an opponent's
campaign headquarters. Although these seem to be pretty mild
jokes played on the opposition, it keeps the other camp off-balance
and suspicious, never quite sure what will happen next. It doesn't
take much for a campaign to progress from these sorts of things
to covert activities like stealing files and records or bugging an
opponent's headquarters.

Distributing bogus leaflets about the opposition alleging some
misdeed or radical policy position is among the dirty tricks most
often employed. These leaflets are usually dropped in mailboxes
late at night or slipped under windshield wipers in parking lots
when no one is looking.

Campaign signs are the object of the most common of dirty tricks, vandalism. Usually this is perpetrated by people who either have nothing at all to do with any election campaign and are having "fun," or by people who have been carried away by rhetoric they have heard from a candidate or campaign worker against another candidate or party. They may even have received the inspiration from something heard at home from an over-zealous parent.

This is not to say that vandalism might not occasionally be an organized activity. There are many cases where the evidence clearly indicates that sign vandalism was part of a deliberate strategy. You can imagine the surprise and dismay of a candidate to learn that all of his or her yard signs had been removed overnight and dumped down a ravine. This not only happened once to Rosemary Brown in B.C., but twice, and in the same campaign.

It is a rare campaign where there are no reports of some kind of sign damage, or "sign rot," as it is called. Widespread destruction of signs can hurt a campaign a great deal. With spending limits in force, there may not be enough money in a budget to purchase more signs, or there may not be enough time to get more printed. There is also a certain loss of momentum for a campaign, since some of the visibility is lost and workers can become discouraged.

Campaigns which have lost a lot of signs try to get some publicity out of their loss by calling the police and media and maybe even posting a reward for the names of the culprits, which just might help get a bit of a sympathy vote.

If sign vandalism is organized, it usually takes place over one or two evenings, and involves only one candidate's signs. A steady attrition of the signs of all campaigns is more likely the result of kids taking a whack at a sign now and then.

Sign damage also has a negative affect on those voters who have had it happen on their property. Having a sign set on fire on your lawn or a 4 x 4 truck roar across your yard to knock down a sign can intimidate voters and many will certainly not want the sign replaced. While these may seem like extreme cases of vandalism, they really are common. Whether a sign is stolen, damaged or has obscenities written on it, it still leaves a powerful feeling with the owners of the property where it has happened which is not unlike the shock of discovering that one's home has been forcibly entered.

There are ways to combat sign vandalism. I call the opponent's campaign manager if I suspect it is coming from them and insist that they stop. At the same time, I ask all campaign staff to tell their volunteers to be sure they do not "liberate" any of the opponent's signs in retaliation. If there is an opportunity to assist an opponent in repairing sign damage and gain positive publicity for my candidate in doing so, then I direct some of my sign crew to help repair all signs, not just ours.

One candidate by the name of Funk found that opponents were changing the letter "n" on his signs, rendering them useless. Because of the great cost of signs, and because they had a limited budget, workers decided to cover the letter "n" on the signs with shellac. This worked, except that the shellac became tacky in hot sun; all manner of leaves, dirt, and refuse stuck to the signs. With the "n"s obliterated by materials stuck to the shellac, the signs accidentally looked the way the vandals were trying to make them look originally with their spray paint!

Campaign foot soldiers often practice some chicanery themselves. Canvassers have been known to bring back a few "samples" of the opponents' campaign material they may have found in mailboxes during their rounds of the polls. When veteran canvassers see workers for the opposition in their area, they double back so that they are travelling behind the others and can see what is being left behind, and get in the last word on the doorstep in order to undo any positive work the others may have accomplished.

Campaign headquarters have been spray painted and candidates have had their homes vandalized and their car tires flattened. Arson is also not out of the question for some people and there have been suspicious campaign fires over the years which resulted in the loss of property and valuable files and records. Very little of this hooliganism and sign destruction ever comes to the public eye, but it is a political reality nonetheless. If it is not happening, then likely the contest is not very competitive.

Falling into much the same category as vandalism are pranks that might be played by campaigns on each other. There are a lot of classic examples of campaign pranks. This happened during an Ontario provincial election, when one campaign manager was trying to book some spots on the local radio station. She was told that there was no available time left during the time slots she wanted but to keep trying in case some became available. One of the competing campaigns had a large amount of time already tied up. She had an associate call back pretending to represent the other campaign and cancel some of the booked time. She then made the media buy she wanted in the first place.

Campaigns try to fool one another about their true intentions when reserving other kinds of advertising space, such as billboards. In some parts of the country, billboards are an important element in an effective advertising strategy, and they are very difficult to get. An ad agency will book several prime billboard locations well in advance of an anticipated election in the name of a client other than the political party or candidate they are working for. This masquerades the state of campaign readiness for the candidate, and keeps billboards that might otherwise be used by the opposition off the market.

Organized telephone harassment of the opponent's volunteer staff is another common practice. Campaigners call and berate people working in their opponent's campaign headquarters about a policy position that the candidate or party has taken. This can be quite disconcerting to a volunteer, and can lead to a reluctance to put in more time on the campaign. That's why telephone receptionists in most campaign headquarters screen each incoming call. This tends to cure the problem.

Election day provides many opportunities for those who want to play tricks on the opposing campaign. I have had people try to tie up the telephone lines at the campaign headquarters, or call in requests for rides to the polls from non-existent addresses. Since election day organizations require incredible energy and concentration, any event that upsets the smooth running of that organization will promote mistakes. Drivers who are sent to false addresses or go to pick up a voter who didn't want a ride at all start to question the campaign leadership. Certainly a few simple controls can be put into place to prevent these problems, but the first time it happens, campaign managers are not always prepared to react quickly enough to avoid the trouble. The second time they may be ready.

Election day harassment might include someone making as

many complaints as possible to the returning officer about alleged misdeeds by another campaign. They might charge that campaigning is taking place within polling stations, or that signs have been erected too close to the building in which the polls are located. Sending troubleshooters out to check on these trivial complaints can keep a campaign distracted from the job at hand.

There have been occasions when one campaign tried to convince their opponent's supporters to vote somewhere other than at the polling station where they were supposed to vote. Also, if one of the parties control the appointment of poll clerks and DRO's in the polling station, they can make it difficult for people of certain ethnic origins or demographics to vote if they feel that that is in their political interest.

One of my favourite election day stories is one told by Dalton Camp about a particular provincial election in Nova Scotia. In the constituency of Hants East, the Tory candidate had won over the Liberal by one vote, 2,249 to 2,248. After the results had been announced, another ballot box was discovered in the shed of one of the Liberal poll workers. When these ballots were counted, the Liberal won. (As you might have expected, this election was voided by the courts, and amazingly, when the by-election was held, the Tory lost by the one vote the Liberal appointed returning officer was required to cast to break a tie. Camp reports that the defeated Conservative commented, "We're pretty evenly divided down here.")

Campaigns usually welcome all offers for help, but from time to time those offers may come from "ringers" who are really supporters of an opponent. Ringers may offer to take on campaign jobs such as delivering leaflets, and never do them. Instead, they throw away the literature, ensuring that some voters never receive the information. Sometimes they only come into the campaign headquarters to hang around and try to overhear important bits of strategy or to sneak a peek into confidential files. Campaign organizations are often so desperate for new blood that they welcome almost anyone who seems eager to help and give them positions of critical importance in the campaign structure. This can lead to an open pipeline to the opposition camp. A saliva test may not be necessary, but a healthy dose of caution should be in order when dealing with new and unknown recruits.

The presence of spies is always difficult to determine until it is too late. During the 1989 provincial election in Alberta, the campaign manager for unsuccessful NDP incumbent John Younie had reason to suspect that the Liberal camp was getting some information straight from the "horse's mouth" because they always seemed able to anticipate each NDP move. The Liberals were able to counter every attack from the Younie team almost instantly, as though they knew in advance what was coming next. This is not to say that each campaign should be suspicious of every stranger who comes in, but they would be wise to be careful of what is said and done in front of enthusiastic newcomers until they have been tried out under battle conditions.

Different people observe campaign practices in different ways. Members of the general public might well classify a lot of campaign activities as "dirty politics," while the campaign practitioners like to refer to them as "hardball" politics. This is political fighting with no punches pulled, and it is characterized by strong attacks against the personal abilities of opposing candidates or by stating that the consequences of certain political ideas would be nothing short of disastrous for people and their futures.

Practitioners of the full-frontal attack are often called "Vego-matic" politicians because they do not hesitate to slice and dice their opponents. Canadians are becoming much more aware of these tactics through exposure to American TV on cable or satellite.

George Bush likes to dignify this kind of campaigning by calling it comparative advertising. He feels that it sets up a comparison in voters' minds between positive and negative ideas. However, rarely do these shots present any positive alternative. The only comparison that is intended is to make the voter feel the opponents are wrong, and in some cases, have destructive ideas.

The best Canadian examples of comparative advertising were campaign ads in the federal election of 1980, which tried to erode the credibility of the Conservative and Liberal leaders. The PCs showed ads of a menacing and arrogant Trudeau in an attempt to remind voters of all the reasons they tossed him out in 1979. The Liberals, for their part, portrayed Joe Clark and the Conservatives as a party too incompetent to govern. The 1988 campaign had some of the same kind of campaigning, centring on the Free Trade debate: the Liberals showed ads of the Conservatives ripping the country apart with help from their American friends, while the PCs, with the aid of their business allies, ran ads that highlighted their notion of Free Trade, that included job creation and prosperity.

This kind of "hardball" is effective when practised at the central levels, party against party or leader against leader, but is hard to duplicate effectively by local campaigns, and can turn voters against a candidate who uses too much of this rough form of politics. Public "hardball," when practised by individual candidates, is usually softened by making direct comparisons between the positions of the candidates on the important issues. Of course, you wouldn't want to apply "truth in advertising" standards to the way one candidate might represent the political program of another.

In fact, providing misinformation is a popular means of running down one candidate or promoting another. Candidates might be creative in describing their own credentials by omitting something in their pasts, or taking credit for experience or accomplishments that are not their own.

Misinformation may also take the form of attributing values or positions to opponents that they do not in fact hold. One candidate may say that another's position would result in some bad situation if it were implemented. A typical example would be saying that an opponent is in favour of more taxation. If challenged to substantiate the charge, the attacker might say he arrived at that conclusion because his opponent is against cutting back on government spending therefore he must want to impose more taxation to keep spending at current levels.

Personal attacks are rare. Now and then a candidate might have some hot information on an opponent, but is unable to do anything with it because it can't be proven. In these circumstances, they might drop off a plain brown envelope containing the facts at a media outlet, hoping reporters will research the story and make it public. They might also leave it with another candidate in the same contest, hoping that even if that campaign can't verify the facts, they will go public with it anyway.

Rumour is a tool that is used a great deal in campaigning. Candidates with strong organizations, with contacts in many groups and community activities, use rumour to spread stories about their opposition. These stories can go undetected for a long time and are very hard to combat. They usually refer to the personal lives of candidates or members of their families. If the rumours are based on infidelity or sexual preference and are untrue, they can be rendered ineffectual by presenting a public image that is designed to debunk the story. Candidates might have spouses share the platform with them more often, for instance.

Rumours can also centre around candidates' business dealings, or focus on their jobs. In fact, a story that was framed in a positive way was my first encounter with the use of a "whisper campaign." The object was a popular teacher, who was well respected in the community, and, because of this, was likely to win the election he was contesting. A lot of voters were willing to break party rank to vote for him. The opponents started a story that said, "John's a great guy and would make a terrific MLA, but I am not going to vote for him because our kids can't afford to lose such a good teacher." The story worked. I think John is superannuated now and only saw the inside of the legislature while taking classes on field trips. I guess you could say he was too good to be a politician.

A good source of ammunition against opposing candidates and parties is their convention resolution books. Some outrageous resolutions have usually been submitted by a riding association that either never got discussed or, if they did reach the convention floor, were soundly defeated. The final disposition of the resolution is of no consequence. The fact that it was submitted to a convention is reason enough to use it against a party, since the general public has little understanding of the niceties of convention procedure.

Some candidates are also vulnerable to attack because they have flirted with another political party. Many successful politicians have been members of other parties before being elected. There is little harm in that. Political parties don't require saliva tests of their candidates, in fact they are proud to point to a recruit from the opposing camp. Those who have considered joining a different party after being elected by another can expect this to have a negative influence on their chances of re-election should it become public. Revelation of such matters leads to party loyalists being less fervent in their work and support, and it also raises doubts in the minds of voters about the politician's reliability and integrity.

Many insiders believe that one House Leader's reluctance to seek his party's leadership was due mainly to the rumour that he had had some tentative discussions with another party about crossing the floor; this would be a source of constant irritation were he to become leader. Some people say that the conversations were even taped and could have been very damaging if they became public, although there is no proof that this is the case.

Here are some of the things that I consider using as part of a campaign against an incumbent politician:

- I make a list of all the important bills he voted on in the legislature or House of Commons to see if I can make a case that will show that he isn't concerned with the welfare of his constituents. I also determine his level of attendance in the house and on committees. Voters don't appreciate a political figure who doesn't show up for work regularly, particularly when he is on the public payroll.
- I like to know how many times he has taken trips paid for with the taxpayers' money. Some political junkets are an important part of the job and are worthwhile expenditures, but not all of them.
- Any time a politician supported a proposal that meant more taxes or more money taken from the wallets of voters, is an occasion for attack. There are few people who appreciate tax and fee increases, no matter how much sense they may make.
- A politician's job is to provide service and representation to his constituents. I like to find out how effective the opponent has been at solving problems for people, how people have felt they were treated by his staff, and what projects he or she might be able to take credit for since last elected. If weaknesses come to light in any of these areas, then they are legitimate targets for attack, particularly the

failure or perceived failure to live up to previous election promises. In this regard, the important rule to follow is that it is what is believable that counts, not necessarily what is true.

- Voters can forgive many shortcomings, even those of politicians, but they are quick to lose confidence in those who lie about their experience and qualifications. I always check out each item of opponents' credentials. Inaccuracies and "little white lies" have been very embarrassing to many politicians.

- There are few full-blown scandals in Canadian politics. Unquestionably there are frequent cases involving some minor misdeeds and cases of questionable judgement, and a growing incidence of violations of conflict of interest legislation. But we have no sizzling sex and drug scandals or even cases of politicians being bought. To whatever extent these things do occur, our Canadian sense of decorum doesn't consider it very proper to be public about them. If an opponent is involved in some sort of scandal, I rarely use it as part of a public message, but I might mention the matter to a few other people. I let the opposing campaign manager know that I know about it too, and do not hesitate to use the information if it becomes necessary.

- The simple response, "I'm sorry. I won't do it again," might well go a long way in restoring an otherwise untarnished political image. If an opponent is caught making the same mistake twice, the accumulated weight of repeated errors may well bring him down. After all, it wasn't one affair that hurt American presidential hopeful Gary Hart. He might have survived one indiscretion, but it was the evidence of repeated events involving poor judgment and outlandish womanizing that put his career on the skids.

- Finally, two points I consider when deciding whether any findings will be used in a campaign: first, I make sure my facts are absolutely correct; and second, I apply the same tests to my own candidate so that I know what warts we might be carrying into the campaign.

Non-political organizations also influence the electoral process in a way that some people might argue is negative. Business groups, trade unions and other organizations representing such widespread interests as seniors, farmers or native people all have something to say during an election. Since most organizations have narrower interests than the parties and candidates, they focus all their attention on one or two issues without consideration of greater factors, such as how to implement or pay for their ideas. They will attack those who are cool to their proposals and embrace those who agree with them, offering things like endorsements, funding and advertising in exchange for the support of politicians.

Many of these groups send out long and complicated questionnaires for candidates to answer, then circulate the answers to their own members, and sometimes publish them. To avoid conflicting replies among candidates of the same party, the central research staff prepare one standard reply to each questionnaire on behalf of all candidates, taking care to craft those replies in a way that best reflects their party's policies and election themes, but at the same time, couching the answers in language that will gain support or limit damage.

There is certainly nothing wrong with organizations using this kind of information to inform their membership about the positions held by candidates on issues that are important to the organization. It helps more voters to make informed decisions, but this is not always the prime motive behind the exercise.

Some organizations are bent on being more manipulative in their election involvement. Candidates from all parties dread the advances made by "Right to Life" organizations, who will not take any qualified answers to questions on abortion. If a candidate attempts to respond that they favour abortion, but only in certain circumstances, they will be reported as being completely in favour of abortion, period. While candidates used to be afraid that their views would hurt their chances of election, more and more candidates are discovering that it makes little difference, and that the abortion issue has little effect on the outcome of an election. If candidates are in favour of a woman's right to choose, they should simply say so. There is no evidence of right to life campaigns affecting the result of an election. Survey research indicates that no more than 5% of the members of the electorate make up their minds solely on a candidate's position on abortion, and that these people are fairly evenly divided on both sides of the issue.

"Right to Lifers" claim to have been instrumental in the defeat of Ray Hnatyshyn in the 1988 federal election. Hnatyshyn was then Justice Minister and was blamed for not having brought forward a definitive piece of anti-abortion legislation. While they may have had some influence in that campaign, it would be as proper to say that Hnatyshyn was on the wrong side of the Free Trade debate in a province where opposition to Free Trade was widespread and deeply felt.

The involvement of business organizations in the 1988 federal election is another case of third party involvement in a campaign. In that campaign, Brian Mulroney was unable to carry the argument for Free Trade by himself. He was losing on it. It was not until the Canadian Manufacturer's Association and other business interests weighed in with an expensive advertising campaign that the tide began to turn enough to ensure another Conservative majority.

Businesses also try to influence voting by threatening layoffs and job losses should the wrong party get elected. It was common practice among lumber companies in the B.C. interior to announce indefinite layoffs a few days before election day. The companies would say that the layoffs would be permanent should the wrong party, i.e. the NDP, were elected.

Rural ridings are more susceptible to bullying. Prominent citizens of a town or district may simply bully people into voting their way. In the case of local church leaders or important merchants who could deny credit or cause other kinds of hardship, such bullies may even hold some financial or moral power over individual voters.

There are lots of popular jokes about vote buying. This was a pretty common practise in many parts of the country for years, but is rarely heard about any more. There are still forms of it used that do not come to the attention of the public. Campaign organizers will use cash or liquor to buy votes. Some use "street cash" to hire all the available transportation to take everyone to the advance polls. Taking advantage of the inner-city poor and others is a sleazy part of our political system that needs to be eliminated.

Nothing, to this point in our discussion has been particularly illegal. Practical politics might violate rules of good taste and offend some sensitivities, but these practises are all part of highly competitive election contests. Unless they are libelous, they are only offensive. However, there have been cases where the law was broken.

The laws governing the conduct of candidates and parties are becoming more strict with the passing of each election, since large sums of public money are now involved in election campaigns. In most jurisdictions, there are rebates of election expenditures available to parties and candidates, depending on how well they do in the election and how much they spend. Also, tax credits are becoming more available to financial contributors. With so much of the taxpayers' money at stake, violation of the laws governing election campaigns carries stiff penalties which include fines, jail, future sanctions against candidacy, or the removal of official party status from a political party that violates the law.

Spending limits that are established for candidates and parties in various jurisdictions are usually adequate to mount a decent campaign. It is in tight races where the law is often broken. In order to get an extra edge, campaigns will hide expenditures. It is almost impossible to prove that a candidate's financial statement is false. Many times, I have been convinced that opponents had far more advertising, signs, and literature than could normally be purchased under expense limits, yet their financial statements revealed no such over-expenditure. These candidates simply did not tell the truth when they were filing their returns. The only way to be sure is to keep an extensive log from day one of the campaign, and even then it would be difficult to prove an infraction without some collaboration from inside the other campaign.

A recent scandal in Ontario centred around a common practice among campaigners. Although few actually go through with plans to manipulate election finance laws, many campaign committees have examined the laws to see how they can get away with hiding expenditures or receiving funds from questionable sources. It seems on the surface that this political supporter, who was charged with contravening election laws, simply went a little farther than most would consider prudent in moving money around, but you can be certain that there is a lot happening in the grey areas of Canadian election laws.

Sometimes election laws are downright foolish and hard not to violate. The Alberta Election Act, for instance, has a provision that prevents anyone who is indebted to any government department or program from being a provincial candidate in Alberta. Many people in Alberta are proud of the Treasury Branches and the symbol of provincial economic freedom they represent. However, if you have a loan with the Treasury Branch, you are ineligible to be a provincial candidate. A lot of people have had to arrange loans and mortgages with other institutions to avoid possible prosecution under this section of the Alberta election law.

Officials in the House of Commons and the various provincial legislatures are beginning to examine their rules concerning the use of the many communication tools given to elected members. It is difficult to determine where the line should be drawn between legitimate expenditure of public money for keeping in touch with constituents and partisan political activity.

Many politicians use mailing and telephone privileges, as well as travel expenses, to advance their party and personal electability. For instance, when a federal election seems near, many MPs will prepare leaflets for distribution to each household in their riding and get it in the mail right at the call of the election; although the brochure might not violate the rules for acceptable content and intent, they do reach beyond the spirit of the rules.

An often-used election day rallying cry is, "Vote Early and Vote Often." Stuffing ballot boxes and resurrecting the dead to vote on election day, just do not happen any more. There are too many independent election officials to allow vote rigging to be organized by any black-hearted politicians. However, people who are not eligible to vote often cast a ballot. Sloppy enumeration leads to non-citizens and other unqualified people being included on the voters' list. If these votes go unchallenged at the polling station on election day, they will be able to vote, and some do, mostly without realizing they are doing wrong. The infraction only comes to light when there is a court challenge to the results and the voting comes under close scrutiny. This is not to imply any wrong-doing by the politicians who might have large numbers of non-Canadians in their constituencies, but, some look the other way if they know this is happening in their favour.

One election, an ineligible voter, Lucy Brook, appeared on the voters' list at my address. The election clerk wouldn't have had to be too sharp to determine that she shouldn't be allowed to vote, though. She's an American Cocker Spaniel! She's smart, but intelligence isn't one of the criteria to determine who can vote and who can't. We had Lucy's name taken off the voters' list, just in case she tried to vote when no one was paying attention.

This chapter has been a brief description of the darker side of politics. We may not like this kind of activity in our democracy, but we need to acknowledge that such things take place. These kinds of tactics do affect election results. It is our job as political consumers to make sure that those who deserve to win do, and that those who should be defeated get their just reward.

Hardball politics are a fact of political life, and will always be with us. Election officials are always reviewing the legislation governing the conduct of candidates and political parties, and this may reduce the number of opportunities for unfair practices. Our only hope is that candidates will treat each other with the respect that the voters deserve.

14. Staying Elected

"We often campaign in poetry,
but we're always required to
govern in prose. In the end,
much of campaign rhetoric proves
to be an impediment to policy
making." *Governor Mario Cuomo*

Candidates need to spend some time after an election getting reacquainted with family, restoring their health and putting their lives back in order. Losers have a lot more time to do this than winners. Political work never stops for successful candidates; little in their previous experience could have adequately prepared them for the rigours of elected office, coupled with the need to stay positioned for re-election.

Those who are elected have to begin preparing for the next election immediately, while at the same time providing service to their constituents. They have to be loyal and partisan team players, while courting people and special interests that may have been fierce opponents during the election. The divergent and competing elements that face each politician make public life a difficult balancing act.

The first order of business after the election is to thank all the people who volunteered time, money and ideas to the campaign. Candidates should not worry if they thank too many people. Just because some people volunteered to phone, but never quite made it to the campaign headquarters, is no reason to exclude them from the list. The fact that they never did any work doesn't change the fact that they volunteered. Some candidates will go as far as to send *thank yous* to people who put signs on their lawns and even those who told canvassers they intended to vote for the candidate... the more thank you notes, the better.

Candidates with an eye to the future use all the lists of supporters, donors, workers and sign locations to build an effective computer database. This becomes the primary source of names for letters on issues, Christmas card mailings and invitations to special events, not to mention requests for political contributions and party memberships. Politicians also consult these lists when a constituent is looking for help with a problem. This is not to exclude someone who is not on the list, but more so the politician knows how to address the voter and, if necessary, help prioritize casework.

Not only do candidates send out hundreds of thank you letters, but if they have any tact at all, they see to it that they pay a little special attention to their chief campaign workers and organizers. Nice gifts and private parties help thank these people for giving so much of themselves during the campaign. Few elected politicians could ever truthfully say that some members of their campaign teams didn't work as hard or sacrifice as much, or more, than the politicians did.

In politics, there is no teacher like experience. The best way to learn the most from the electoral process is to take sufficient time to preserve all the campaign records and conduct a meaningful post-mortem of the election strategy and tactics.

Preserving the election records means more than cleaning out the campaign headquarters and throwing all the junk into someone's garage or basement. It means putting it all in some useable form so that it can be used to help prepare for future elections and keep the legislator in touch with his or her supporters.

In spite of all the paper and files that accumulate during an election, the real records of a campaign end up being a few file folders plus a set of voters' lists which indicate known supporters. Three or four computer disks later, all the sweat and tears of a month or more of flat-out campaigning can be reduced to a size small enough to tuck into a shirt pocket.

Many candidates have gone into a re-election campaign with the prospect of having to rebuild all their lists from scratch, simply because they didn't take time to make sure that all the important documents from the previous election were stored properly and in a useable form.

Winners and losers alike should take time while the campaign is still fresh in their memories to conduct a serious post-mortem of their efforts. The immediate tendency of winning candidates is to assume that they did everything correctly; losers feel they did everything wrong. Neither is true, of course. A frank session that avoids finger-pointing and accusations but also pulls no punches is the best way for campaign teams to leave a helpful blueprint for the next election. Making mistakes in one campaign is bad enough without compounding the sin by repeating them.

Another post-campaign matter that requires the immediate attention of candidates is campaign finances. Not all campaigns deficit finance, but few raise all the money they need by election day. Elected politicians need to protect their reputations in the local business community; they don't need a debt lingering too long after a campaign. Successful politicians have little trouble establishing or extending a line of credit for their campaign organizations with financial institutions. Therefore, their first job is to ensure that all individual accounts are paid off. Then all their fund raising efforts can be directed toward a single debt.

A manageable election deficit can be politically useful. It gives a solid reason to keep a campaign organization together and gives the team something to work toward without the pressure of an actual election. Campaign victories followed by a series of well-planned and rewarding financial drives and events keep a team pumped up and looking forward to the next election.

Once the debt for one campaign is retired, it is time for politicians to start raising the money they need for the next electoral fight. Even candidates without any financial shortfall in their campaigns won't wait long to begin building a war chest for the next trip to the polls. Campaigns don't get any cheaper, and given the Canadian electoral system, only municipal politicians can be dead certain when the next election day will be coming. The longer a politician remains in office, the easier it becomes to raise money for the subsequent election. They get to know more people who are capable of making and soliciting contributions. As well, over time, more people feel they owe something to a politician who has helped them with some problem or has shown special interest in their affairs.

Successful candidates need to take care to avoid "sleepy hollow syndrome," which is characterized by a lazy and moribund party organization at the constituency level. Politicians who feel that they were elected on their personal appeal, and fail to spend time providing leadership to their own riding organizations, will have machines that barely pass as skeletons when needed most, at the next election. Careful nurturing and regular watering builds a healthy team. Therefore, politicians devote a lot of energy to recruiting new members, holding policy conferences, and similar events throughout the term in office.

Official constituency organizations occupy a lot of the attention of elected politicians. The people who make up the local party leadership may not all have been hard workers in the election campaign; they may not even have supported the incumbent during the nomination process. Regardless, local associations must be massaged and never ignored by politicians, in case they should rise up and bite politicians when least expected. As much as possible, politicians want campaign loyalists filling executive positions so that support can be counted on in difficult situations, including everything from not scheduling meetings at an awkward time to active support should there be a challenge in a future nomination. The next election may be just around the corner; successful politicians know the importance of keeping the best cogs in their election machine well-oiled and in campaign-readiness.

Len Evans, the long-time MLA from Brandon East, appointed poll captains in every poll in his riding. He provided them with scrolls to put on their walls, visited them regularly, and had them host neighbourhood coffee parties and deliver his legislative reports in their area. This attention to detail ensured Evans a tough fighting machine in every election, including two campaigns when his party was thrown out of provincial office. He weathered the storm each time.

Most politicians take a "hands on" approach when dealing with recruiting their constituency executive, to make sure there are no loose cannons who might embarrass them by making an untimely public statement about policy or the politician's performance.

Keeping the local rank and file in line is not the easiest job. Politicians usually have some form of minor patronage they can dispense; but the luckier elected officials are on the government side of the house. There they can make recommendations for appointments to important boards and commissions and arrange employment for supporters and their friends. Even opposition backbenchers have invitations to special government dinners or social events they can hand out during their terms, in appreciation for work and support in past elections. And, of course, opposition members can also hold out the hope of rewards in the future.

In the first few days after they are elected, new politicians must select support staff. Most jurisdictions have some funds allocated for elected members to hire staff. These funds are usually for staff in a constituency office, or for legislative research, and often for both.

Many politicians don't take enough care when they first hire staff. An effective staff person needs to have a proper balance between the ability to organize and an aptitude for serving the public on behalf of the politician. Too often, politicians exercise poor judgement. They believe that once the last ballots are counted, they are no longer politicians. They frequently hire people with no political experience whatever, and then wonder why their campaign supporters are angry at them for not considering partisan priorities and their future re-election.

In 1975, the Manitoba NDP had a policy that whenever a person came into the provincial headquarters looking for party information, they were to be referred to an organizer. (This was because the party was broke and any unsuspecting prospect was a prime target for money.) One well-dressed young man was sent down to my office for the treatment. I took time to explain the policies and structure of the organization as well as the need for finances. He seemed quite interested in it all. When I asked him why he wanted this information, he told me it was because he had just been hired by one of the cabinet ministers, and he felt he should know a little more about the NDP, maybe even join!

There are other errors of judgment made by politicians when hiring staff. There was the Edmonton MLA who hired a constituency secretary who, after hours, worked on behalf of someone who was challenging her boss for the nomination: her husband. A Toronto Liberal MP watched his constituency assistant file nomination papers against him in an election, as a candidate for another party. Other incumbents use government funds to reward their relatives and friends rather than partisan activists who have worked hard to get them elected. No party is immune to this foolishness.

This is not meant to leave the impression that politicians' offices are filled with appointees who are there only to sabotage their bosses at the first opportunity, either wittingly or otherwise, or that the payrolls are treated like a patronage slush fund.

The importance of finding capable staff quickly was driven home for freshman MP Cid Samson. You can imagine his relief at being able to hire an experienced staff person shortly after his 1988 election, when he went to the post office to look for his cheque, and found a twenty pound box full of mail instead.

Most political staff work many hours more than any regular work day, for less pay than similar jobs in the private sector, and they are subject to a demanding public who expects instant resolution to difficult problems. Not the least of the pressure comes from bosses, who expect the same Herculean effort every day between elections on their behalf that they received in the four or five weeks of the election campaign.

In fact, most casework that finally arrives in a politician's office can't be resolved. The complainant has probably been through all the bureaucratic hoops, and the case just does not fit into the tidy rules of government. These problems take special skills to solve because they often require delicate negotiations with hide-bound public servants who are unwilling to consider special circumstances. At times, the only thing that will move recalcitrant civil servants is the threat of censure from the politicians.

The problems that politicians' staffs deal with daily can range from garbage pickup to a culvert on a side road to arranging passage for political refugees from another country. Most people who work for politicians are public servants in the truest sense. In addition, they portray the incumbent as an ombudsman ready to go to bat for citizens who are confused, frustrated and even intimidated by government procedures. The resulting good will pays off in the ballot box the next time out.

MP Les Benjamin is one example of many who were not given "star" status during his political life, but who always got the job done for people. He can count many thousands of successful conclusions to casework problems, and this helped him weather even the toughest challenges with apparent ease, election after election. The real credit goes to dedicated constituency staff.

In making their personnel decisions, legislators must make sure that their people are capable of following the priorities that are established by politicians, and that they can operate within pre-determined rules designed to govern the accessibility of the member to the general public and the amount of time he is prepared to devote to constituency matters. These guidelines are then applied to scheduling the legislator's time. Staff members do not agree to a meeting or schedule attendance at an event or turn down an invitation without first consulting the member.

Politicians often forget who sent them to St. John's, Victoria, Ottawa or wherever the seat of government is located. They get wrapped up with the grandeur of it all. The perquisites, the officiousness of senior civil servants, and the media attention all make it difficult for many incumbents to remember they were sent to serve and represent the people in their ridings. Politicians have to work hard to maintain profile in their home ridings. The last thing any of them needs is to earn the reputation of being too important to care about the folks back home.

Parliamentary duties transform a simple ward politician into a statesperson, filled with heady ideas of justice, fairness and the law. Almost all elected officials are assigned some additional legislative job, whether it is in the Cabinet, serving as a parliamentary or legislative assistant to a Minister, serving on committees, or acting as a spokesperson in some critic area as a member of the opposition. In addition, there are positions such as House Leader, Whip and Caucus Chair, all of which carry a measure of prestige, and, for some, an extra salary. When a legislator gets lost among all these trappings, the Smiths on Main Street at home can seem a long way away.

The pecking order within an opposition caucus is established no differently than that on the government side. The assignment of administrative jobs and critic areas take on the same importance as the appointment of cabinet ministers. The Finance critic has a higher profile and more favour with the Opposition Leader than the critic for Youth and Culture, for example.

At the same time, legislators are mindful of how their caucus responsibilities are viewed back home. One Saskatchewan MLA, Dwain Lingenfelter, who represented a very conservative rural riding was the Minister of Social Services in the Blakeney government. After his government's defeat in 1982, he was the logical choice to be the opposition critic for social welfare issues, but taking a high profile on these issues without the power of a cabinet portfolio to bring benefits to his riding likely contributed to his personal defeat in 1986.

Of course, these parliamentary responsibilities are part of the job. But they shouldn't overpower the primary need to serve those who elected the politician. When service to the voter is neglected or takes a lower priority, the seeds of defeat are being sown.

Within a few weeks of being elected in 1988, one MP I know had already started to establish a reputation for taking himself too seriously. He had been invited to a conference where about thirty long-time friends from the trade union movement were discussing current issues. Instead of being the old buddy they all knew, he proceeded to deliver a formal speech that lasted one hour and thirty-eight minutes. No one was impressed.

Some politicians start to lose their partisan edge after being elected. Drawing significant differences between themselves and their opponents' ideas helps to attract votes, but once they become parliamentarians those lines can start to become less distinct. When Alberta Premier Don Getty was first elected as part of Peter Lougheed's six-man opposition to then Premier Ernest Manning and the Social Credit government, Getty was so taken by the logic and power of Manning's arguments in debate that he was often seen nodding in agreement to his foe's speeches. He was finally sent a note by Lougheed which simply said, "Stop nodding!"

Caucus discipline is an important part of our system of government. It is not always to the liking of every politician, since it means having to walk a fine line between the wishes and needs of the voters at home and the larger political picture. Legislators have the opportunity of making their points in caucus meetings which provide direction to the leadership and help form the stand their caucus will take on important legislative issues, but once a decision is made, caucus solidarity demands that each member accept the decision and support it. As a result, it often falls on the shoulders of the individual member to sell an unpopular political position to supporters and constituents. It may even be a position with which the member does not agree. Sometimes members have to apply unusual powers of persuasion and live through some temporary strain on local relationships.

The whole area of caucus discipline is coming under attack in Canada. Individual Conservative MPs are receiving a lot of abuse from their constituents for supporting the Goods and Services Tax. This is a classic example of what many feel is wrong with our system of parliamentary democracy. There is a definite conflict between the idea of an MP or MLA being a representative of the people who elected him or her, and the need to support a party and its position on various issues. For the individual politician, all power and influence flows from caucus and crossing colleagues can only diminish the ability to be an effective representative. Most politicians take the attitude that these hard feelings over issues will blow over after a while. There is some doubt that the anger over the G.S.T. will pass before the next federal election. Time will tell.

Elected politicians quickly learn that each action causes some reaction, and that they can expect to lose some battles and supporters over time. It's only normal, and their success can be measured as much by how they can minimize damage as on how many times they win.

Up to the time of his departure from the PC Caucus, David Kilgour often spoke against his party's policy positions, particularly those which seemed to treat the West with indifference. This probably harmed his constituents in the long run. This is because other Alberta Conservative MPs and cabinet ministers who worked hard to sell PC policies in their own ridings might be very reluctant to recommend programs to benefit Kilgour's constituents.

On most issues, politicians manage to keep their balance while juggling these responsibilities. Maintaining the respect of fellow caucus members is important to most politicians. Breaking rank with their colleagues can bring sanctions that only make their jobs harder.

Keeping in touch with constituents and explaining the reasons for taking various positions becomes a lot easier if politicians have used all the vehicles available to them to remain in touch with the electorate. Extensive use of mailing and postage allowances help to maintain credibility with local voters. Being able to mail a letter or leaflet on a regular basis to the constituency allows members the chance to put their point of view across, usually without any competition from political adversaries who do not have the same resources as those provided by the public purse.

These mailings are used to highlight various current public issues and the member's stand on them, and there is often an opportunity to take shots at those who support the other side of those issues as well. Not many people pay a lot of attention to this material from local representatives, unless they follow legislative affairs closely. The real value of these mailings is in the way they show the politician in action, working on behalf of constituents. Having voters receive the material is as important as their actually reading it. Outside of the local news media, this is the main vehicle for maintaining name recognition and a positive image at home.

While staff do most of the casework for legislators, smart politicians will take the time to draft replies to letters they receive from the public themselves. There are two advantages to taking the time to do this, even if it means carrying a lot of correspondence on a plane or home in the evening. First, it keeps the politician in touch with reality, and secondly, it helps to build a reputation for the "personal touch." The personal signature tells the voter that the busy member has taken the time to deal with the problem. In casework, one MP I know will never sign replies to voters that are not a positive resolution to the problem. Staff are left to sign letters if the case cannot be resolved.

Another MP of my acquaintance does not involve himself in casework at all. Everything is done by his lone constituency office staff member who is not very comfortable dealing with most matters and puts off cases that are too difficult or require more than a simple phone call. This MP is steadily losing votes because he is not paying attention to what is happening at home.

Politicians can have mountains of mail to process. Peter Lougheed had an interesting system for prioritizing replies to his correspondence: handwritten letters first, typed letters with a postage stamp second, and metered mail and form letters last.

Mail is very important in keeping politicians "up to speed" with what is happening in their constituencies or areas of policy specialization. The opinions and attitudes that are expressed in correspondence provide an important barometer, from the grassroots, of changing times and ideas. Legislators who dismiss most of their correspondence as a nuisance miss a real chance to keep in touch.

Former PC Member of Parliament from Hamilton, Lincoln Alexander, has been widely quoted as saying if he received more than four letters on any one topic, he considered that an avalanche. These days, organizations and special interests are better equipped to mount letter writing lobby campaigns than they once were. As well, more individual citizens are less in awe of their representatives and more prepared to approach them with problems, suggestions and comments. Elected officials at every level still measure the relative importance of the issues by the amount of mail or number of calls they receive on a particular topic.

Provincial and federal elected officials also have to be prepared to answer a lot of phone calls, probably more than they ever did before, because voters now feel far less removed from their representatives than they once did. Political staff screen calls, so politicians know what the call is about and what problem may be involved, before they speak to constituents, if they do.

John Turner never waited to hear from people. He would get on the phone every day and inquire about opinions, ideas and solutions his friends and acquaintances might offer on various topics.

People may be impressed by politicians who answer their phone calls and mail, but politicians do this with varying amounts of diligence. With cynicism about the motives and dedication of elected officials growing, these personal touches surprise many voters, and they are likely to let their friends and neighbours know about it when it happens. This goes a long way in building a positive reputation and image for that politician as a person who cares about peoples' problems and appreciates their ideas.

Pressing the flesh doesn't end on election day. Once elected, candidates find they are frequently guests at a host of events sponsored by organizations and individuals who may not even have given them the time of day before the election. It is important to keep a profile in the community and these events are a big help in doing that. Besides, they are an opportunity to be seen by large numbers of constituents without expending the kind of time and energy that door to door canvassing requires and few politicians can resist a free meal.

MLA John Younie took a unique approach to these events. Very early in his first and only term in the Alberta Legislature, he told the president of a prominent community organization that he wasn't going to be a "rubber chicken MLA." John's sentiments might have been noble enough, he didn't want to take advantage of his position to advance his personal political fortunes, but his reasons were certainly difficult for those who were offering the hospitality to understand.

Most politicians develop a formal or informal outreach plan to make new contacts among organized groups within their ridings. They do this by providing regular information to these groups on issues that concern them, providing access to government officials and generally, giving them a conduit so their points of view are heard at the legislative level. At the same time, incumbents take care to make sure that they also maintain the close relationship they developed with organizations that helped during the election campaign. It is critical for the chances of re-election not to leave the impression that these groups were used only to elect the politician, and that they have no further worth.

The importance of these outreach activities is growing. Canadians are becoming increasingly identified with single issues such as the environment, education and human rights and it is through their local organizations that they get information about the matters that concern them most. That is why the politicians have to stay in touch.

Endorsements from organizations also carry responsibilities for politicians, who need to show continued interest about those issues that concern these groups the most. Some elected members invite representatives of important groups in their ridings to sit on formal or informal advisory committees in order to provide direct input on those issues. This affords the opportunity for people who may have been cool to the politician during the election to come to know them better and perhaps become supporters in the future, a part of the "defanging" process.

Being a legislator is not an automatic ticket to more news coverage. Politicians still have to work at getting space and time with local media. When legislatures are in session, cabinet ministers and high profile opposition members get most of the coverage. Backbenchers need to develop the reputation that they are capable of giving articulate and newsworthy responses to questions asked by reporters.

Being outspoken and controversial will help build this reputation, but if the politician is not also giving information that is useful to the reporters, who are trying to get all the angles to a story, then the comments will get less coverage. After a while, the only image that emerges is that of being a bit of a lightweight with nothing significant to add to the public debate. Such politicians may even end up being embarrassments to the voters back home if their reputations start to show flaky sides. Few have the wit and charm of a John Crosbie or the reasoned and logical views of Herb Gray or Bill Blaikie. A positive post-election media image has to be cultivated and earned, and quickly.

Those politicians who represent ridings which receive their news coverage from the same city where the seat of government is located have little opportunity to put a local spin on the news coming out of a legislative session. People in Toronto, for instance, have a keener sense of the happenings at Queen's Park and are more able to draw conclusions based on first hand knowledge of what their own MPP's are doing than someone from Sarnia, Ottawa or Thunder Bay. This means the politicians from outlying ridings are more able to influence the way the news is reported with less fear of contradictory evidence.

The federal Conservatives leave nothing to chance with "PCTV." This is their news service to smaller stations that do not have ready access to the Ottawa Press Gallery. This news package is controlled by the PC's and beamed out to stations who want coverage of the House of Commons. Subscribing stations also get clips of their own MPs speaking on current issues, as long as the MPs are Conservatives, of course. Clearly this is an operation that is designed to manipulate and control the quality and content of media coverage. However, don't be fooled by the protests from the other parties. They would all like to have the money to do the same thing.

Increasing television coverage of the proceedings of legislative bodies gives incumbents another opportunity to play to the folks back home. Important speeches or penetrating questions will be broadcast on the news, and members of the public who have the inclination can watch events unfold live. In fact, the number of people who tune in the local cable channel to catch the action in the House of Commons or local legislatures is increasing every year. More and more politicians are hearing from people who watched their latest speeches on TV.

The main feature of legislative broadcasts is the daily question period. This provides the bulk of television news coverage and becomes the basis for political reporting in the other media. In fact, during other debate and proceedings there is rarely more than a corporal's guard, if that, in the press seats.

Legislators face twin dilemmas when preparing for their turn in front of the cameras, if they are in the opposition. They have to ask relevant questions, but if they concentrate on the hottest daily news items, they are accused of relying on the *Globe and Mail* or some other media outlet for their political agendas. At the same time, if they bring to light issues that do not have a high profile in the public domain, they are criticized for not dealing with important issues.

Regardless of the method of arriving at a theme for the daily questions, the guiding principle behind any question asked is, "never ask a question unless you know the answer." Since few government ministers ever give a direct answer to the questions put to them, the politician asking the question needs to know what the answer really is so that he or she can pursue the issue in follow-up questions or in media interviews. This has the effect of raising doubts about the particular minister's credibility and elevating the image of the questioner.

David Lewis was as good as anyone at asking effective questions in the House of Commons. He would start out innocently enough, but by the time he had finished his second or third supplementary question, he would have a cabinet minister dangling at the end of a rope of his own construction.

When live broadcasting from the House of Commons was first

introduced, political parties hired consultants to teach their members how to dress properly for the electronic eye and how to use body motion to emphasize debating points. Colourful wardrobes of plaids and checks were dispatched to the Goodwill Store and carefully co-ordinated blue, black and grey ensembles took their place in the closets of our legislators. A refresher course might be useful though. During a recent broadcast, I saw a Liberal MP who violated almost every known rule of gentle haberdashery. He wore a broadly striped shirt, polka-dot tie and a green jacket.

When television came to the House of Commons, seating arrangements took on new importance to backbenchers on both sides of the House. A seat within the camera angle of an important frontbench member meant frequent exposure, even if the backbencher rarely got the opportunity to get on his or her feet. Those who sit close to the politicians getting most of television time are chosen because they are among the few women elected or because they are youthful and attractive, rather than because they have seniority.

The only chance an individual politician has to have any personal impact on the federal or provincial legislative process, other than by supporting or opposing government bills or opposition motions is through the introduction of Private Member's Bills. A certain amount of time is set aside during sessions for these bills to be introduced and debated by a member and others who wish to join the debate. The fate of these well-intentioned actions is almost always failure. Sometimes a politician may be unable to get a seconder, or, when the bill finally reaches the order paper, it may be "talked out" so that it never comes to a vote.

The value of these motions for legislators who introduce them is that they can point to something concrete they have tried to achieve; they cannot be blamed if the bills are not passed.

This is not to say that these bills are always condemned to a certain death. Former Toronto MP Lynn McDonald introduced worthwhile legislation with regard to smoking that was passed into law. Others have had their work plagiarized and re-introduced in amended form by a government which could see the good sense in the initiatives of an individual member, but didn't want to give credit to anyone else.

Membership on important legislative committees is another advantage available to elected politicians that helps maintain an edge in the next election. The committee system is most developed at the federal level, where MPs can be assigned to high profile committees such as Finance, Health or Transportation. Membership on these committees gives an MP the opportunity to develop a national profile and a platform from which to speak on important issues even when the House of Commons is not in session. Finance Committee Chair Don Blenkarn is probably better known than many cabinet ministers.

Provincial legislatures do not have as many committees with the same public presence as those in Ottawa. They tend to be more administrative in nature. Still, service on committees such as Public Accounts helps provide the same benefits to provincial politicians that they do for their federal counterparts.

Only under the most unusual circumstances are politicians acclaimed to office; almost every politician intends to be a candidate again. The success of their terms in office can sometimes be measured by the quality of candidates who challenge them in the next election. The better the job they do, the less likely the opposition will be able to attract heavyweight candidates to try to snatch their jobs away. Going into an election, being either an incumbent or a challenger carries distinct advantages and disadvantages.

Incumbents have the advantage of ready access to the media. They are more newsworthy and can generate news on their own. As well, they get a lot of secondary exposure. For instance, the main story might be the opening of a new hockey rink or senior citizens' centre, but the incumbent is always on the platform or cutting the ribbon in plain view of voters.

Being a provincial or federal member brings with it stature in the community. Politicians can show that they have been entrusted with important responsibilities and have carried out their duties well.

Having staff to handle casework, write press releases, research issues and schedule events is a powerful advantage. These are paid employees to do the bidding of the politician and not just well-meaning and sincere volunteers. As well, elected office brings with

it the other advantages of mail and phone privileges, travel allowances and permanent offices in the constituency.

Incumbents can have a record of achievement to point to when
the time for re-election rolls around. I once advised a Maritime
candidate to take advantage of the fact that he had worked hard
to get a hospital built in a town in his rural constituency. He refused
to take credit for his efforts because he felt that the town deserved
the hospital and that it shouldn't be turned to his own political
advantage. It was a close election and he lost largely because he
would not blow his own horn.

Even if they have been members of the opposition, politicians
can still point to projects and grants they worked to obtain for their
ridings. If the government has been particularly hard-nosed about
refusing to put money into an opposition member's constituency,
that too, can become a debating point for the incumbent seeking
re-election.

Since one of the factors used by voters to decide who to vote for
is the amount of experience the various candidates have, the
incumbent has a natural advantage. Even if the challengers have
also had experience at the same or different levels of government,
the incumbent has the most recent and therefore most relevant
knowledge of what it takes to perform the tasks the position
requires.

Even the most timid incumbent has the advantage of a higher
level of name recognition among the general public. Name recognition is a central part of any election campaign and recall is
normally high for politicians seeking re-election. In polls I have
conducted, the normal level of incumbent recognition among
voters is about 65% to 75%; and after those who could not name
their member were prompted with the name, the total level of
recognition is normally 90%. Anything lower than 65% for initial
recognition spells trouble or should be cause for concern about
the re-election prospects of an incumbent, and means he or she
hasn't taken as much advantage of the position as was necessary.

However, a history as an elected representative can also be the
source of many disadvantages when it comes time to seek a new
mandate from the voters. Incumbents can seem invisible, particularly if their constituencies are a long way from where the parlia-

mentary action is taking place. This impression is enhanced when the member has been unable to generate regular and sustained media coverage at home. This opens an area of vulnerability and, in addition, if they work hard to cover themselves at home, they may be accused of shirking their legislative duties.

An effective election campaign can help create this attitude by building false expectations among voters who may think, "We elected him and haven't heard from him since." It's very common for people to compare the visibility of their legislator during an election period with later levels of exposure. It's an unfair comparison, but one that is made nonetheless. Not maintaining residence in the constituency after winning an election also fuels the feeling that politicians have dropped out of sight. The obligations of official business become a serious impediment to keeping a distinct profile in the riding. There comes a time when smart politicians simply drop all the extra tasks and get out and meet people in the ridings and hope they haven't left it for too long.

The perquisites of office also become sources for attacks on incumbents. Special privileges and compensation packages can reflect on politicians. The general public becomes cynical over huge pay increases, free dental plans and cheap meals and haircuts. Trips to exotic destinations and exorbitant travel bills are bound to receive media attention. In many cases, politicians are forced to justify a lot of the money spent on them from the public treasury.

Probably the biggest handicap for the incumbent is potential association with problems people may be facing at election time. This is more a problem for those who represent the government side, but is not restricted to them. Even opposition members can be accused of not having done enough to help the local area, and many voters may view an opposition member as the prime cause for not receiving adequate government attention.

While politicians have a better opportunity to establish public records than their challengers, these may not be the kinds of record that are positive factors in re-election campaigns. Their records are open for all to see, and are open to both opponents and the media to criticize and attack. Records may include a lot of unkept or broken promises from a previous election. This is made worse if politicians make the mistake of promising more than they can possibly deliver. All any politician can really promise is to work hard on behalf of constituents. To avoid disappointing voters, politicians need to work from a point of promising a lot, and then delivering even more. This was part of the success formula of the Schreyer governments in Manitoba.

Being a politician also brings with it an "establishment" image. While there may be no real harm in that, there can be times when the collective attitude of the voters will cause a rebellion against those they feel are standing in the way of real growth and realization of their hopes. In his successful bid for the Democrats' Presidential Nomination, Jimmy Carter ran against the establishment and machine politicians of Washington with great success. The success of so many NDP challengers in the recent Ontario election can be traced in part to the feeling that many of them were not considered typical politicians.

Naturally, incumbency brings with it the most advantage when the next election is called. Under normal electoral circumstances, each re-election comes easier than the one before. Barring disastrous elections like the New Brunswick election where every one of Richard Hatfield's PC members and candidates were defeated, the success rate of those seeking re-election is extra-ordinarily high.

Canadian elections are not becoming as predictable as those in the U.S., where a decreasing number of seats can be expected to change hands when incumbents seek re-election. In the last U.S. House of Representatives series of elections, 402 of 408 incumbents were re-elected. In fact, 89% of these winners had at least 60% of the vote. The main reason given by observers for this declining number of marginal seats is the political and financial advantages that incumbents enjoy.

Those who wish to defeat incumbent politicians also have an assortment of advantages and disadvantages. Challengers can be active in the riding, while the incumbent is performing his job elsewhere. They can attack the legislator's record and can be on the offensive without offering solutions to current problems. Challengers also have the advantage of not having a record to defend, and they can stress their "concerned underdog" status versus the "professional politician."

The disadvantages for an incumbent's opponents are obvious.

Without records, they likely have little experience to offer voters. They also find it difficult to attract any meaningful media attention, and, as a result, they may not be able to build strong name identification and a visible presence in the community. Even if local groups and opinion leaders are reluctant to support the incumbent, they may not want to risk the sitting member's wrath by publicly supporting a challenger. As a result of all this, it takes a very special person to build an effective team and raise the kind of money necessary to mount a serious challenge.

Author Ronald Moran, a politician himself, in his fine book on municipal politics, had sound advice for elected officials. Moran cautions that leaving no time for enjoyment of family, work, or personal pursuits in a blind chase for votes can of itself cause dissatisfaction. He suggests that the best form of campaigning is good performance in elected office. A careful and intelligent politician who responds to the needs of the electorate will build a reputation that precedes him or her to the polls.

That advice, as much as anything, should be the basis of the way a politician conducts his or her activities between elections in the ultimate drive towards re-election.

15. Getting Out of Politics

"One day you might be the
prized piece of china and
the next day you're Tupperware."
A Minnesota TV News Anchor

At some point before every election, incumbents take personal stock of themselves and their political futures. They do this in much the same way they conducted a self-evaluation when they decided to run in the first place. Some decide to continue, while others make up their minds to return to private life.

Family, friends and political colleagues are all useful sources of advice for incumbents as to whether they should seek re-election. If the advice is honest, it becomes the basis for making the final decision. It's hard to say what constitutes honest advice in these matters, but most experienced politicians know who they can rely on to be straightforward and bloody-minded on personal matters.

As part of this process, most politicians take time to measure their accomplishments against their own personal expectations of what they thought they could achieve during their terms in office. If they are satisfied that they are doing a good job and have had a positive impact for their constituency and its voters, they will likely decide to run again.

Some politicians first ran for public office because they were concerned about a certain issue. They need to consider whether there are any more windmills to tilt at, or whether their own goals and objectives have changed over the years. If there are no more battles to fight, incumbents need to consider whether or not to get out while they are on top.

Incumbents need to consider their health and general frame of mind. Public life can take its toll on the most healthy of people, and it may be a matter of self-preservation for an elected official to consider leaving office. Some of the legislators I know tell me that even though the pay, benefits and status that come with the job are considerable, and hard to ignore or duplicate, they will consider quitting as soon as they no longer enjoy the job. As far as they are concerned, the long hours and hard work cannot be offset by pay and perks alone.

Some of the most successful politicians that I know have a terrific sense of humour and a zest for the competition of politics. Whether it is in trading barbs back and forth in the legislature or meeting people and solving problems, they say they wouldn't be able to survive without the extra edge they get from the joy of being a politician. Some call it "fire in the belly," others call it enthusiasm. Whatever it is, they say they would quit if they lost it.

One factor that weighs heavily in decisions to seek re-election is the politician's performance and standing in caucuses and assemblies. Legislators who have risen through the ranks and have been given major responsibilities are reluctant to leave those behind. Besides, there is always the expectation of even more prestige if they are re-elected, since many of these rewards are based at least in part on seniority.

From time to time, the boundaries of constituencies are redistributed and some politicians find that a constituency that was once a pretty safe bet may suddenly be much tougher to win. During redistribution, others may find that their ridings have been wiped out altogether, or that the boundaries have changed so radically that they have to face a popular incumbent from their own party for a nomination. Rather than face the uncertainty of a new constituency, some politicians will take advantage of the situation and retire.

Another factor facing an incumbent who is trying to decide whether to seek re-election may be his or her family. Politics can be dangerous to marriage, and does not promote a happy family lifestyle. Politicians who find themselves away from home for long periods of time may slide into habits that include infidelity and too much liquor. So, the politician may feel it is not worth the potential of marriage breakdown to continue in office.

It may also be that what a family might have seen as a glamorous future was far less than that in reality. A politician's family not only gets to share centre stage on occasion, and has a lot of stature in the community; family members are also exposed to a great deal more stress. They can count on dealing with angry constituents at all hours of the day or night, postponing holiday plans because of emergency legislative debates, or having to attend social events in the constituency, when they would far sooner sit at home and relax.

Popular Saskatchewan Tory politician and now Senator, Eric Berntson, summed up the trials of a family when he ended a long career on both sides of the Saskatchewan Legislature. He said that because of his profile, people either loved or hated him. He could take it, but it was very hard on his children and they suffered because of it.

Of course, the most important consideration for any hard-nosed politician is a simple assessment of whether he or she can win another election. If their party is in disfavour or they have been discredited during the previous term, re-election might be difficult or impossible. Even if things are relatively stable politically, they may find when consulting campaign activists, that there may be a lot of trouble recruiting volunteers or that it might be difficult to raise money. The quality of the candidates that the other parties can be expected to nominate for the next election is a further consideration in determining how tough the contest might be. These might just be reasons enough to pause for careful reflection, if not opt for retirement.

As we know, few incumbents retire from office. Most hang in as long as they can. There are a host of reasons for this. The most obvious reason is that the answers to all of the questions they have asked their families, campaign activists and themselves all point to renewed support for their candidacy, the likelihood that re-election will be a fairly simple matter and that they still have zest for the job.

Some office holders get a little too caught up with the trappings of office. They can't imagine a life without all the extras. They become too accustomed to power. There are some who even feel it is their right to occupy their seats as long as they choose. The idea of stepping aside would never occur to these politicians and they rarely retire unless given a direct order from their leaders or are challenged from within their own ranks.

The status that association with an elected official brings in the community also sometimes rubs off on the spouses of politicians; there are times that it is family members who do not want to withdraw from public life.

For some, there is simply no graceful way to leave office. They have no other job to take up after political office. If they haven't negotiated for an appointment to a government agency or looked for some position in a corporate boardroom or community agency, these retiring legislators have no way of maintaining their dignity while adjusting to the real world.

Some may simply forget that they don't like public office, or at least the politics that go with it, and forget to retire. One Manitoba PC cabinet minister who was known to have a healthy disdain for politics offered the following excuse when asked why he had decided to run for re-election, "I don't know what came over me when they asked me to run. I guess I went brain-dead again."

For a person with years in the public eye, a retirement with dignity doesn't mean just a comfortable pension, since that is already assured, but usually means some sort of continued public presence. Even retired politicians who have a profession or occupation to fall back on tell me their jobs rarely replace the experience of holding public office. They have a continued need for public recognition in order to be validated as people.

In fact, some legislatures have an area in the chamber where previous members are allowed to sit while the house is in session. It's not uncommon to see these seats as well used as those of the active politicians.

The parties generally have a habit of ignoring the needs of veteran politicians. While party hierarchies expect some veterans to step aside for new blood, they have no history of honouring their retirees, other than former leaders, in any meaningful way. The parties are run by young people who never have time to seek counsel and advice from experienced legislators, a fact that doesn't escape the notice of these veterans as the years go by, so for them, the only way to keep a feeling of being useful and wanted is to remain in office.

Still other incumbents run one more time because they simply don't take the time to consider and evaluate their careers. They never bothered to plan for the future, and when an election becomes imminent, there is not enough time to make any preparations to leave office, nor is there time to prepare the riding association to look for a competent successor and plan an election around a newcomer. No matter how obvious an impending election seems, a lot of politicians are caught by surprise. For this reason, thoughtful incumbents plan their personal careers well in advance. Those who are in control of their lives decide soon after an election whether or not they intend to seek re-election. With that out of the way, they can spend their terms in office self-assured in the knowledge that their careers are planned.

Leaving politics is a lot harder than entering the field. There is a lot more support and advice offered to the novice, and veterans are left largely on their own, because people feel they are capable of making up their own minds. This is surely not the case, since it is a certain fact of political life that the longer people have been in office, the farther removed they probably are from daily reality.

For that reason, friends, relatives, and colleagues must be prepared to offer the support, advice, and encouragement politicians need to make the right decision when it is time. Family and friends of politicians should not shake their heads from the wings, wondering why the politician carries on, when what may be ahead is the possibility of ruined health, loss of respect, and defeat.

If politicians were given a little more respect, in and out of office, it would be easier for them to make decisions about whether to remain or retire. It is a common sport to beat up on politicians, in the same way we dump on the Toronto Maple Leafs or complain about the weather. It becomes easy for legislators to escape the slings and arrows of public criticism and seek the comfort and security of their legislative chambers and perks of office. Certainly, some office holders have given us a lot of good reasons to question their motives, but that is no reason to tar them all with the same brush. Most legislators, from all the parties, work hard to provide decent representation for those who elected them, and discharge their responsibilities as best they can.

Former Prime Minister Lester Pearson thought that if politicians were more highly regarded by the general public, it would be much easier for our governing bodies to go through renewal and welcome fresh ideas and approaches to the problems that face us all.

Politicians and the politics they practise require far more respect than they receive today. Yes, we send politicians to represent us in our legislative bodies. We expect them to give voice to our personal concerns and their votes to the issues that affect us; we are always disappointed if their final decisions and votes are against those things we feel are important. Rather than grumbling, however, we must stay in touch with these people so that they know what the grassroots is thinking. That communication with elected officials is what makes democracy work between elections, and is an essential responsibility of citizens, voters, political workers, and supporters.

Without our participation and input, we leave our representatives hanging out to dry; our ultimate response is to criticize government, aided in our poor opinion of politicians by media that are more than willing to focus public scrutiny on the shortcomings of those who represent us. That scrutiny of decisions, as well as personal and public actions and behaviour is far more intense than that we apply to CEOs or VPs of major corporations, whose decisions and subsequent waste and mismanagement can cost each of us far more in money, job security, and lost opportunities than most political decisions.

It is true that politics and democracy are diminished by those politicians who, through unwise decisions or indiscretion, betray the trust of those who elected them. Yet, there can be no prouder achievement than to be chosen by one's neighbours to represent their hopes and aspirations, and to speak on their behalf freely in an elected assembly.

I have always felt proud and privileged to work beside so many men and women who were willing to serve, or seek to serve, in Parliament, or any other legislative body.